RALPH STORER is an experienced [illegible] has hiked and backpacked extensively [illegible] a Sassenach by birth, he has lived in Scotland [illegible]gy at Dundee University and has a great affinity for the Highlands, where he can be seen in all weathers roaming the glens and tramping the tops. As well as disappearing into the hills for a regular fix of nature, he also writes novels and sexological non-fiction, and produces dark-wave music on his home computer.

The Ultimate Guide to the Munros, Volume 3: Central Highlands North is the third volume in a series that draws on his decades of adventures in the Scottish Highlands.

Praise for *The Ultimate Guide to the Munros, Vols. 1 and 2*

This is a truly indispensible guide for the Munro-bagger. Bursting with information, wit and a delightful irreverence rarely found in this type of guide, it's a joy to read. Ralph and his motley crew are the perfect companions on a great day out. An absolute gem! ALEX MACKINNON, Manager, Waterstone's George Street, Edinburgh

The Ultimate Guide to The Munros *picks up where others – including my own – leave off, with lots of nitty-gritty information on alternative routes, levels of difficulty and aids to navigation, all in a very up-beat style... I look forward to seeing the rest of his fun-packed Munros series.* CAMERON MCNEISH

Fabulously illustrated...Entertaining as well as informative... One of the definitive guides to the Munros. PRESS & JOURNAL

Irresistibly funny and useful; an innovatively thought-through guide-book that makes an appetising broth of its wit, experience and visual and literary tools. Brilliant. OUTDOOR WRITERS & PHOTOGRAPHERS GUILD

After much praise and cult following from avid Munro baggers following the first book comes the second volume in The Ultimate Guide to the Munros *series... Ralph Storer preserves the quirky charm that made the first book a loveable essential for hill walkers... the book is as fun as it is practical...* EDINBURGH EVENING NEWS

While most climbing authors appear to have had their funny bones surgically removed, Storer is happy to share numerous irreverent insights into the hills, and this acts as a timely reminder that walking should, after all, be primarily about enjoyment of the great outdoors. A further advantage is that the book will easily fit in a rucksack and does not require SAS *training to lug it up the slopes.* SCOTTISH FIELD

With the winning combination of reliable advice and quirky humour, this is the ideal hillwalking companion. SCOTS MAGAZINE

His books are exceptional... Storer subverts the guidebook genre completely... Storer's effort would be the bedtime reading, the one where I might laugh out loud, and it contains the passages to quote to the fearful Mrs Warbeck – who would of course be memorising every pronouncement by Baffies. THE ANGRY CORRIE

BY THE SAME AUTHOR:

100 Best Routes on Scottish Mountains (Warner Books)
50 Best Routes on Skye and Raasay (Warner Books)
50 Classic Routes on Scottish Mountains (Luath Press)
Exploring Scottish Hill Tracks (Warner Books)
The Joy of Hillwalking (Luath Press)
Mountain Trivia Challenge (Cordee)
The World's Great Adventure Treks (contributor) (New Holland)
Trekking Atlas of the World (contributor) (New Holland)
The Rumpy Pumpy Quiz Book (Metro Publishing)
Love Scenes (a novel) (Birlinn)

Also in *The Ultimate Guide to the Munros* series:

Volume 1: Southern Highlands
Volume 2: Central Highlands South (including Glen Coe)

Route-based iPhone apps, containing route maps and descriptions derived from the contents of the books in this series, are also available through the Outdoors app on iTunes

The Ultimate Guide to the Munros

Volume 3: Central Highlands North

RALPH STORER

Boot-tested and compiled by
The Go-Take-a-Hike Mountaineering Club

Luath Press Limited

EDINBURGH

www.luath.co.uk

For Sandi

Hillwalking and mountaineering are not risk-free activities and may prove injurious to users of this book. While every care and effort has been taken in its preparation, readers should note that information contained within may not be accurate and can change following publication. Neither the publisher nor the author accept any liability for injury or damage of any kind arising directly or indirectly from the book's contents.

First published 2010

ISBN: 978-1-906817-56-5

The paper used in this book is recyclable. It is made from low-chlorine pulps produced in a low-energy, low-emission manner from renewable forests.

Printed and bound by Bell and Bain Ltd., Glasgow

Typeset in Tahoma by Ralph Storer

All maps reproduced by permission of Ordnance Survey on behalf of HMSO. © Crown copyright 2010. All rights reserved. Ordnance Survey Licence number 100016659.

Front cover artwork by Sinéad Bracken

All photographs by the author, including front cover (Lancet Edge on Sgor Iutharn of Geal-Charn), except that on page 7 by Allan Leighton.

The author's right to be identified as author of this book under the Copyright, Designs and Patents Act 1988 has been asserted.

© Ralph Storer

CONTENTS

INTRODUCTION

The north face of Ben Nevis towers over Coire Leis

We must be humble...
these stones are one with the stars

Hugh MacDiarmid 1892–1978

Written at the Site for Contemplation, Glen Nevis Visitor Centre

The Go-Take-a-Hike Mountaineering Club

Ralph Storer President

Compiler of routes, penner of words, stopper of bucks, all-round good egg. His favourite campfire reading: *The Outsider*.

GiGi Custodian of the Common Sense

Farer (fairer?) of the Ways, arbiter of disputes, friend to all. Named after the two embarrassing grooves occasioned by too much fence-sitting. Her favourite campfire reading: *Fear of Flying*.

F-Stop Controller of the Camera

Advisor of the Aperture. Recorder of the Ridiculous. So-named because he's always f***ing stopping to take photographs. His favourite campfire reading: *A Room with a View*.

Needlepoint Companion of the Compass

Wary Watcher of the Weather. Finds featureless plateaus intimidating, doesn't understand GPS, barely understands a compass. Her favourite campfire reading: *Long Day's Journey Into Night*.

Committee Members

Chilly Willy Keeper of the Cool

AKA Snowballs. Peely-wally, estivates during summer, has never seen a midge, likes his toast crisp and even. His favourite campfire reading: *The Bumper Pop-up Book of Snowflakes*.

Torpedo Expender of the Energy

Bald and streamlined. Loather of laziness. Scorch marks on boots. Ascends as fast as a falling Munro bagger descends. His favourite campfire reading: *The Guinness Book of Records*.

Terminator Raveller of the Rope

Grizzled, monosyllabic, self-taught suicide commando. Hater of the horizontal. Measures his life in scars. His favourite campfire reading: *The In-depth Guide to Thin Cracks*.

Baffies Entertainments Convenor

Allergic to exertion, prone to lassitude, suffers from altitude sickness above 600m, blisters easily, bleeds readily. His favourite campfire reading: *The Armchair Guide to Munro Bagging*.

Route Quality Ratings

*****	**Outstanding**
	The best. Outstanding routes in every respect. The reason we climb mountains. The stuff of memories.
****	**Excellent**
	Still great, but just lacking that extra something that would make them outstanding.
***	**Very Good**
	Maybe not the best, but still commendable, perhaps outstanding or excellent in parts.
**	**Good**
	Nothing to prise the uninitiated off the couch, yet still good enough to provide a satisfying hillwalk that brings a smile to the visage.
*	**Fair**
	Could be better, but all Munros are worth booting up for, aren't they?

Route Rage Alert

Flagged on routes where 'challenging' terrain makes a beach holiday seem not such a bad idea after all.

Route Difficulty Grades

G1 **Mostly good going**

Mainly on good paths or good terrain. There may be occasional steep or rough sections, but not for long.

G2 **Appreciable awkward going**

Notably rough or steep terrain, perhaps prolonged, but not involving handwork on rock.

G3 **Minor handwork required**

Use of hands required on rock, e.g. for balance or a step-up, but not difficult or prolonged enough to constitute scrambling.

G4 **Easy scramble**

Includes one or more sections that require movement on rock with good holds.

G5 **Hard scramble**

One grade below a rock climb for which a rope would normally be required. Compared to G4, holds are often smaller and exposure is often greater.

OF MOUNTAINS AND MUNROS

It's a big place, the Scottish Highlands. It contains so many mountains that even resident hillwalkers struggle to climb them all in a lifetime. How many mountains? That depends...

If two summits 100m apart are separated by a shallow dip, do they constitute two mountains or one mountain with two tops? If the latter, then exactly how far apart do they have to be, and how deep does the intervening dip have to be, before they become two separate mountains?

Sir Hugh Munro (1856–1919), the third President of the Scottish Mountaineering Club, tackled this problem when he published his 'Tables of Heights over 3000 Feet' in the 1891 edition of the SMC Journal. Choosing the criterion of 3000ft in the imperial system of measurement as his cut-off point, he counted 283 separate Mountains and a further 255 Tops that were over 3000ft but not sufficiently separated from a Mountain to be considered separate Mountains themselves.

In a country whose vertical axis ranges from 0ft to 4409ft (1344m) at the summit of Ben Nevis, the choice of 3000ft as a cut-off point is aesthetically justifiable and gives a satisfying number of Mountains. A metric cut-off point of 1000m (3280ft), giving a more humble 137 Mountains, has never captured the hillgoing imagination.

Unfortunately Sir Hugh omitted to leave to posterity the criteria he used to distinguish Mountains from Tops, and Tops from other highpoints over 3000ft. In his notes to the Tables he even broached the impossibility of ever making definitive distinctions. Consider, for example, the problem of differentiating between Mountains, Tops and other highpoints on the

Sir Hugh Munro himself never became a Munroist (someone who has climbed all the Munros). Of the Tables of the day, he climbed all but three: the Inaccessible Pinnacle (although that did not become a Munro until 1921), Carn an Fhidhleir and Carn Cloich-mhuilinn. The latter, which he was saving until last because it was close to his home, was ironically demoted to Top status in 1981.

Cairngorm plateaus, where every knoll surpasses 3000ft.

The Tables were a substantial achievement in an age when mapping of the Highlands was still rudimentary, but no sooner did they appear than their definitiveness become the subject of debate. In subsequent years Munro continued to fine-tune them, using new sources such as the Revised Six-inch Survey of the late 1890s. His notes formed the basis of a new edition of the Tables, published posthumously in 1921, which listed 276 separate Mountains (now known as Munros) and 267 Tops.

The 1921 edition also included J. Rooke Corbett's list of mountains with heights between 2500ft and 3000ft ('Corbetts'), and Percy Donald's list of hills in the Scottish Lowlands of 2000ft or over ('Donalds'). Corbett's test for a separate mountain was that it needed a re-ascent of 500ft (c150m) on all sides. Donald's test was more mathematical. A 'Donald' had to be 17 units from another one, where a unit was one twelfth of a mile (approx. one seventh of a kilometre) or one 50ft (approx. 15m) contour. We can assume that, however informally, Munro used some similar formula concerning distance and height differential.

Stob Coire Easain

Over the years, various developments have conspired to prompt further amendments to the Tables, including metrication, improved surveying methods (most recently by satellite), and a desire on the part of each succeeding generation of editors to reduce what they have regarded as 'anomalies.' For example, the 'mountain range in miniature' of Beinn Eighe was awarded a second Munro in 1997 to redress the balance with similar but over-endowed multi-topped ridges such as the seven-Munro South Glen Shiel Ridge. Changes and the reasons for change are detailed individually in the main text (see Peak Fitness for details).

The first metric edition of the Tables in 1974 listed 279 Munros and 262 Tops. The 1981 edition listed 276 Munros and 240 Tops. The 1990 edition added an extra Munro. The latest (1997) edition lists 284 Munros and 227 Tops, but Sgurr nan Ceannaichean was demoted to Corbett status following re-measurement in 2009, leaving 283. Watch this space.

The first person to bag all the Munros may have been the Rev Archibald Robertson in 1901, although his notebooks bear no mention of him having climbed the Inaccessible Pinnacle and note that he gave up on Ben Wyvis to avoid a wetting.

The second Munroist was the Rev Ronald Burn, who additionally bagged all the Tops, in 1923, thus becoming the first 'Compleat Munroist' or Compleater. The third was James Parker, who additionally bagged all the Tops and Furths (the 3000ft summits of England, Wales and Ireland), in 1929. The latest edition of the Tables lists 1745 known Munroists.

THE SCOTTISH HIGHLANDS

The Scottish Highlands are characterised by a patchwork of mountains separated by deep glens, the result of glacial erosion in the distant past. On a global scale the mountains reach an insignificant height, topping out at 1344m/4409ft on Ben Nevis. But in form they hold their own against any range in the world, many rising bold and beautiful from sea-level. For hillwalkers they have distinct advantages over higher mountain ranges: their height is ideal for day walks and glens give easy road access.

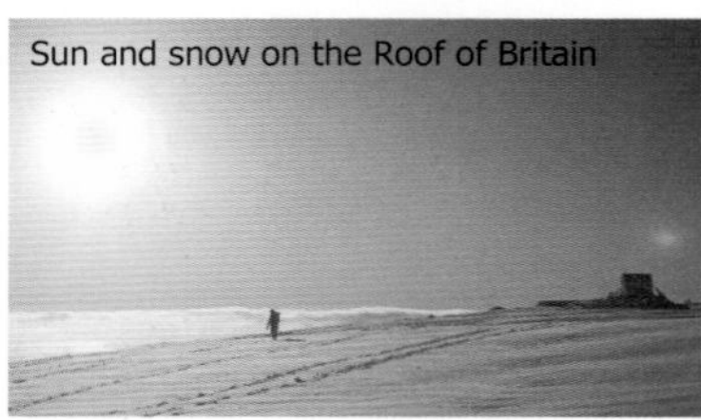
Sun and snow on the Roof of Britain

Moreover, the variety of mountain forms and landscapes is arguably greater than in any mountainous area of equivalent size. This is due to many factors, notably differing regional geology and the influence of the sea.

In an attempt to give some order to this complexity, the Highlands are traditionally divided into six regions, as detailed below. The potted overviews mislead in that they mask the variety within each region, ignore numerous exceptions to the rule and reflect road access as much as discernible regional boundaries, but they serve as introductory descriptions.

The Southern Highlands 46 Munros	Gentle, green and accessible, with scope for a great variety of mountain walks.
The Central Highlands 73 Munros	A combination of all the other regions, with some of the greatest rock faces in the country.
The Cairngorms 50 Munros	Great rolling plateaus, vast corries, remote mountain sanctuaries, sub-arctic ambience.
The Western Highlands 62 Munros	Dramatic landscapes, endless seascapes, narrow ridges, arrowhead peaks, rugged terrain.
The Northern Highlands 39 Munros	Massive, monolithic mountains rising out of a desolate, watery wilderness.
The Islands 13 Munros	Exquisite mountainscapes, knife-edge ridges, sky-high scrambling, maritime ambience.

THE CENTRAL HIGHLANDS

The Central Highlands is the smallest of the six regions of the Highlands and Islands, yet it is packed with more Munros and a greater variety of scenery than any of the other five.

On the north and west the region is bounded by the great fault line that runs through Loch Linnhe and continues up the Great Glen from Fort William to Inverness. On the east it is bounded by the A9, which runs north from Perth over Drumochter Pass to Aviemore and Inverness. The southern boundary runs along the A85 from Oban to Tyndrum, up the A82 to Rannoch Moor, then east beside Lochs Rannoch and Tummel to Pitlochry.

From Scotland's populous Central Belt, two main arteries lead north and west through the region. From Dalwhinnie on the A9, the A86 runs west along Loch Laggan through Glen Spean to Spean Bridge and Fort William, at the entrance to Glen Nevis. From Crianlarich, where the Edinburgh and Glasgow roads meet, the A82 runs west to Tyndrum, then north-west through Bridge of Orchy and across the edge of Rannoch Moor to Glen Etive and Glen Coe.

As you travel along the roads, you'll be aware of a changing landscape that reflects a varied underlying geology, from the granite of Cruachan in the south to the mica-schist of the Monadh Liath in the north, from the sandstones of Loch Ericht in the east to the quartzite of the Mamores and Grey Corries in the west.

Erupting through this geological base, volcanic extrusions have created the most dramatic scenery of all, around Glen Coe and Glen Nevis, where world-famous mountains such as the Three Sisters of Glen Coe and Ben Nevis vie for attention.

Fault lines and depressions, often paralleling the Highland Boundary Fault to the south, further divide the region into mountain groups. Lochs such as Loch Etive and Loch Ericht fill some of these depressions and create barriers to land access. Yet more sculpting of the landscape occurred during the Ice Ages. The effects of glaciation are everywhere: ice-gouged geological faults, U-shaped glens, hanging corries, erratic boulders, kettle holes, parallel roads...

The end-result is a region of more rugged scenery and starker contrasts than the neighbouring Southern Highlands, but one in which complexity of landscape still leaves room for individual Munros of great presence.

Owing to its size and diversity, the region is covered by two volumes – Volume 2: Central Highlands South and Volume 3: Central Highlands North. In total the region boasts 73 Munros, together with 64 associated Tops and 35 Corbetts. Following on from the 46 Munros of the Southern Highlands, Central Highlands South contains 36 Munros (Nos. 47-82) and Central Highlands North contains 37 Munros (Nos. 83-119).

CENTRAL HIGHLANDS NORTH

The Munros in this volume fall into eight groups, presented in roughly west-to-east and south-to-north order. They are numbered 17-24, following on from groups 1-8 in the Southern Highlands and groups 9-16 in the Central Highlands South.

Some of the groups constitute named mountain ranges, others are named after the glen, loch or area on which they are centred:
17 The Nevis Range, 18 The Grey Corries, 19 Corrour, 20 Culra, 21 Drumochter West, 22 Laggan and Spean, 23 The Creag Meagaidh Group, 24 The Monadh Liath.

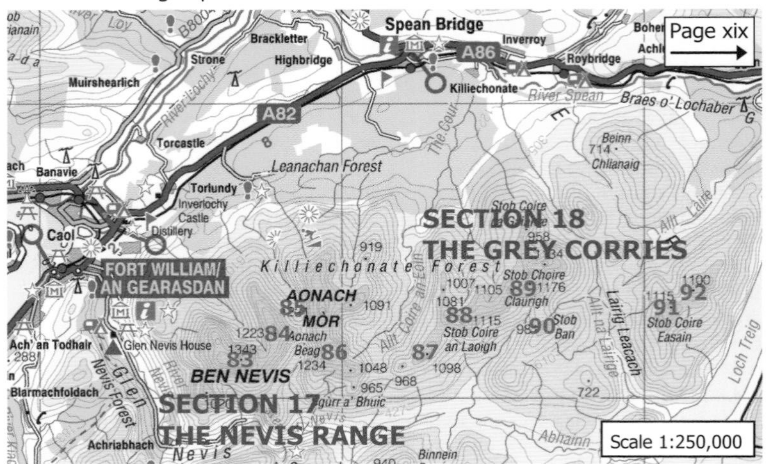

If the Central Highlands South are epitomised by the soaring rock peaks of Glen Coe, the Central Highlands North are characterised by plateau summits indented by Alpine-style corries. Ben Nevis, Ben Alder, Creag Meagaidh… this is scenery on the grand scale, often hidden from the roadside and revealed only to those prepared to boot up and walk.

At the heart of the **Nevis Range**, Ben Nevis is not only the highest and most popular mountain in the land, but it is of a stature that makes it a worthy 'rooftop of Britain'. Mechanised uplift in the nearby Nevis Range ski area makes the neighbouring Munros similarly busy.

Moving east, the **Grey Corries** are a ridge walker's dream to rival the Mamores on the south side of Glen Nevis. Although there are only four Munros here, their narrow connecting ridge, reached by long approaches and dotted with intervening Tops, makes them challenging objectives.

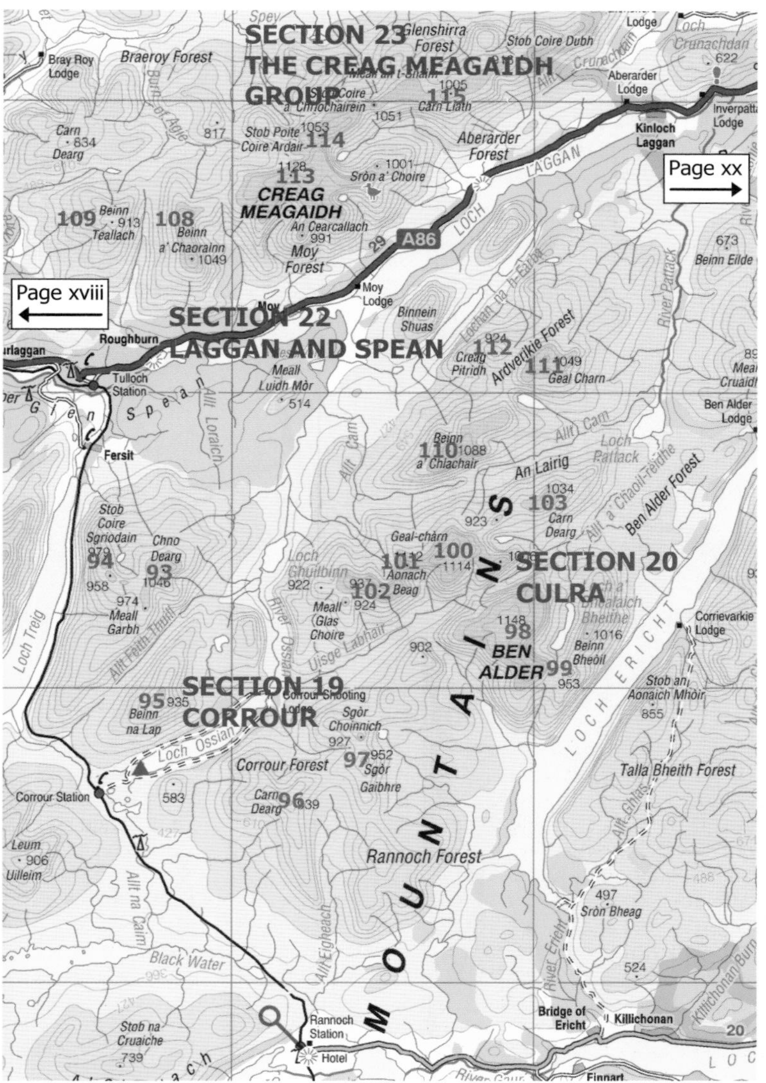
SECTION 23
THE CREAG MEAGAIDH
GROUP
SECTION 22
LAGGAN AND SPEAN
SECTION 20
CULRA
SECTION 19
CORROUR
Page xx
Page xviii
CREAG
MEAGAIDH
BEN
ALDER
Braeroy Forest
Bray Roy
Lodge
Glenshirra
Forest
Stob Coire Dubh
Aberarder
Lodge
Kinloch
Laggan
Aberarder
Forest
LOCH LAGGAN
A86
Moy
Lodge
Roughburn
Tulloch
Station
Fersit
Ardverikie Forest
Loch Pattack
An Lairig
Ben Alder Forest
Ben Alder
Lodge
Loch Treig
Corrour Station
Loch Ossian
Corrour Forest
Rannoch Forest
Talla Bheith Forest
LOCH ERICHT
Corrievarkie
Lodge
MOUNTAINS
Black Water
Rannoch
Station
Hotel
Bridge of
Ericht
Killichonan
Finnart

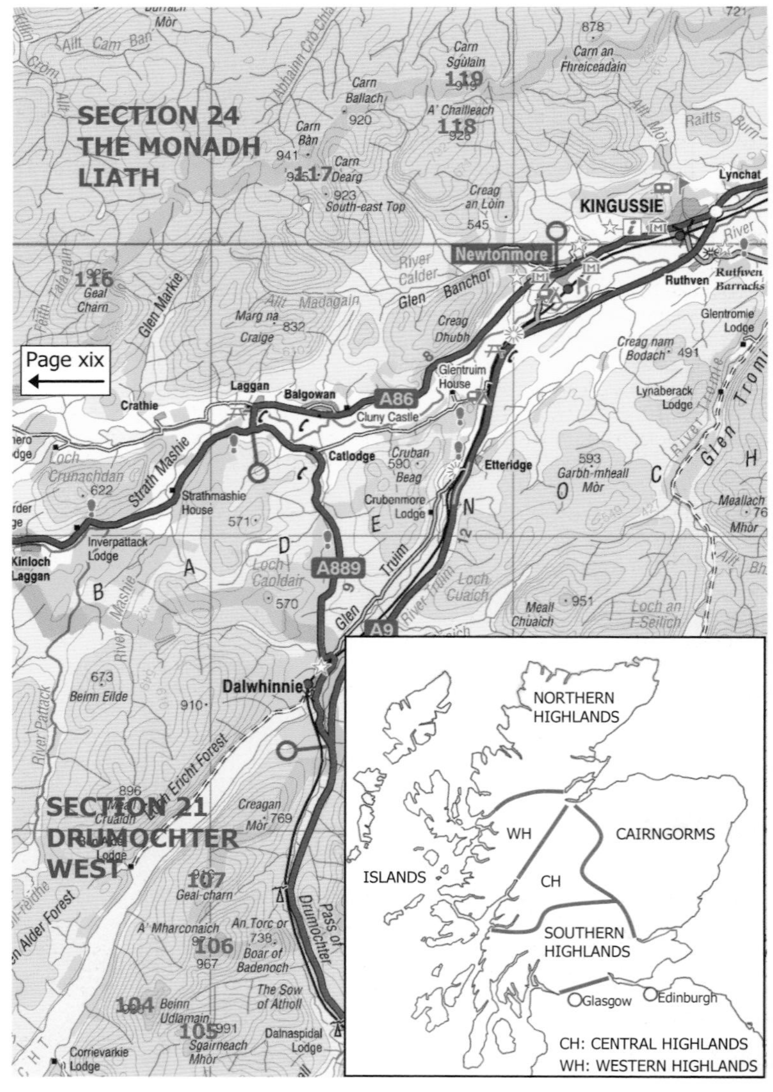
SECTION 24
THE MONADH
LIATH
SECTION 21
DRUMOCHTER
WEST
Page xix
Carn Sgùlain
Carn an Fhreiceadain
Carn Ballach
A' Chailleach
Carn Bàn
Carn Dearg
South-east Top
Creag an Lòin
KINGUSSIE
Newtonmore
Lynchat
Ruthven
Ruthven Barracks
Glentromie Lodge
Glen Banchor
River Calder
Creag Dhubh
Geal Charn
Glen Markie
Allt Madagain
Marg na Craige
Laggan
Balgowan
Crathie
Cluny Castle
Glentruim House
A86
Catlodge
Cruban Beag
Etteridge
Strath Mashie
Strathmashie House
Loch Crunachdan
Crubenmore Lodge
Creag nam Bodach
Lynaberack Lodge
Garbh-mheall Mòr
Glen Tromie
Meallach Mhòr
Inverpattack Lodge
Kinloch Laggan
Loch Caoldair
A889
Glen Truim
Loch Cuaich
Meall Chuaich
Loch an t-Seilich
A9
River Mashie
Beinn Eilde
Dalwhinnie
River Pattack
Ben Alder Forest
Creagan Mòr
Geal-charn
A' Mharconaich
An Torc or Boar of Badenoch
The Sow of Atholl
Pass of Drumochter
Beinn Udlamain
Sgairneach Mhòr
Dalnaspidal Lodge
Corrievarkie Lodge
NORTHERN HIGHLANDS
WH
CAIRNGORMS
ISLANDS
CH
SOUTHERN HIGHLANDS
Glasgow
Edinburgh
CH: CENTRAL HIGHLANDS
WH: WESTERN HIGHLANDS

Further east still, and presenting an even greater logistical challenge, a group of remote Munros inhabit the roadless country around the railway station at **Corrour** and the bothy at **Culra**. Using the morning train for access, day walks from Corrour back to the car make for unique point-to-point Munro bagging trips, but the Culra Munros require a long walk-in or cycle-in.

To make the most of Culra's scenic setting, many choose to backpack in and stay overnight. The mountains themselves do not disappoint, with extensive summit plateaus approached by ridges that are in places narrow and exciting. Welcome to a Walk on the Wild Side.

To the north of these four areas, across the A86, lies more accessible but still big country, where **Creag Meagaidh** rivals even Ben Nevis for the grandeur of its scenery. On its eastern flank, Coire Ardair is one of *the* great corries of the Highlands. The neighbouring Munros in Glen **Spean** and by Loch **Laggan** are a mixed bunch that suffer by comparison, yet they are by no means without interest if you choose good routes up them.

If only the same could be said for the Munros of **Drumochter West** and the **Monadh Liath**... These two most easterly areas of the Central Highlands lie close to the Cairngorm plateaus and lack the rugged scenery found further west. Unfortunately they also lack the character of the Cairngorms. There is plenty of high-level tramping to be had here, atop broad, rolling ridges that perhaps deserve more merit than they receive, but the summits themselves lack distinction.

Like the Central Highlands South, the Central Highlands North are more rugged than the Southern Highlands, with mountains that generally require more effort and more commitment. Compared to the Central Highlands South, summits are generally higher and approaches longer. The Munros here are not to be taken lightly, but they are all eminently baggable.
If you like your hillwalking high and wild, you've found the right place.

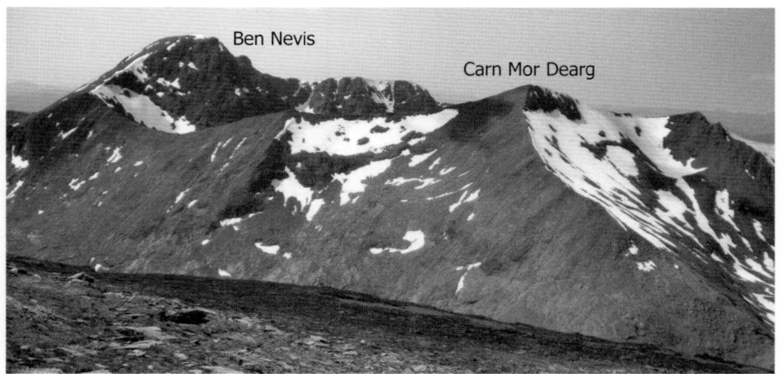

SEASONS AND WEATHER

From a hillwalking perspective, the Highland year has two seasons: the snow season and the no-snow season. The length of these seasons varies from year to year and from place to place.

From May to September, snow is rarely a problem. Historically, May and June have the greatest number of sunny days, with the air at its clearest. July and August are the hottest months but are also more prone to rain and haze, not to mention that blight on the landscape, the Highland midge. The biting season begins in mid to late June and lasts until the first chills of late September. By October it is colder, the hills get their first dusting of winter snow and good days are few and far between.

The months from November to April, though sometimes earlier and later, are characterised by short days, cold and snow. March and April are transition months, with little or lots of snow. In some years, snow can last into early summer and be a nuisance on some routes. If you are unequipped for it, turn back. Snow is more treacherous to descend than ascend, and spring snow often has a crystalline quality that makes it behave like ball-bearings.

In a normal winter (whatever that is, these days), conditions vary from British to Alpine to Arctic. An easy summer route can be made life-threatening by icy conditions and severe winter weather. When paths are obliterated by snow, hillsides become treacherous and walking becomes difficult and tiring.

On a clear winter's day the Scottish mountains have an Alpine quality that makes for unforgettable days out, but no-one should attempt a Munro in winter without adequate clothing and equipment (including ice-axe and crampons), and experience (or the company of an experienced person). The number of accidents, some of them fatal, that occur in the Highlands every winter should leave no doubt as to the need for caution.

Evening descent of Ben Nevis Mountain Track above Loch Linnhe

Sample weather forecasts:
www.metoffice.gov.uk/loutdoor/mountainsafety/ Tel: West (09068-500442), East (09068-500441)
www.metcheck.com/V40/UK/HOBBIES/mountain.asp
www.mwis.org.uk
www.sais.gov.uk (avalanche conditions)

Webcams may be available for specific mountain areas. Useful webcams at the time of writing can be found at:
http://visit-fortwilliam.co.uk/webcam/
www.webcam-ski.com/webcams/interfaces/nevis-range/
http://trafficscotland.org/lev/index.aspx

USING THIS BOOK

Position in Munro's Tables (1 = highest)   OS 1:50,000 map number   Grid reference

▲84 Carn Mor Dearg 9 1220m/4003ft (OS 41, NN 177721)
Carn Mor Jerrak, Big Red Cairn

Many Munro names are Gaelic in origin. We give approximate pronunciations but make no claim to definitiveness. For example, the correct pronunciation of Ben is akin to *Pyne*, with a soft *n* as in the first syllable of *onion*, but it would be pedantic to enforce a purist pronunciation on a non-Gaelic speaker. The name Bealach, meaning Pass, is pronounced *byalach*, but many find it hard not to call it a *beelach*. And if you're one of those unfortunates who appear congenitally incapable of pronouncing *loch* as anything other than *lock*, you're in trouble.

In connection with the phonetic pronunciations given, note that Y before a vowel is pronounced as in *you*, OW is pronounced as in *town* and CH is pronounced as in Scottish *loch* or German *noch.*

Route 116a Geal Charn from Spey Dam
G1 *** NN 584937, 10ml/16km, 710m/2350ft M212 —— Page number of map

The maps used in this book are reproductions of OS 1:50,000 maps at 75% full size (i.e. 1:66,667 or 1.5cm per 1km).

Route distances are specified in miles (to the nearest half-mile) and kilometres (to the nearest kilometre). Short distances are specified in metres (an approximate imperial measurement is yards). Total amount of ascent for a route is specified to the nearest 10m (50ft) and should be regarded as an approximation only.

To calculate how long a route will take, many begin with Naismith's Rule (one hour per 3ml/5km + half-hour per 1000ft/300m). This can be adjusted by an appropriate factor to suit your own pace and to cater for stoppages, foul weather, technical difficulty, rough terrain, tiredness and decrepitude. (Bill Naismith, 1856–1935, was the 'father' of the SMC.)

River directions, left bank and right bank, refer to the downstream direction. When referring to the direction of travel, we specify left-hand and right-hand.

The symbols ▲ and Δ indicate Munros and Tops. An ATV track is an All-Terrain Vehicle track, rougher than a Land Rover track.

ACCESS

Land access was revolutionised by The Land Reform (Scotland) Act 2003 and the accompanying Scottish Outdoor Access Code (2005), which created a statutory right of responsible access for outdoor recreation. It is recommended that anyone walking in the Scottish countryside familiarise himself/herself with the Code, which explains rights and responsibilities in detail. Further information: www.outdooraccess-scotland.com.

Deer stalking considerations: Most of the Scottish Highlands are privately owned, and non-compliance with stalking restrictions is likely to be counter-productive and cause aggravation for all concerned. If revenue is lost because of interference with stalking activities, estates may be forced to turn to afforestation or worse, thereby increasing access problems.

The red stag stalking season runs from July 1 to October 20 but actual dates vary from locality to locality. Access notices dot the roadside and information on stalking activities can be obtained from estate offices and head stalkers.

An increasing number of estates contribute to the Hillphones service, which provides daily recorded messages of where stalking is taking place. Further information can be found on the Outdoor Access website or on the Hillphones website: www.snh.org.uk/hillphones. Alternatively, obtain a leaflet from The Mountaineering Council of Scotland, The Old Granary, Perth PH1 5QP.

It is worth noting that there is no stalking on a Sunday and that land belonging to public bodies such as the National Trust for Scotland and the John Muir Trust is normally not subject to stalking restrictions. See main text for specific access considerations.

TERRAIN

There are boot-worn paths on most of the standard ascent routes, but don't expect the kind of manufactured paths to be found in the Alps, Rockies or even the Furth of Scotland (England and Wales). Rough or boggy ground may sometimes preclude the formation of a path at all.

On the more popular routes, path restoration continues apace. The boggy morass of the former Coire Ardair path, for instance, is now a beautiful approach route. In general, however, be prepared always for rough, rugged terrain and wear appropriate footwear.

A wobble on Stob Choire Claurigh

17 THE NEVIS RANGE

The Nevis Range is a group of massive **Alpine-like mountains** that dominate the landscape east of Fort William. Here stand four of the nine Munros that top 4000ft (1220m): Ben Nevis itself, the highest mountain in the British Isles, and three others that rank 7th, 8th and 9th highest in Munro's Tables. The remaining five 4000ft Munros are in the Cairngorms.

The quartet divides naturally into two pairs. Ben Nevis and Carn Mor Dearg are connected by a high 1058m/3472ft bealach, while Aonach Mor and Aonach Beag are connected by an even higher 1090m/3578ft bealach. The two pairs are separated by a lower 830m/2725ft bealach. This can be crossed on a long day in order to bag all four Munros together, but it is more normal to climb the two pairs separately and, of course, Ben Nevis is most often climbed on its own.

Three of the four mountains (Ben Nevis, Aonach Mor and Aonach Beag) are characterised by plateau summits edged by huge corries and crags. Carn Mor Dearg is a more conical peak that, although little more than a satellite of Ben Nevis, holds its own in such exalted company by sporting one of the most famous scrambling ridges in the country: the CMD Arête.

Roads to the north-west (the A82 between Fort William and Spean Bridge) and the south-west (the Glen Nevis road) make access easy. Ben Nevis is usually climbed by the Mountain Track from Glen Nevis (Route 83a). Scramblers use this as a descent route and approach via the Carn Mor Dearg Arête (Route 83b).

The Aonachs are most easily climbed from the Nevis Range ski centre near Spean Bridge to the north (Route 85a), although they can also be reached by a scenic route from Glen Nevis to the south (Route 85b) and by an interesting off-the-beaten-path route that takes in their north-west Tops (Route 85c). Adventurous walkers can bag the Aonachs and continue to Carn Mor Dearg and Ben Nevis (Route 85a Extension 1).

The Nevis Range from the west

Tourist activity in the Nevis Range forms an important part of the local economy and there are no access restrictions during the stalking season.

Glen Nevis

Glen Nevis is the nearest geographical feature Scotland has to an Alpine valley, with green riverside pastures flanked by high mountains – the Mamores on one side and Ben Nevis on the other. As the glen is almost at sea level, and Ben Nevis is almost half as high again as some Munros, the view up the glen could be said to be the most mountainous that the Highlands have to offer.

A 7ml/11km road runs up the glen, becoming increasingly scenic as it progresses. On the left, Ben Nevis hides its great northern cliffs behind a huge, uniform mountainside, but the view ahead more than compensates, with the gleaming quartzite summit caps of Sgurr a' Mhaim and Stob Ban forming a prominent backdrop. These two Munros and others in the Mamores, on the south side of the glen, are described in *Volume 2: Central Highlands South*.

After 5ml/8km the road reaches Polldubh Falls, where a mid-river rock splits the Water of Nevis into two 12m/40ft waterfalls. The road crosses the river on two adjacent bridges and becomes a single-track road that climbs to a car park at the entrance to the Nevis Gorge. In summer, arrive early if you intend to park. Above the car park, the longest waterslide in Britain tumbles no less than 460m/1500ft down the great southern hillside of Ben Nevis, but the gorge itself is the primary attraction.

Baffies: The Visitor Centre (NN 123728) is open daily 9-5 but opening hours are subject to change, especially out of season. Call 01397-705922 to verify.

Section 17 Short Walk: The Nevis Gorge and Steall

G1 ***** NN 168691, 2ml/3km, 80m/250ft M13
used by Route 85b & Route 87a
(and Route 75a Extension 2 & Route 78a in *Central Highlands South*)

At the head of Glen Nevis, the great mountain ranges to the north (the Nevis Range) and the south (the Mamores) close in to form the Nevis Gorge, a deep ravine where the combination of crags, mixed woodland and rushing waters give it an almost Himalayan character (admittedly, on a somewhat smaller scale).

As if this wasn't lure enough, beyond the head of the gorge lies a hidden mountain sanctuary that rivals the Lost Valley of Glen Coe for scenery and serenity. It even has something to make its Glen Coe counterpart green with envy – 110m/350ft **An Steall** (*An Shtyowl*, The Waterfall), the third highest waterfall in Scotland. And for a spot of fun/terror, you'll also find here a wire tightrope that bridges the river and gives a bigger adrenaline rush than anything you'll find in an adventure playground...

From Glen Nevis road-end car park, a renovated path, sometimes carved out of the rock, runs the whole length of the gorge high above the Water of Nevis. The foaming torrent drops steeply from the plain at its head and is known as Eas an Tuill (*Ess an Too-il*, Waterfall of the Hole). As you progress it rises to meet the path, bringing you ever closer to its enormous water-worn boulders and the potholes gouged out of its flanking rock walls.

Many consider the gorge walk to be **the most outstanding short walk in the Highlands**. It is little more than a rocky promenade, although you'll probably want to use hands for balance in places, especially when the path crosses polished or wet slabs above considerable drops.

The rocky path through the Nevis Gorge

Baffies: A superb jaunt before afternoon cappuccino at a Glen Nevis watering hole. And after seeing that bridge, I'll have an extra shot of caffeine, please, garçon.

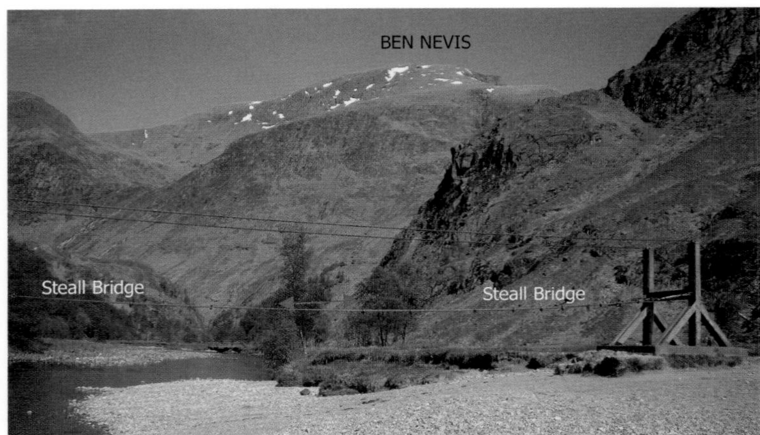

All and sundry make their way up the gorge in summer in all manner of footwear, but accidents happen, so take heed of the warning sign at the start. Hillwalkers should have little difficulty except in winter, when iced rocks can prove treacherous. Go see it in autumn, when the birches are golden and the rowans heavy with red berries.

You emerge from the gorge onto the Plain of Steall, where the Water of Nevis flows peacefully between grassy haughs beneath An Steall, which tumbles down from the Mamores. Go see it after rain, or in springtime when swollen with snowmelt, when the crashing cascade is a spectacular sight. Go see it in the evening, when the westering sun illuminates the spray between flanking buttresses of shining quartzite. In the past there have been

Crossing Steall Bridge in the 1960s, before the transverse cables were removed to make it even more exciting

The high-wire act today

The Plain of Steall

plans to turn the plain into a reservoir by damming the head of the gorge. May it never happen.

Across the river stands Steall private climbers' hut, reached by a wire bridge of three strands: one double cable for the feet and higher single cables on each side for the hands. When tackling the Mamore Munros across the river, some find that crossing the bridge is the hardest part of the route! Certainly it's not for the fainthearted, with the river racing gorge-wards beneath the swaying tightrope...

Beyond Steall, the path continues along upper Glen Nevis, penetrating remote country that will fill you with as much peace as you can handle, to Corrour, Culra and all points east. See route descriptions for further details.

Two faces of An Steall

▲83 Ben Nevis 1 1344m/4409ft (OS 41, NN 166712)
Meaning obscure. A 17th century map names the mountain Ben Novesh. An 18th century description refers to Beniviss. Possible meanings include: Ugly Mountain (from Gaelic *ni-mhaise*), Venomous Mountain (from Gaelic *neimh*), Heavenly Mountain (from Gaelic *neamh*), Mountain with Keen Atmosphere (from Gaelic *neamh*), Cloud -capped Mountain (from Gaelic *neamh-bhathais*), Terrible Mountain (from old Irish *neamheis*). Note also that *nieves* is Spanish for snows. It is also possible that the mountain is named for the glen.
∆Carn Dearg (south-west) 1020m/3347ft (OS 41, NN 155701)
Carn Jerrak, Red Cairn
∆Carn Dearg (north-west) 1221m/4407ft (OS 41, NN 159719)
Carn Jerrak, Red Cairn

▲84 Carn Mor Dearg 9 1220m/4003ft (OS 41, NN 177721)
Carn Mor Jerrak, Big Red Cairn
∆Carn Dearg Meadhonach 1179m/3869ft (OS 41, NN 176726)
Carn Jerrak Mee-onach, Middle Red Cairn

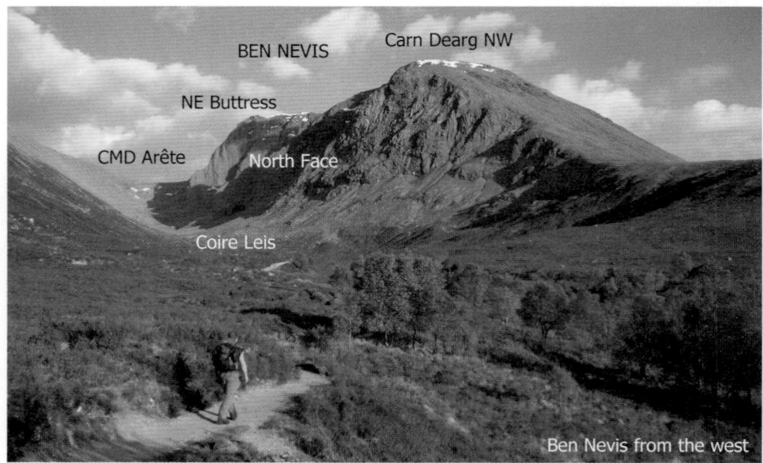

Ben Nevis from the west

Peak Fitness: No change to existing Munros and Tops since 1891 tables. Carn Beag Dearg (NN 171737, *Bake*, Little) was an additional Top until 1981.

Ben Nevis is some mountain. If you were going to choose a mountain that, as the highest in the land, was going to represent your country, you could do worse than choose the Ben*. For a start, it's a big mountain, not only because of its height, which almost pushes the summit up to the snowline for its latitude, but also because of its huge bulk. When viewed from sea-level at Fort William or in Glen Nevis, its massive dome-like appearance will leave you in no doubt as to the effort required to climb it.

The normal route is the Mountain Track, which winds its seemingly endless way up the enormous, convex hillside above Glen Nevis (Route 83a). But this is only half the story, because in reality the Ben is only a *half*-dome. On its hidden north side, fringing the deep bowl of Coire Leis (*Corra Laish*, Sheltered Corrie), is a 1ml/1½km-long, 600m/2000ft-high north face that has **Alpine scale and presence**. Here, where snow often lies all year round (or at least used to), are rock and ice climbs of world-wide significance. You'll get close-up views of the face from the summit plateau.

And there's more. The Ben is connected to the adjacent summit of Carn Mor Dearg by a graceful arête that curves around the head of Coire Leis. Carn Mor Dearg itself is easily reached from Coire Leis (Route 83b) or via its east ridge (Route 83c), but the arête is the main draw. Affectionately known as the CMD Arête, its traverse is nowhere harder than a G4 scramble and gives an exciting ridge walk that ranks alongside any in Scotland (Route 83b Extension 1).

In short, the Ben fittingly encapsulates every aspect of the Highland walking and climbing experience. Does size matter? Is biggest best? We'll let you decide. One thing's for sure: Respect is due.

Summit cornice

* You are allowed to refer to the mountain in such familiar fashion only after you have climbed it. Beware: we license Terminator to enforce strict adherence to this rule.

Terminator: On a mountain as complex as the Ben, there are bound to be a number of off-the-beaten-path routes in addition to the ones described in this section. None of them are easy.

One relentlessly steep way up begins at Glen Nevis road end, climbs to the east rim of Coire Eoghainn and finishes up the rockpile of the Ben's south-east slopes. Unsurprisingly, few people venture here.

Expert scramblers have other options. Carn Dearg Meadhonach's east ridge gives an exposed but relatively easy scramble above the little visited glen of the Allt Daim. Ledge Route, which finishes up the narrow crest of Carn Dearg Buttress, is a harder scramble above awesome drops.

There are still harder routes on the Ben's north face that blur the boundary between scrambling and rock climbing. Apparently, such routes are outwith the remit of a Munros hillwalking guide.

A Potted History

The earliest recorded ascents of Ben Nevis took place in the eighteenth century to aid research into developing sciences such as botany and geology. Interest in climbing the mountain for its own sake gathered pace only after a series of fortuitous events a century later. In 1883 a meteorological observatory was built at the summit, together with a pony access track that is now the route taken by the Mountain Track. In 1889 the Scottish Mountaineering Club was formed and in 1894 the West Highland Railway reached Fort William.

As a result, the last decade of the nineteenth century became a Golden Age of Scottish Mountaineering. As the major lines on the great buttresses, ridges, faces and gullies of the north face were picked off, it became obvious that Scotland had climbs to rival those being pioneered in the Alps.

For English mountaineer and SMC member Norman Collie, Tower Ridge resembled the Italian side of the Matterhorn. After Collie's first ascent of it in 1894, Scot Bill Naismith (of Rule fame) wrote of his achievement, 'This is truly a sad day for auld Scotland. Flodden or even Culloden was nothing to this'. Over the years such friendly cross-border rivalry has continued to characterise much of north face climbing. When Joe Brown and Don Whillans beat Scottish rivals to a much-coveted line on Carn Dearg Buttress above the CIC Hut in 1954, they incorrigibly named it Sassenach.

In the early days the person who made most ascents was Clement Wragge. In the two years preceding the opening of the observatory, he climbed to the summit every day between June and October to take meteorological measurements. For the state in which this endeavour sometimes left him, he earned the nickname Inclement Rag.

The observatory was built to record 'the diversity of the mountain environment'. It operated from 1883 to 1904 and was later used as part of a summer 'hotel' that lasted until the end of the First World War. At that time there was a toll-gate where walkers ascending the newly-built pony track paid a fee: one shilling (5p) on foot, three shillings (15p) on horseback and twenty-one shillings

(105p) for hire of a pony and guide.

In 1929 access to the north face was improved when the SMC built a hut in Coire Leis. It was named the Charles Inglis Clark Memorial Hut for a club member killed in the First World War. The modern CIC Hut, still in private SMC hands, is more popular among climbers than ever.

Throughout the twentieth century, Ben Nevis continued to be at the forefront of rock and ice climbing advances, while the post-Second World War explosion in hillwalking saw it become ever more crowded.

In 2000 the summit area was purchased by the John Muir Trust and given a clean-up. Volunteers removed tons of litter and a clutter of personal memorials, which were replaced by a collective memorial built near a new Visitor Centre in Glen Nevis in 2006. Designated a Site for Contemplation, the memorial stands in the woods just beyond the north end of the car park.

All cairns except the summit cairn, a Peace Cairn war memorial and others used to aid navigation were removed. Uninformed visitors still erect more that have to be dismantled to prevent routefinding confusion.

The ruined walls of the observatory still stand. The remains of its tower are crowned by an emergency bivouac shelter, raised high above winter snows. Other emergency shelters near Carn Dearg North-west (NN 158718) and in upper Coire Leis (NN 174714) were removed in 2004 as they were often buried in snow and difficult to locate when most needed. Aluminium markers at the head of No. 4 Gully (a traditional climbers' descent route to Coire Leis) and on the CMD Arête (see Page 23) were also removed.

In 2003 the JMT and other bodies formed the Nevis Partnership. Great progress was made in path restoration and environmental and visitor management, but lack of funding caused the body's closure in 2011. Let us hope that, under the continuing stewardship of the JMT, the Ben is nevertheless finally in hands that will ensure its continued well-being for those who come after us.

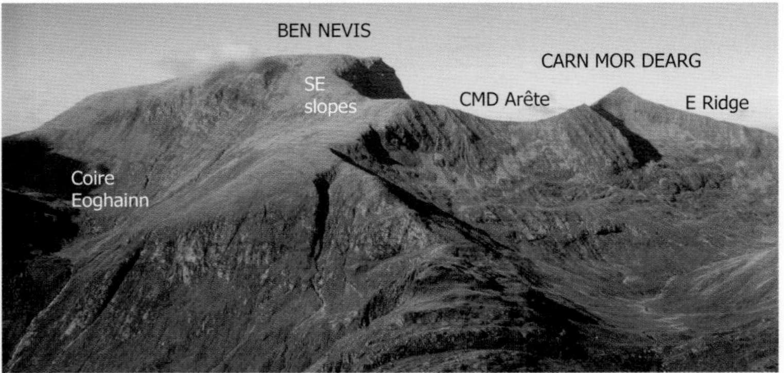

Route 83a Ben Nevis from Glen Nevis: The Mountain Track

G1 **** 9ml/14km, 1340m/4400ft M12 Starting points: Visitor Centre (NN 123731), Achintee (NN 126729), Youth Hostel (NN 128718)

This seemingly interminable manufactured highway to the heights isn't everyone's bowl of porridge. Pejoratively known as the 'Tourist Path', it has misled many a tourist into underestimating the effort required to ascend it.

Not only is Ben Nevis almost a Munro-and-a-half in height, but the ascent begins virtually at sea level. The height to be climbed is twice as much as on many inland Munros. Then there's the nature of the path – a 4½ml/7km ribbon of stone and rubble up a vast mountainside that is as wearisome to descend as to ascend and which hides the summit until the very last.

Some may think it deserves a Route Rage Alert, but that would be too churlish. Without its staircases and switchbacks of rock and rubble, the track would become dangerously eroded (as it was before restoration) and unable to withstand the 160,000+ ascents it currently receives each year.

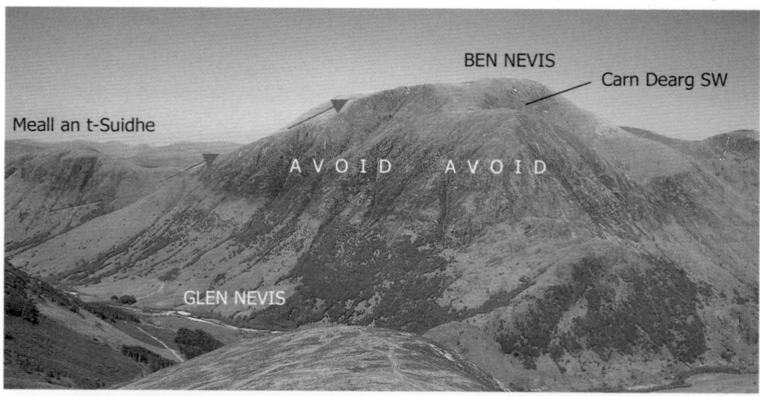

Terminator: The south-west slopes of Ben Nevis above Glen Nevis are the longest and steepest in Britain. Above Polldubh they rise some 1200m/4000ft at an average angle of 35° and are riven by giant gullies. Coire Ghaimhnean is split by Five Finger Gully. To its right are Antler Gully and Surgeon's Gully, which gives the longest and most continuously difficult gully climb in Scotland. To the right again are more deep gullies. The convex slopes above descend benignly from the summit plateau before funnelling into the gullies and trapping anyone who has strayed off-route in cloud. This is the major cause of accidents on the mountain.

Baffies: After the main railway reached Fort William in 1894, there were plans to build a rack railway up Ben Nevis to service the observatory. If it's good enough for the highest peak in Wales...

At the summit 'hotel' that replaced the observatory at the start of the twentieth century, lunch cost three shillings (15p) and an overnight stay cost ten shillings (50p). Now that's what I call civilised.

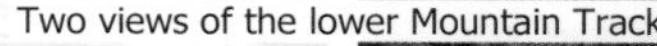

Two views of the lower Mountain Track

Although a prolonged slogathon, it does provide an easy way up the highest Munro of all, its completion engenders a rare feeling of accomplishment, and the summit is an amazing place whichever way you get there. Controversially, we award the route as many as four stars.

The track has three starting points. One begins at the Ben Nevis Inn, at the end of the short road to Achintee on the north side of the River Nevis. This is the time-honoured approach, following the line of the observatory pony track. A newer second approach begins across the River Nevis from Achintee, at a bridge near the Visitor Centre on the Glen Nevis road. The third approach begins a short distance further down the road at the bridge opposite the Youth Hostel.

Despite a small parking fee and the unavailability of refreshments (apart from a vending machine), the Visitor Centre, with extensive parking and toilet facilities, is the normal starting point nowadays. The path bridges the River Nevis at the north end of the car park and joins the Achintee path 120m beyond its start, adding negligible distance to the day.

The Ben Nevis Inn has free parking and refreshments. The YH path, from very limited roadside parking, climbs steeply up the hillside to join the main path at the 170m/550ft contour.

Torpedo: To add interest to an ascent of the Mountain Track, why not go for a record? The fastest time for the Ben Nevis Race, up and down from Claggan Park in Fort William, stands at under 1½ hours (that's right – one and a half hours).

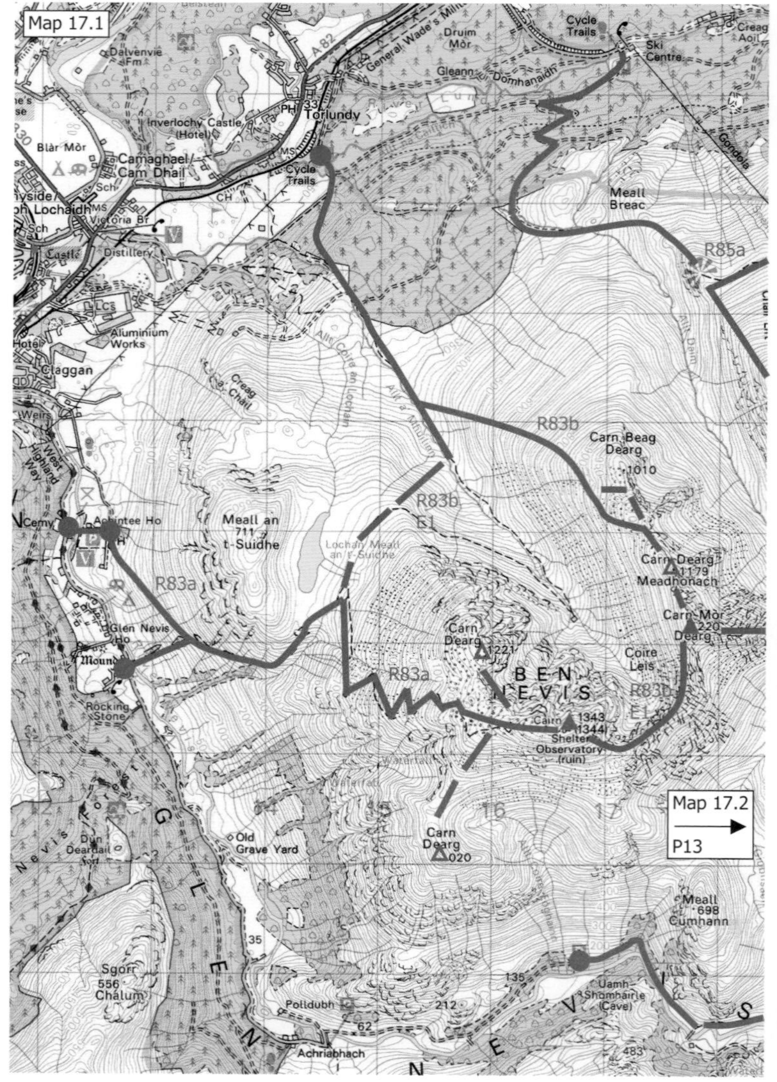
Map 17.1
Map 17.2
P13
R83a
R83b
R83b E1
R85a
BEN NEVIS
Torlundy
Cycle Trails
Ski Centre
Meall Breac
Carn Beag Dearg
Carn Dearg Meadhonach
Carn Mòr Dearg
Coire Leis
Carn Dearg
Meall an t-Suidhe
Lochan Meall an t-Suidhe
Achintee Ho
Glen Nevis Ho
Inverlochy Castle (Hotel)
Aluminium Works
Claggan
Gondola
Observatory (ruin)
Old Grave Yard
Polldubh
Achriabhach
Sgorr Chalum
Meall Cumhann
Uamh-Shomhairle (Cave)
Dun Deardail fort
Rocking Stone

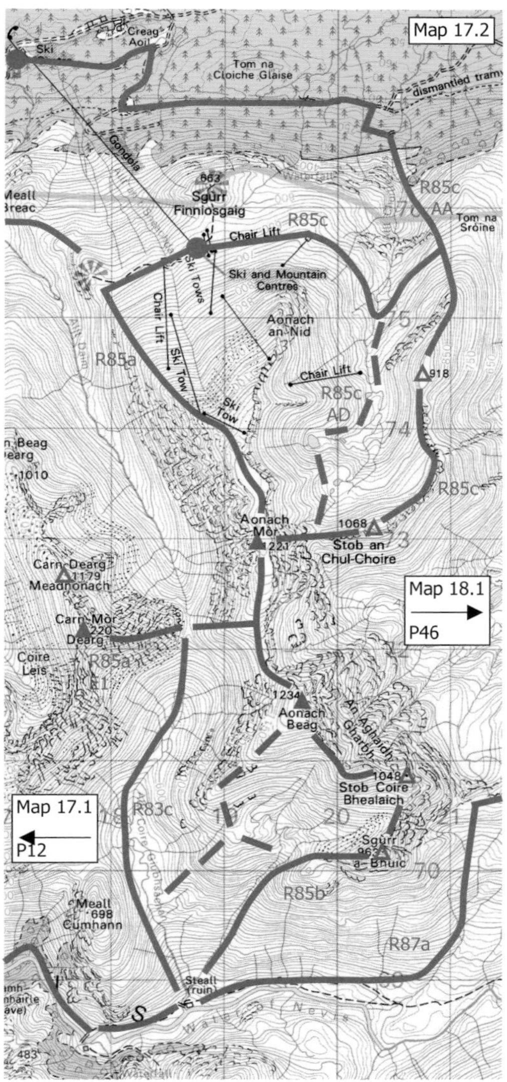

For further directions we could offer you the same advice as for Ben Lomond and suggest that you simply follow the person in front of you. But even if you find yourself in the newsworthy position of being the only person on the mountain, it would require negligence in the extreme to stray off-route on a clear day.

In its lower half, the track curves upwards around the south and east slopes of Meall an t-Suidhe (*Myowl an Tu-ya*, aka *Melon Tea*, Hill of the Seat), a lowly hill on the Ben's north-west flanks. The surface has been 'stabilised' to such an extent that it is more a rock staircase *cum* boulder hop than a path.

The angle eases as it climbs onto the saddle east of Meall an t-Suidhe, where Lochan Meall an t-Suidhe nestles beneath Carn Dearg North-west. At a height of 630m/ 2050ft on the saddle, a T-junction marks the approximate half-way point.

The left branch crosses the saddle to Coire Leis (see Page 22). The Mountain Track cuts back sharp right across the stony slopes of Carn Dearg to the Red Burn (*Dearg* is Gaelic for Red). This is the more common name for the Allt na h-Urchaire, which tumbles down from Coire h-Urchaire (*Corra na Hoora-churra*, Corrie of the Shot) above.

Beyond the Red Burn the track reaches a sharp left-hand bend that marks a major turning point. Above here, it deteriorates into a stony

Descending the zigzags

GiGi: We hope you have better weather than poet John Keats did when he climbed Ben Nevis in 1818. As he wrote wistfully in a sonnet he composed at the summit, 'I look into the Chasms and a Shroud Vaprous doth hide them'.

MacLean's Steep

highway that zigzags up the Ben's north-west shoulder. As height is gained, views expand over Glen Nevis to the Mamores, but in reality you're likely to have eyes only for the next rubbly zig or zag and wonder if the summit will ever hove into sight.

Four major zigzags (follow the track left and right four times) take you up to a stone windbreak at the 1200m contour. Here the track turns left to begin the crossing of the wilderness of broken rock that forms the Roof of Britain. N.B. Ignore a side path that goes straight on above the depths of Five Finger Gully, which has claimed many lives (see Needlepoint).

A series of pyramid-shaped stone cairns, each 1.8m tall, now line the track at 50m intervals to aid foul-weather navigation. After 400m, and now less than 600m from the summit, you reach the last steepening, known as MacLean's Steep (for the local contractor who built the observatory). Cairns 8 to 11 take you up MacLean's

Summit architecture

GiGi: There is much to see on the summit plateau, including the Peace Cairn, the ruins of the observatory, the emergency shelter and, of course, the north face with its monumental crags and gullies. Gardyloo Gully was the gully into which observatory staff tipped their rubbish, the name deriving from the warning shout used in old Edinburgh when rubbish was tipped out of the window onto the street. 'Gardyloo' is an Anglicisation of the French *Garde de l'eau*, meaning Beware of the Water.

Steep, then the remaining cairns veer right, away from the track (but useful when it is snow-covered).

Above MacLean's Steep the track tops out on the Ben's summit plateau close to the edge of the north face. The ▲summit itself is now close at hand, seen across the rim of Gardyloo Gully, the north face's most deep-cut indentation. It is necessary to go around the rim of this gully to reach the summit plinth. If there is snow on the ground, give the rim a wide berth as its enormous cornice can be mistaken for solid ground. Take especial care in cloud. A triangle of three cairns beyond the lip marks the presence of solid ground.

After suitable R&R, pick your way back down the Mountain Track with care, especially the rocky lower half. Its unrelenting nature is such that anyone with dodgy knees can expect to lose any remaining cartilage.

GiGi: Even the summit plateau holds little respite for weary hillwalkers as it is covered by *felsenmeer* or *blockfield* – a patchwork of broken rocks and boulders formed by a series of freeze-thaw cycles during the last Ice Age. For easy walking, it does not make. The sharpest rocks, on which a slip would be painful, lie east of the summit cairn and therefore must be crossed only when approached from the CMD Arête.

The summit in spring

F-Stop: The best roadside views of Ben Nevis, with light on the north face, are obtained from the west in the evening, e.g. the B8004 north of Corpach. The best viewpoints on the hill are Carn Mor Dearg and the entrance to Coire Leis.

The view from the summit is as extensive as you would expect, there being no point higher in the whole country. But for that very reason it loses its power, because neighbouring mountains seem less imposing.

To compensate, there's more than enough wow factor in the immediate vicinity, courtesy of the cliff edge of the north face. The most prominent feature on the face is the classic Tower Ridge. The notch behind the Great Tower is Tower Gap, the crossing of which gives many a climber pause for thought.

If you have time, pick your way across the blockfield to the east end of the plateau, where the top of the North-east Buttress gives superb views back along the cliffs and from where you can look down on the seeming tightrope of the CMD Arête.

Finally, for a scenic viewpoint above Fort William that also gives good views of the upper Mountain Track, Meall an t-Suidhe makes a great evening objective.

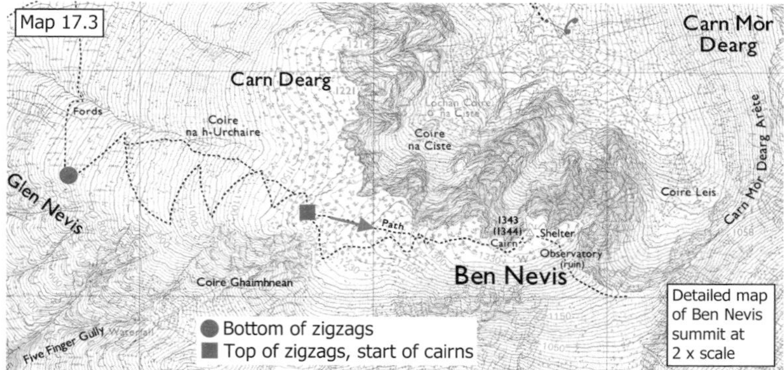

Needlepoint: Don't let the Mountain Track fool you into thinking that the summit of Ben Nevis is an easy target. It is in cloud for 70% of the year, annual rainfall (4300ml+) is more than twice that at the mountain's foot, the old observatory recorded 261 gales per year and the average temperature is below freezing.

Not only that, but the summit plateau is notoriously dangerous to get off in cloud. So many people have been killed here (mostly in winter) that in 1994 the Ben had the dubious distinction of overtaking the Eiger as the most lethal mountain in Europe. Of course, it doesn't help that you'll see attire here more suited to Fort William High Street than the roof of Britain.

The Mountain Track is pretty obvious most of the way but near the summit it is indistinct among rocks, and it may also be obscured by snow even in summer. On descent, it is important to avoid Gardyloo Gully on the right (north), but take care not to veer too far left (south), into the steepening confines of Five Finger Gully, the top of which lies c.800m from the top of Gardyloo Gully. If you find yourself on steeper ground dropping away to the south or west, you're too far left.

To clear the plateau from the summit, the correct initial grid bearing is 231° (+ magnetic variation, which was 3° west in 2007 years, i.e. 234°), decreasing by 1° every six years. Follow this bearing for 150m, to clear Gardyloo Gully, then follow 282° (+ magnetic variation) to clear the summit plateau. After 300m level going on this bearing, a steeper section of 100m (MacLean's Steep) leads down to easier ground and then, after another 400m, to the windbreak at the top of the zigzags (NN 157713).

To ease routefinding, a line of pyramid-shaped stone cairns, placed at c.50m intervals, has been constructed to mark a safe route off the plateau. From the summit, two cairns point the way to a triangle of cairns near the lip of Gardyloo Gully. The remaining cairns take you down to the top of the zigzags. However, even though 1.8m tall, these cairns may disappear beneath snow.

If the zigzags are under snow, keep to the 282° bearing until you can follow the track right (north) across the Red Burn to the Meall an t-Suidhe saddle. Avoid a diagonal short cut as this may lead you onto steep ground around the Red Burn.

A leaflet 'Navigation on Ben Nevis' is available locally (e.g. at the Visitor Centre) or visit www.mountaineering-scotland.org.uk/ben-nevis-navigation.asp

Torpedo: The Ben has two lower Tops, both confusingly called Carn Dearg. Would a tad more nomenclatural imagination have been too much to ask for?

ΔCarn Dearg South-west lies at the end of a broad ridge that curves southwards from the west end of the summit plateau, forming the dividing line between Coire Ghaimhnean and Coire Eoghainn. It's a good viewpoint over Glen Nevis, requiring only a 30m/100ft ascent from the intervening bealach, but it is rarely visited owing to the 360m/1200ft return climb back up to the plateau.

ΔCarn Dearg North-west is the highpoint at the north-west end of the summit plateau, near the top of Carn Dearg Buttress, and is a much more interesting spot to visit. The walk to it along the cliff edge of the north face, again requiring an ascent of only 30m/100ft, gives ever-changing views of matchless crag and corrie scenery. Walk a further 300m, to the top of Carn Dearg Buttress, and you can look down Ledge Route (see Page 7).

From here, it is tempting to make a direct descent to the Mountain Track, but the steep slopes that fall to the south-west are best avoided. Instead, return south, towards the Ben's summit, and contour across flatter ground in upper Coire na h-Urchaire to join the track higher up.

The Roof of Britain

Viewed across Gardyloo Gully

Chilly Willy: In winter the summit is a spectacular but dangerous place because of enormous, overhanging cornices that accumulate above north face gullies. The cornice above Gardyloo Gully has been known to extend horizontally for five metres, a phenomenon that enabled pioneer climbers tunnelling through it to stop for a sheltered brew-up.

Much to the astonishment of innocent tourists, these cornices often survive well into early summer. In such conditions, and especially in poor visibility, stay well back from the edge. Venture to what you think is the edge and you may well find space beneath your feet (but not for long).

Routefinding problems on the summit plateau are multiplied when the Mountain Track is obliterated by snow. On good days it is usually possible to follow footprints in the snow, but blizzards can cover tracks in a remarkably short space of time. In such conditions, it would be prudent to reverse tracks before they disappear.

Route 83b Carn Mor Dearg via Coire Leis from North Face car park (Torlundy)

G2 **** NN 144764, 8ml/13km, 1350m/4450ft M12

Far from the Glen Nevis crowds on the south side of the mountain, the Ben reveals its true stature to those who approach from the north via Carn Mor Dearg and the CMD Arête. You can, of course, climb Carn Mor Dearg alone, return without crossing the arête and climb Ben Nevis by the Mountain Track on another day. This is certainly the easiest way to climb both Munros but, once up Carn Mor Dearg, that curving arête is very tempting...

The approach route to Carn Mor Dearg begins at the north face car park near Torlundy (signposted off the A82). The formerly notoriously boggy path was fully renovated in 2007 and now gives excellent walking.

From the far end of the car park, take the track signposted 'Access to the north face'. Leave it after c.130m for a path on the right that climbs steeply through the forest to join a Land Rover track. Follow this uphill for 150m to a T-junction, then turn right (still signposted) to reach the track end at the upper forest boundary after another 150m. Here, at the entrance to Coire Leis beside the Allt a' Mhuilinn (*Owlt a Voolin*, Mill Stream), you'll want to pause to take in your first view of north face architecture (picture on Page 6). Privileged individuals who belong to the right organisations can drive to this point on forest tracks.

A stile gives access to the continuing excellent path, which runs up the corrie beside the stream. After around 1000m or so, the muddy path to Carn Mor Dearg branches left. It is easy to miss so keep an eye out for it. When the main path rises left around a hillock and bends back right just beyond a couple of rowan trees, the Carn Mor Dearg path goes straight on at the right-hand bend.

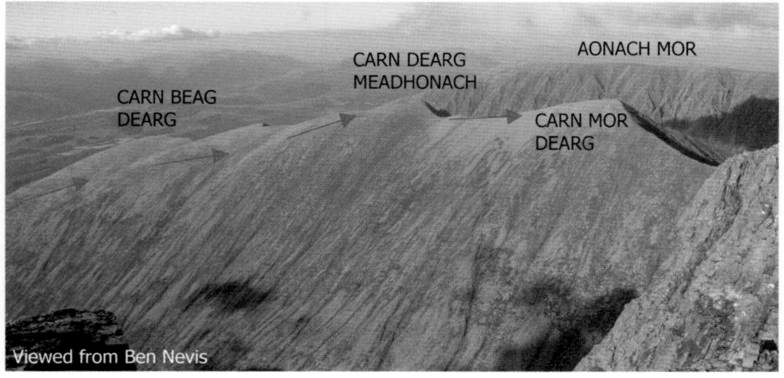

Viewed from Ben Nevis

The path is very boggy at first but improves with height on slopes of grass and heather. You'd think it would head straight for Carn Beag Dearg, but instead it contours right to reach the skyline further along, at a brief levelling just below Carn Dearg Meadhonach.

As the path eventually becomes steep and eroded, you may well decide to climb easy grass slopes to reach the skyline earlier and obtain more panoramic views. Whichever way you go, the ascent is one considerable slog. Before leaving ΔCarn Dearg Meadhonach, take a peek down the pinnacled east ridge, the final rock tower of which provides a challenge for experienced scramblers.

A shallow, bouldery dip of only c.30m/100ft (but enough for Carn Dearg Meadhonach to retain its Top status) is now all that separates you from ▲Carn Mor Dearg itself, whose pink granite boulders give all the Carn Dearg peaks their name.

The summit is a viewpoint eyrie at the apex of three ridges. Apart from the north ridge by which you have arrived, the south ridge leads down to the CMD Arête and the narrow east ridge offers an alternative ascent route (Route 83c). But it is the Ben's towering north face crags, seen to perfection across Coire Leis, that hold the gaze.

Route 83b Extension 1: Ben Nevis via the CMD Arête

G4 ***** Carn Mor Dearg + Ben Nevis: 9½ml/15km, 1650m/5400ft M12

The CMD Arête is sometimes spoken of in the same breath as Aonach Eagach (Route 71c) but it is nowhere near as hard. Sassenachs who have crossed Striding Edge on Helvellyn in the English Ponds (aka the Lake District) will find this of a similar standard.

Much of the crest is formed of jumbled andesite blocks, sometimes exposed but requiring little handwork. A few spots demand easy G4 scrambling while a path below the crest takes a line that is barely more than G3. Despite the lack of any great difficulty, the arête nevertheless has a justified reputation for excitement. With the Ben's north face looming across Coire Leis, and big drops all round, it has a real mountaineering flavour. If you thrill to such challenges, we suspect the CMD Arête will come to rank highly on your all-time list of favourite routes.

The CMD Arête beckons

We describe the route in some detail so that you can decide if it's a viable option for you. From the summit of Carn Mor Dearg to the summit of the Ben, the 1½ml/2km route can be viewed as having four sections.

1. A gritty path descends c.100m/330ft among rock rubble to the start of the ridge proper.

2. A level section of andesite blocks runs out to a point where the ridge turns sharp right. If you have sufficient nerve and balletic prowess, this section resembles a roof-top boulder-hop, punctuated by an occasional easy scramble. A path below the crest takes an easier line. Whichever route you choose, the proximity of the Ben's north face, and of the towering North-east Buttress especially, begins to give the traverse an air of seriousness out of all proportion to its difficulty.

3. After the ridge turns right, the going eases for a while on a 70m/250ft descent to the low point of the arête at 1058m/3472ft. Then things become rockier again on ascent to a prominent point, where the arête abuts against the Ben's sprawling south-east slopes. Just before the point, the path stays well down on the left to avoid a nerve-testing section atop a wall of rock on the crest.

4. Just beyond the point, with all scrambling now over, a small saddle is reached at the foot of the rockpile that forms the Ben's upper south-east slopes. The 250m/800ft ascent from here to the ▲summit is a tough slog. It may not require scrambling ability, but you'll be unlikely to maintain an upright posture throughout.

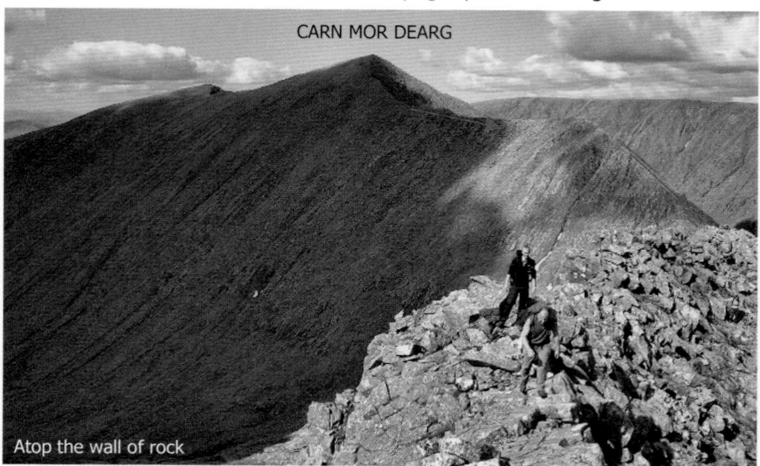

Atop the wall of rock

Having taken your fill of the summit environment, descend the upper half of the Mountain Track. Leave it at the T-junction above Lochan Meall an t-Suidhe (NN 147724) for the path that crosses the saddle to descend to the CIC Hut in Coire Leis.

Stay right at a fork after 400m. The left branch, dubbed the Path to Nowhere at the time of writing, ends at the mouth of the lochan. It is to be hoped that it will be extended in the

! Until it was removed by the JMT, there was a marker post on the saddle indicating a line of abseil posts down into Coire Leis. Although it is *possible* to make a way down the steep headwall of loose rock and hidden crags, you'll probably agree, once you look over the edge, that any attempt to do so would probably land you in more difficulty than you bargained for. Avoid.

Awkwardly soft snow conditions on Section 3 of the CMD Arête

future to form the Ben's Missing Link – a connecting path between the Mountain Track and the Torlundy path.

Currently, unless you wish to make a long detour via the CIC Hut, it is necessary to leave the Coire Leis path to descend a 200m/650ft hillside of tangled grass and heather to reach the Torlundy path on the far side of the Allt a' Mhuilinn. Then, finally, if you still have the energy, you can motor back down to the north face car park.

Needlepoint: Even if you lose the path, finding your way up and down Carn Beag Dearg should remain easy in cloud. Ditto the narrow ridge leading to Carn Mor Dearg and the continuing CMD Arête. You'll have more difficulty navigating across the boulders that litter the eastern end of the Ben's summit plateau. As always at the summit of the Ben, take especial care if there is any snow around.

Chilly Willy: In winter, the ascent of Carn Beag Dearg remains easy. The connecting ridge to Carn Mor Dearg has no technical difficulty but big drops all around may unnerve some. The CMD Arête is a different matter. With the requisite ability and equipment, its traverse is **an Alpine outing**. At its finest it becomes, in places, a knife-edge of snow. Compression caused by the passage of boots creates a narrow sky-high walkway in a superb situation.

However, conditions on the arête vary considerably and it is certainly no place for anyone lacking winter experience. Whether there is soft snow on the path and the rocks, or less snow and more ice, or so much snow that the path is obliterated, the traverse is a serious proposition.

Note also that the final bouldery ascent to the Ben's summit plateau becomes an infinitely more serious proposition in winter than in summer. Because the slope faces south-east, freeze/thaw cycles can turn it into a dangerously smooth ice sheet. This situation can prevail into early summer, even when the CMD Arête itself is snow-free. If unsure of conditions, carry ice-axe and crampons in case.

The slog up the Ben's SE slopes

Route 83c Carn Mor Dearg East Ridge from Glen Nevis

G3 *** NN 168691, 9ml/14km, 1170m/3850ft M12

Carn Mor Dearg's east ridge is by far the best ascent route on the mountain. Unfortunately, reaching its foot is such a hassle that it can hardly be recommended over the standard route from Coire Leis. It also leaves you with no easy return route if you cross the CMD Arête to Ben Nevis (but see Route 85a Extension 1 on Page 30). We describe it for the sake of intrepid souls who are not dissuaded by a rough approach.

From Glen Nevis road end, take the path through the Nevis Gorge to the bridge over the Allt Coire Giubhsachan, as described on Page 32. Leave the main path here for another that climbs the left-hand side of the stream onto the flats of hidden Coire Giubhsachan, sandwiched between the huge mountainsides of Ben Nevis and Aonach Beag.

If the path were in a better state, this would be an approach to rival that of Coire Leis. But it isn't. It is so rough and boggy that you'll spend more time off it than on it, resulting in slow and tiring progress.

Not until you reach the 830m/2725ft bealach at the head of the corrie and the foot of Carn Mor Dearg's east ridge do matters improve. But at least they improve dramatically. The 390m/280ft ascent to the ▲summit manages to be both easy and exhilarating. Broad broken slopes rise to a narrow, curving ridge whose crest of shattered rocks and grass requires no more than a spot of handwork in places. The upper section is a scenic aerial highway that finishes all too soon.

Picture of E Ridge on Page 31

▲85 Aonach Beag 7 1234m/4048ft (OS 41, NN 196715)
Ernach Bake, Little Ridge (not to be confused with namesake ▲101)
∆Stob Coire Bhealaich 1100m/ft (OS 41, NN 202709)
Stop Corra Vyalich, Peak of the Corrie of the Pass
∆Sgurr a' Bhuic 963m/ft (OS 41, NN 204701)
Skoor a Voo-ichk, Peak of the Roe Buck)

▲86 Aonach Mor 8 1221m/4006ft (OS 41, NN 192729)
Ernach Mor, Big Ridge
∆Stob an Cul Choire 1068m/ (OS 41, NN 203731)
Stop an Cool Corra, Peak of the Back Corrie)
∆Tom na Sroine 918m/3012ft (OS 41, NN 207745)
Toum na Strawna, Knoll of the Nose)

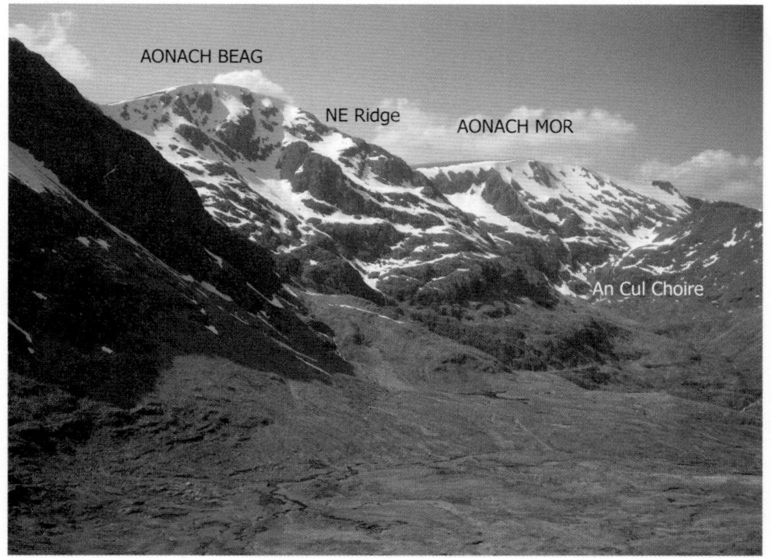

Peak Fitness: No change to existing Munros and Tops since original Tables. Stob Coire an Fhir Dhuibh (*Stop Corran Eer Ghoo-y*, Peak of the Corrie of the Black Man, NN 208735) was also a Top from 1891 to 1981.

Immediately east of Ben Nevis and Carn Mor Dearg lie two more big mountains that would be better appreciated were it not for the commanding presence of the Ben. Their Cairngorm-like summit plateaus would certainly win no prizes in a beauty contest yet they have immense presence and stand atop some colossal scenery. Interestingly, the so-called Little Aonach is higher than the Big Aonach, probably because the mountains were named from below for their bulk rather than their height.

The two summits rim an immense eastern wall, over 3ml/5km long, that rivals the Ben's north face for **Alpine scale and grandeur**. The cliffs are indented by a series of huge corries named the Back Corries after the most outstanding of them – An Cul Choire (*An Cool Chorra*, The Back Corrie).

Access to the summits has been revolutionised in recent years by the Nevis Range ski development in Aonach Mor's north-west corrie (Coire an t-Sneachda, *Corran Trechka*, Snowy Corrie). The usual approach is now from the Nevis Range car park, using the gondola to gain 550m/1800ft of initial height and start the walk 650m/2150ft above sea-level (Route 85a). You may think that's cheating, but at the time of writing there is no dedicated path for walkers between the base station and the top station.

A southern approach from Glen Nevis is now understandably less popular, even though it approaches along the edge of the eastern cliffs, bags Aonach Beag's two satellite Tops *en route* and is infinitely more scenic (Route 85b). For those in search of even more adventurous fare, there's a third approach from the east that takes you to the heart of the Back Corries via Aonach Mor's two satellite Tops (Route 85c).

The Aonachs are linked to Carn Mor Dearg by an 830m/2700ft bealach, making it possible for fit and adventurous types to bag all four Nevis Range Munros in one memorable expedition (Route 85a Extension 1).

Terminator: The formidable headwall of An Cul Choire boasts climbs to rival those on the north face of Ben Nevis. Their remoteness ensures that they will always remain less popular, but for that same reason they retain a real pioneering flavour. The classic NE Ridge beneath the summit of Aonach Beag was first climbed in winter conditions in April 1895 by a party that included Bill Naismith of Rule fame.

Route 85a Aonach Beag and Aonach Mor from Nevis Range car park via Coire an t-Sneachda

G1 ***** NN 172774 M13
Using gondola: 6ml/10km, 880m/2900ft
Avoiding gondola: 11ml/18km, 1430m/4700ft
(includes Aonach Mor to Aonach Beag return: 2ml/3km, 290m/950ft)

The Nevis Range ski development is friendlier to mountain bikers than it is to hillwalkers. A purpose-built mountain bike trail, which has obliterated the former path, runs from the gondola top station to the car park, but at the time of writing its use by walkers is severely restricted.

During the biking season (mid-May to mid-September) walkers are allowed to use the trail only outside operational hours (around 9.30 to 18.00), which leaves little room for manoeuvre.

Eschewing the gondola, you can use forest tracks to reach open hillside under your own steam, but respect is due to anyone who has the motivation to do so. Make a note of the following directions anyway, in case the gondola is closed.

From the car park, follow forest tracks into the glen of the Allt Daim, aiming for the track-end at NN 167757. From here, climb to the ridge on the left, which separates the Allt Daim from Coire an t-Sneachda, then continue up to a bump on the ridge called Meall Beag (*Myowl Bake*, Little Hill, NN 178753, named only on OS

GiGi: Coire an t-Sneachda's spring snowfield melts into the shape of a goose, hence the name of the top station restaurant.

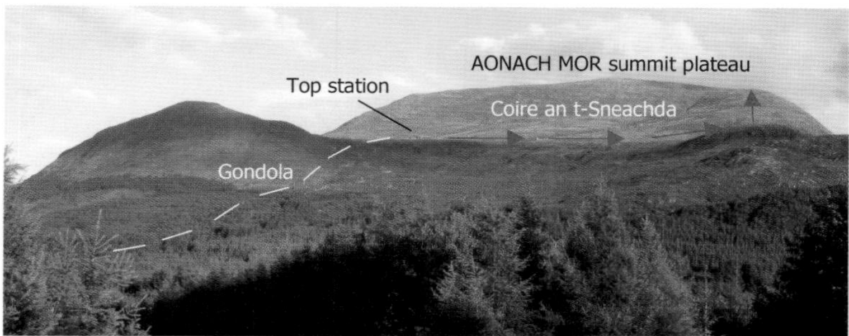

Baffies: This is more like it! As on the best Alpine walks, you can obtain refreshment at the foot of the mountain in the Pinemarten Coffee Shop and half-way up (and down) at the gondola top station in the Snowgoose Restaurant, where there's also a shop and a mountain discovery centre. Don't forget to carry pocket money.

Nevis Range information. The gondola runs all year round, except mid-November to mid-December, when it is closed for annual maintenance. During the skiing season it runs from 9.00 (8.30 at week-ends) to dusk (around 16.00). During July and August it runs from 9.30 to 18.00. At other times it runs from 10.00 to 17.00. In winter, a chairlift can be used to gain more height (see Chilly Willy). Verify this information and view a webcam at www.nevisrange.co.uk or call 01397-705825.

AONACH MOR

1:25,000 map). If using the gondola, a dirt road contours across Coire an t-Sneachda from the top station to Meall Beag.

Above Meall Beag, the broad ridge forms the corrie's west-bounding rim and gives an easy ascent to Aonach Mor's summit plateau. With height, a path becomes increasingly distinct on grass among boulders. At a height of 1100m/3600ft (NN 188741) you'll reach a ski tow and associated snow fencing that can be followed all the way up to the plateau. The tow tops out right at the rim of the east face above Coire an Lochain, the first of the Back Corries.

N.B. From the dirt road that crosses Coire an t-Sneachda from the gondola top station, it is possible to take a diagonal short cut up to the ridge to avoid the dog-leg via Meall Beag, but any line here (even on traces of paths) is likely to enmesh you in bog and snow fencing.

Aonach Mor's tundra-like summit plateau is virtually level for hundreds of metres. Simply follow the cliff edge or take a more direct line to reach the ▲summit cairn, set 100m back from the edge. Note the rugged rib that descends below the cairn to Stob an Cul Choire (Route 85c).

Continuing to Aonach Beag on mossy terrain, an earthy path descends gently to the intervening 1080m/3550ft saddle, rimming the vast hollow of An Cul Choire. The corrie's huge crags rise to Aonach Beag's summit and a zigzagging path picks out the easiest line up steep slopes of rock and rubble beside them.

Torpedo: If you need a cure for a Hogmanay hangover, the annual Ne'er Day Aonach Mor Uphill Race could be just the tonic you're looking for. Base station to top station via the mountain bike track in under half an hour. How could one resist?

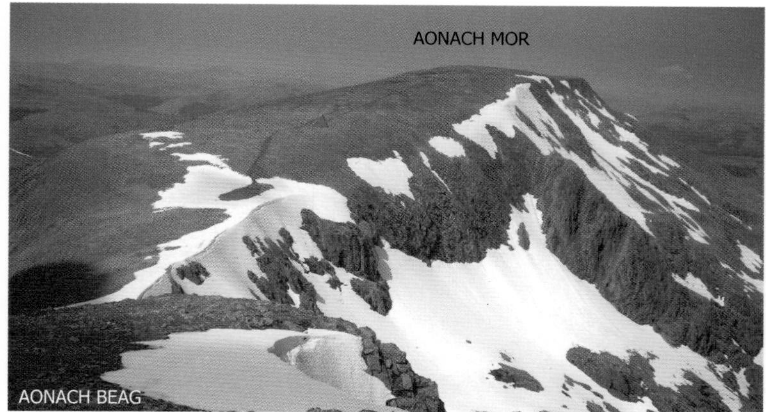

There's a brief section at the start where you may use hands to aid uplift. Above here, easy ground returns for the short walk onto ▲Aonach Beag's bare summit dome.

To descend, reverse the route over Aonach Mor. Remember that, if the gondola is closed, you are allowed to use the mountain biking path. On World Cup days, expert cyclists hurtle down here in under five minutes, but you are likely to take a tad longer.

See also picture on Page 26

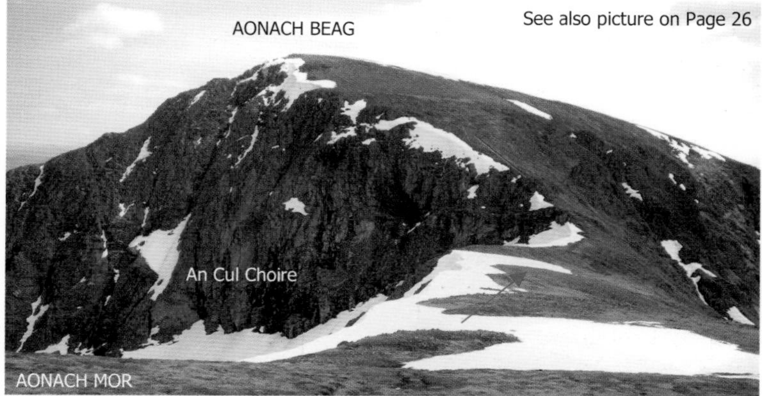

F-Stop: As the Aonachs' major corries face east, you'll have to start early in the day to photograph them before the sun leaves them. On Aonach Beag, it is worth going a short distance beyond the cairn to obtain reverse views of the summit crags.

Needlepoint: Although the path that links the two Aonachs is for the most part easy to follow, it becomes indistinct on their flat summit plateaus, so navigation in cloud will require closer attention than you might expect. In particular, when leaving the summit cairn of each Munro, make sure you are heading in the right direction.

Chilly Willy: If you welcome a summer ascent by gondola, you're gonna love the place even more in winter, when, if you can stand fraternising with the sliding brigade, you can be chairlifted to a height of 920m/3020ft on the ridge leading to Aonach Mor, only 300m/1000ft below the summit.

The climb to the summit is an easy, scenic snow plod, although the mossy terrain, so easy in summer, requires care when iced. In hard winter conditions the crossing to Aonach Beag is more awkward. The narrow, rocky section above the connecting saddle, which you will have to descend as well as ascend, may sport iced rock or steep snow, exposed above the depths of An Cul Choire.

An Cul Choire is a fantastic sight in spring, when huge cornices overhang the rim. Take extreme care at the summit of Aonach Beag, which lies close to the cliff edge. When the cairn is under snow, the highest point may be the tip of a cornice.

To add fun to the descent, Coire an t-Sneachda holds snow late into the year (hence the skiing). Check the Nevis Range website for conditions.

Route 85a Extension 1: Carn Mor Dearg and Ben Nevis via the CMD Arète: The Nevis Four

All four Munros using gondola: G4 ***** 13ml/21km, 1410m/4600ft M12/13

The Aonachs are separated from Carn Mor Dearg by an 830m/2725ft bealach. On the west side, Carn Mor Dearg's narrow east ridge makes a fine ascent route, but on the east side the very steep spur of grass and loose rocks that drops from the Aonachs somewhat spoils the crossing.

The descent of the spur isn't something you'd want to recommend to friends, but it *goes*. And it *is* the only awkward spot on an otherwise superlative four-bagger that, if you use the gondola, requires only 70m/250ft more ascent than the Ben Nevis Mountain Track alone. Mind you, it's more than twice as long.

After climbing Aonach Mor and Aonach Beag, return to the intervening saddle, climb a short distance back towards Aonach Mor and seek out the spur that descends to the bealach. Beginning at NN 192722, an old path zigzags down the steep slope, now so eroded, loose and slippery that its negotiation requires care. This is not a descent to be rushed.

Once down, the re-ascent to Carn Mor Dearg, described in Route 83c on Page 24, is infinitely more enjoyable. Once up, continue across the CMD Arête to Ben Nevis and descend to the Torlundy path in Coire Leis as per Route 83b Extension 1. When the Torlundy path reaches the forest at NN 148750, go right along a forest track to reach the network of tracks above the Nevis Range car park.

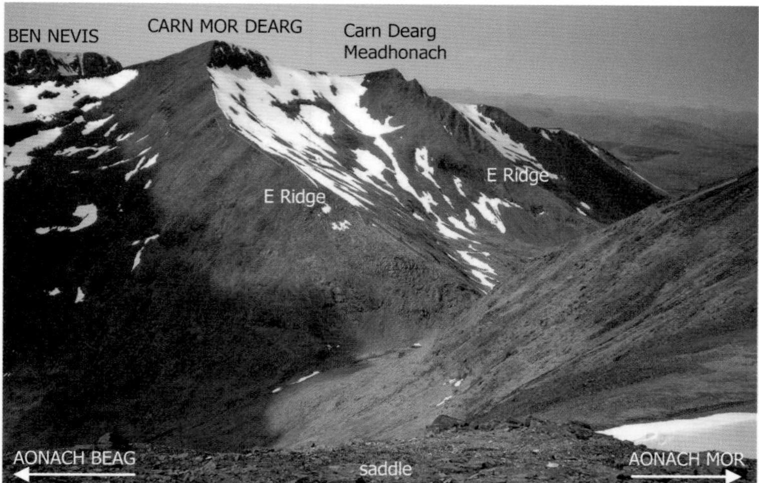

Needlepoint: In cloud, precise navigation is required on descent from the Aonachs if you hope to land on the bealach rather than to either side of it. But why you'd want to do the route in cloud is best left as a secret between you and your therapist.

Chilly Willy: The climb up Carn Mor Dearg's east ridge can approach a similar winter standard to the traverse of the CMD Arête. Moreover, the slopes that drop from the Aonachs to the intervening bealach are extremely steep and exposed under snow or ice. The complete route is a big winter's day for experts only.

Route 85b Aonach Beag and Aonach Mor from Glen Nevis

G2 ***** NN 68691, 10ml/16km, 1450m/4750ft M13
(including Aonach Beag to Aonach Mor return: 2ml/3km, 290m/950ft)

On its south side, Aonach Beag throws out two ridges, south-west and south-east, around a southern corrie (Coire nan Laogh, *Corra nan Leu-y*, Calf Corrie, named only on OS 1:25,000 map). The ill-defined corrie is no match for the majestic Back Corries, but the round of the corrie skyline, crossing Aonach Beag's two satellite Tops, and with Aonach Mor as a return add-on, is as spectacular as any in the Nevis Range.

The approach walk through the Nevis Gorge is perhaps the most scenic in the Central Highlands, while the cliff-top walk over the two Tops, rimming the Aonachs' great eastern face, has claims to being its high-level equal. Plus you get to feel smug at not having used mechanical uplift to reach the summits.

Begin at Glen Nevis road end and take the path through the Nevis Gorge, as described on Page 3. Beyond Steall Waterfall, the Plain of Steall forms a marshy basin hemmed in by steep mountainsides. Paths circumvent it on both sides. The main path appears to stay left on higher ground, but you'll find a more congenial path if you keep right along the bank of the Water of Nevis.

As you progress, Munro after Munro comes gloriously into view, each revealed to perfection in some new photogenic composition. On the right, the peaks of the Mamores are revealed one by one, culminating in volcano-like Binnein Beag (which can be reached by this same approach – see Route 81b in *Central Highlands South*). The left side of the glen is dominated by

Upper Glen Nevis

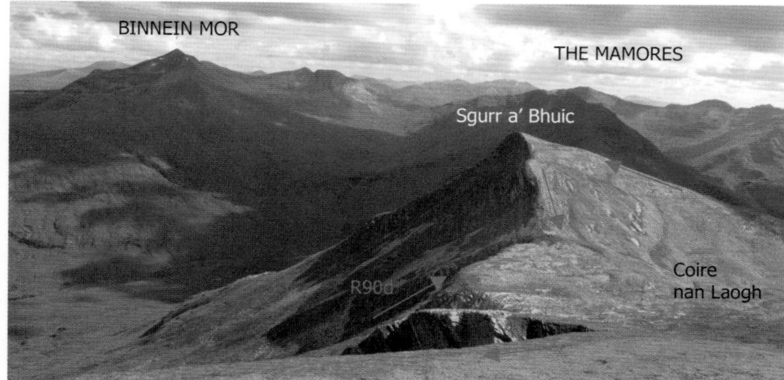

Aonach Beag and its two Tops, with the whole route to the summit laid out for study.

The two paths rejoin at the far end of the plain and reach a bridge over the Allt Coire Giubhsachan (*Owlt Corra Gyoosachan*, Stream of the Corrie of the Fir Trees). This stream descends from the deep corrie between Ben Nevis and Aonach Beag and has considerable force in spate. On the far side of the bridge are some ruined dwellings, in a spot also known as Steall. The path continues eastwards along the glen towards Sgurr Choinnich Mor (Route 87a), but it is time to leave it now for Aonach Beag.

The most direct ascent route is the south-west ridge on the left-hand side of Coire nan Laogh, but it is steep and tedious. A more well-graded route, with a useful path, climbs the south-east ridge on the corrie's right-hand side. Once on the skyline at the head of the corrie, the route curves back left, along the eastern cliff edge and over the two subsidiary Tops, to Aonach Beag's summit. The line is so much easier and more scenic that it would be perverse not to take it, so leave the south-west ridge as a possible descent option.

From the bridge, take the serviceable path along the right-hand side of the Allt Coire Giubhsachan then the Allt Coire nan Laogh, climbing north-east into Coire nan Laogh. The path climbs mostly dry ground beside the picturesque stream, whose waterfalls and siren pools provide ample distraction on a hot summer's day. Regular pauses will be required to take in expanding views of the Mamores and nearby Ben Nevis, punching skywards to the west.

The path deteriorates temporarily when it leaves the streambank to climb steeper ground, but try not to lose it as it soon improves again. It avoids a direct ascent of the crest of the south-east ridge, which rises very steeply further right, and instead makes a rising traverse across the hillside below the skyline. Eventually it rounds a corner into a shallow upper corrie, where it finally disappears.

F-Stop: On any ascent of the Aonachs, the most dramatic views are all to the west, so start early while the sun is still in the east. The view of Sgurr a' Mhaim over Steall Waterfall, seen on ascent, approaches photogenic perfection, but you'll need to move fast to catch the Back Corries and Ben Nevis at their best.

Now a choice has to be made. Stob Coire Bhealaich, which must be crossed *en route* to Aonach Beag, lies to the left of the bealach at the head of the corrie. Sgurr a' Bhuic lies to the right. Both stand at the edge of the still hidden eastern cliff face. One option is to make a rising traverse up grassy slopes on the left-hand side of the corrie to gain the shoulder of Stob Coire Bhealaich.

An easier option is to aim directly for the bealach, to pick up a cliff-edge path. For the sake of a mere 60m/ 200ft of extra ascent, however, we'd go over Sgurr a' Bhuic to add a sense of completeness to the route and for the immense view from the cliff-top Δsummit. Bear right up gentle slopes of boulder-strewn heath to get there.

From hereon, the cliff edge is followed all the way to the summit of Aonach Beag. A stony path makes the short descent down quartzite rubble (the only quartzite of the day) to the rocky bealach at the head of Coire nan Laogh. Note the grassy gully that descends from here to connect to the Grey Corries (Route 90d). The rock strata on the bealach are folded almost flat, giving easy walking. They rise gradually up the corrie from the west, flatten at the skyline and end abruptly to form the eastern cliff face.

On ascent to Stob Coire Bhealaich, initial bouldery ground at the cliff edge can be avoided on grass to the left. Soon the rocks are left behind and a pronounced path appears to make the remainder of the ascent easy. At one point the cliff edge makes a sharp left turn and the path bypasses the highpoint on the corner. Note the cliff-edge cairn that marks the top of the scramblers' route to/from the Grey Corries (Route 90d).

After turning left, the cliff top becomes more ridge-like as it crosses ΔStob Coire Bhealaich, giving great views of the Aonach summits across the Back Corries. The craggy wall that flanks the ridge is well named An Aghaidh Gharbh (*An Eu-y Gharrav*, The Rough Face).

Beyond Stob Coire Bhealaich, the ridge descends to another

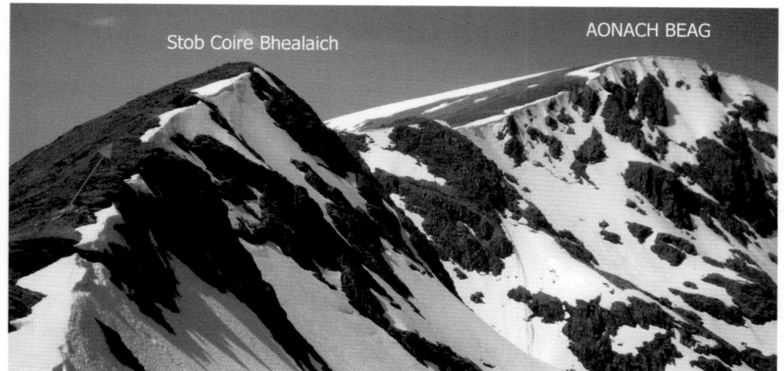

corner, where the cliff edge turns sharp right again. This corner, which marks the low point between Stob Coire Bhealaich and Aonach Beag, lies only c.10m/30ft below the summit of the Stob, which makes it a very lucky summit indeed to find itself listed as a Top in the Tables.

Above the corner, easy slopes of grass and heath broaden onto Aonach Beag's spacious summit plateau. The main path appears to contour left across the hillside, but stay right near the cliff edge and you'll find another that climbs directly to the ▲summit. Continue to ▲Aonach Mor and return as per Route 85a, then decide on a descent route.

The least aggravating way down is to reverse the route of ascent, bypassing Sgurr a' Bhuic. Some guidebooks suggest a return via the bealach to the west, between Aonach Mor and Carn Mor Dearg. This looks attractive on the map as it obviates the need to climb back over Aonach Beag, but the awkwardly steep and loose descent to the bealach (see Page 30), followed by a boggy walk down Coire Giubhsachan (see Page 24), is a poor way to end the day. Take a look and see what you think.

For the sake of an extra 160m/550ft climb, we'd go back to the summit of

Aonach Beag. From there, if you can handle steep, off-path terrain, consider a descent of the south-west ridge, which completes the round of Coire nan Laogh and gives close-up views of the Ben's enormous east face. You can recce this route on the way up Coire nan Laogh on the outward trip.

Once off Aonach Beag's summit plateau, the grassy ridge begins in fine fashion, with a path along the crest and excellent views of the Mamores, bathed in westerly light (hopefully). Unfortunately the good going doesn't last. When the ridge loses definition and the path disappears, bear left down broad grass slopes that descend more steeply to a flattish section, right of a basin full of small lochans. Stay right of the basin to reach the top of a shoulder on its far side.

Steep slopes, beset by small but avoidable crags, continue the descent. You can go more or less straight down, veer left to join the outward path along the Allt Coire nan Laogh or bear right to gain the path along the Allt Coire Giubhsachan. If you decide to go right, don't try to descend before you reach the shoulder beyond the flat section, as the hillside harbours hidden crags. The path beside the Allt Coire Giubhsachan, such as it is, runs along the far bank, so you may have to ford the stream if water levels are high.

Ascending Coire nan Laogh in winter

One way or another, we trust you'll make it down to the bridge at Steall ruins with time and energy enough to enjoy the walk back down the Nevis Gorge to the car park.

Needlepoint: On ascent in cloud, the shallow expanses of upper Coire nan Laogh can be very confusing, but keep heading north-east up the bowl of the corrie and you should reach the skyline at some point between Sgurr a' Bhuic and Stob Coire Bhealaich. From there, a path follows the cliff edge to the summit of Aonach Beag.

Chilly Willy: Upper Coire nan Laogh's height and situation turn it into a snow bowl in winter, which makes for scenic but tedious going. You'll encounter steep snow on ascent to it, and also on the ensuing route around the eastern cliff top.

Stretches of hard-packed snow beside a corniced cliff edge can give a feeling of great exposure, so this is not a route for beginners. For the competent and well-equipped, big mountains, big drops and superb snow scenery give the route an Alpine ambience out of all proportion to its technical difficulty.

Route 85c Aonach Beag and Aonach Mor from Nevis Range car park via the Back Corries

G3 **** NN 172774 Using gondola: 6ml/10km, 680m/2250ft M13
(plus Aonach Mor to Aonach Beag return: 2ml/3km, 290m/950ft)

Although Route 85a is shorter and Route 85b boasts great views of the surrounding mountains, the best ascent route for views of the Aonachs themselves approaches via a ridge to the east. This ridge crosses Aonach Mor's two satellite Tops and gives matchless views over the Back Corries to the Munros' craggy eastern wall. That wall looks impregnable but it is breached in one place only by a steep spur immediately below the summit of Aonach Mor, and it is this breach that makes the route possible. You won't meet many people here. It's a real Walk on the Wild Side of the Aonachs.

Beginning at Nevis Range car park, your first task is to head east around the sprawling northern slopes of Aonach Mor to reach Coire Choille-rais (*Corra Cullya-rash*, Corrie of the Shrub-wood, named only on OS 1:25,000 map). The ridge on the far (eastern) side of this corrie climbs to Tom na Sroine, the first of Aonach Mor's two Tops. N.B. Don't be misled by the OS map's placing of Tom na Sroine's name a mile to the north of the summit.

The traditional approach route uses forest tracks to reach the mouth of the corrie but the usual approach route nowadays uses the gondola to gain initial height before contouring into the corrie half-way up. You may regard gaining height in a seated position as cheating, but the alternative 3ml/5km forest approach march and ensuing trudge up Tom na Sroine's featureless slopes are so dispiriting that we have no hesitation in recommending initial mechanical uplift.

If ethical qualms persist, console yourself with the knowledge that you are (a) merely 'following orders' or (b) contributing to the local economy (whichever works for you). For times when the gondola isn't running, we describe the forest route as an Alternative Approach.

From the gondola's top station at 650m/2150ft, follow the line of the Great Glen Chairlift left across the tussocky, virtually level hillside. In winter (and perhaps in summer – check the website) you can ride the chairlift to further delay the prospect of scuffing your boots.

At the far end of the chairlift bear right and, losing as little height as possible, contour into Coire Choille-rais. Large swathes of craggy ground dot the hillside, obstructing a direct line. Some loss of height is probably unavoidable, so keep your wits about you to minimise effort.

F-Stop: To maximise available time between gondolas and catch the east-facing corries and crags at their best before the sun leaves them, take the earliest gondola possible.

It is normally possible to cross the Allt Choille-rais dryshod on boulders to reach Tom na Sroine on the far side. Steep slopes of grass among craglets rise to the summit and can be tackled direct, but you'll find easier going by climbing diagonally left to gain the skyline lower down.

From the Δsummit, the route to Aonach Mor can be seen in its entirety. An undulating ridge runs across the former Top of Stob Coire an Fhir Dhuibh and the still extant Top of Stob an Cul Choire to a dip, from where a steep spur climbs to Aonach Mor's summit plateau.

After the moorland and thick grass that has characterised the going so far, the terrain at Tom na Sroine's summit is a joy to walk, with short grass and flat quartzite rocks underfoot. On the short descent to the next bealach, a path stays below the crest on the right to avoid a bump on the ridge and awkward quartzite rocks on the crest. As you approach the bealach, if you take a peek over the crest, you'll unexpectedly find yourself atop considerable crags – Tom na Sroine's laudable effort to mirror its parent Munro's eastern wall.

The ridge then rises to Stob Coire an Fhir Dhuibh, where it makes a sharp right turn above yet more crags. Ironically, the corner makes this former Top a more shapely highpoint than either of its two flanking current Tops, but attractiveness has never

Viewed from Tom na Sroine

been a criterion for Munro's Tables.

The path again stays below the crest and curves right to bypass Stob Coire an Fhir Dhuibh. As this is a great viewpoint above the Back Basin, however, and as there is barely a dip between it and Stob an Cul Choire, it does no harm to climb it. As you progress, note the lochan-studded upper reaches of Coire Choille-rais below (see Alternative Descent).

Between Stob Coire an Fhir Dhuibh and Stob an Cul Choire the ridge becomes quite narrow along the rim of a wall of rock that drops abruptly from the crest, but there is no difficulty. Stay right of the crest to avoid exposure. Over the summit of ΔStob an Cul Choire the terrain becomes much rockier. Progress is slowed by awkward quartzite, so sharply upturned that a slip would be painful. The ridge descends over a bump to the 1000m/3300ft bealach at the head of Coire Choille-rais, above which a steep spur rises to the summit plateau of Aonach Mor.

The foreshortened view of the spur, to say nothing of an imposing rock tower half-way up, makes the ascent appear intimidating. Fortunately it's easier than it looks, requiring only occasional handwork for balance on mildly exposed grass slopes. Traces of path rise to the tower, bypass it on the right and continue up the crest. You top out on the plateau almost directly at Aonach Mor's ▲summit. Continue as per Route 85a, making the return trip to ▲Aonach Beag before descending to the gondola top station.

To find the correct line down off the plateau, follow the cliff edge to the first ski tow, which descends the west-bounding rim of Coire an t-Sneachda.

The route up the spur

The Spur from below

The Spur from above

Needlepoint: Apart from routefinding problems on the summit plateaus of the Aonachs (see Page 30), the main difficulty in cloud is finding an optimal line across the pathless mountainside from the Great Glen Chairlift into Coire Choille-rais.

Chilly Willy: For winter considerations on the summit plateaus of the Aonachs, see Page 30. On the Back Corries' approach, the main additional problem in winter is the ascent of the spur to Aonach Mor. This becomes a steep and exposed snow climb that is no place for walkers. Snow can lie late on the upper section and cause problems into early summer. If there is still snow around, avoid the spur, leave the Aonachs for another day and take the Alternative Descent.

Route 85c Alternative Approach: Leanachan Forest

G3 *** Route Rage Alert, Add-on: 5ml/8km, 550m/1800ft M13

From Nevis Range car park, follow forest tracks eastwards through Leanachan Forest to the Allt Choille-rais. The number of tracks around the car park can be confusing. The easiest way to begin is to take the track that runs under the gondola on the south side of the base station. This is soon joined by another from the car park and heads eastwards into the forest.

Branch right at a first junction (NN 184775) to climb back right (in the wrong direction!) to a second junction (NN 181769). Branch left here to take a level route through the forest to another junction (NN 203769). Branch right here to follow the steep track to its end at a small dam on the Allt Choille-rais (NN 205766).

Cross the dam and climb left of the stream through sparse but awkward tree cover to the upper forest fence, then continue up the grassy hillside right of another fence. Clamber through a small rock band (brief hand-work required) and continue up slopes of thick grass to the summit of Tom na Sroine to join the gondola route.

Route 85c Alternative Descent: The Four Lochans

G2 **** Total mileage: 6ml/10km, 470m/1550ft M13

We describe this entertaining descent route for those who do not wish to clamber up the spur to Aonach Mor. Perhaps you have already climbed the Munro and have come this way only to bag its two 'lost' Tops, explore the Back Corries and enjoy the views. Or perhaps you have decided to opt out of climbing the spur because it is snow-covered or looks too steep. By descending Coire Choille-rais from its head (the dip between Stob an Cul Choire and the spur), you can visit no less than four attractive lochans on the way back to the gondola.

From the dip, grass slopes descend easily to Lochan No. 1 (NN 200735). Cross a short rise and zigzag down steep grass among outcrops to Lochan No. 2 (NN 198739), nestling in its own craggy little corrie (Coire an Lochain). From its outlet, follow waterslides down to Lochan No. 3 (NN 200739). Continue down beside the stream to a smaller lochan (Lochan No. 3½?) then contour left to Lochan No. 4 (NN 203744), situated just above the Allt Choille-rais. The rectangular outline of this last of the quartet gives it the appearance of a swimming pool.

Below here, because of rock outcrops, you'll find easier going on the right bank of the Allt Choille-rais than on the left. If you cross to the right bank, you'll have to re-cross lower down, but you'll know from the outward journey whether this is possible dryshod. The only problem that remains then is when to leave the streamside to cross the hillside to the Great Glen Chairlift and gondola. Of course, being an exemplary hillwalker, you will have made a note of landmarks on the outward journey.

The Four Lochans

18 THE GREY CORRIES

East of Ben Nevis and the Aonachs, there is a dramatic change in the character of the mountains as massive plateau summits give way to sharp-pointed peaks, linked by a slender 5ml/8km-long ridge. The mountains are collectively known as the Grey Corries on account of the pale quartzite slopes that give them their characteristic appearance when seen from afar. Of the twelve peaks in the Tables, eight are Stobs and two are Sgurrs. Both names imply rocky terrain and sharp summits, and give some indication of the nature of the range.

The main spine boasts no less than three Munros and six Tops, which give outstanding ridge walking and easy scrambling to rival anything on the nearby Mamores. Lateral ridges to the north sport a further two Tops, while a deep bealach to the south isolates the fourth Munro (Stob Ban).

Each of the two central Munros (Stob Coire an Laoigh and Stob Choire Claurigh) can be climbed separately by a variety of interesting routes (Routes 88a-88d), although the long approach walk and the justly famed Grey Corries Traverse along the ridge that links them ensure that they are usually climbed together (Route 88a Extension 1). The two outlying Munros (Sgurr Choinnich Mor and Stob Ban) also have much to commend them as individual goals (Route 87a and Routes 90a & 90b), while those in search of greater challenges can append either or both to the Traverse (Route 88a Extension 1 & Route 90a Extension 1).

Finally, for the benefit of those who just can't get enough of Grey Corries ridge walking, we'll also tell you how to make a Grand Traverse of the whole shebang (Route 90c)... and even add the Nevis Range for good measure (Route 90d).

The Grey Corries from the Mamores

Access restrictions may apply during the stalking season (start of August to middle of October, excluding Sundays). Consult www.snh.org.uk/hillphones.

▲87 Sgurr Choinnich Mor 52 1094m/3589ft

(OS 41, NN 227714) *Skoor Choan-yich Mor*, Big Mossy Peak, probably named for its boggy southern slopes.

△Sgurr Choinnich Beag 963m/3160ft (OS 41, NN 220710) *Skoor Choan-yich Bake*, Little Mossy Peak

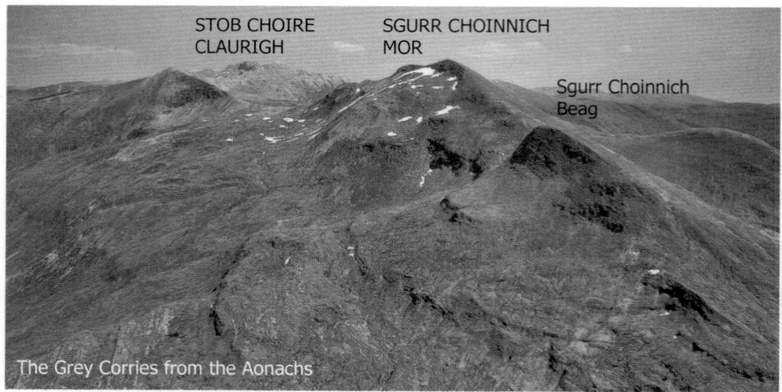

The Grey Corries from the Aonachs

Peak Fitness: No change since 1891 Tables.

Sgurr Choinnich Mor's tapering summit, separated from the central Grey Corries by a deep bealach, makes it the most shapely Munro in the range. It is neither the highest nor most characteristic, being thankfully bereft of ankle-twisting quartzite, yet its distinctive pyramid summit, far from any starting point and guarded by rough terrain, makes it a challenging goal.

For an extra 160m/500ft of ascent (and a long walk back), it can be appended to an east-west Traverse of the two central Munros from Coirechoille (Route 88a Extension 1), but it is more normally climbed on its own from the nearer starting point of Glen Nevis further west (Route 87a). An approach from this direction has an additional advantage for non-scramblers in that it involves no rock work, although the narrow roof-like summit ridge may still unnerve anyone prone to vertigo.

Unusually among the peaks that flank Glen Nevis, the summit remains out of sight atop rough hillsides for much of the approach, such that finding the optimal ascent line becomes difficult. To compensate, views are nothing short of exceptional, so we refuse to award the route any less than four stars.

Route 87a Sgurr Choinnich Mor from Glen Nevis

G2 **** NN 168691, 10ml/16km, 1020m/3350ft M46

Begin at Glen Nevis road-end and take the path through the Nevis Gorge, past Steall Waterfall and the Plain of Steall to the footbridge over the Allt Coire Giubhsachan at Steall ruins. This is already a wonderfully exciting and scenic walk, described in detail in Route 85c to Aonach Beag.

Beyond Steall ruins a rougher path continues the journey eastwards. It goes all the way to Corrour Station, 14ml/23km from Glen Nevis road-end, and beyond, and there's a feeling now of heading deep into wild country. The path contours across the hillside, well above the river, and rises gently to a shoulder above a waterfall, where it divides (NN 194690).

Keep to the main (high) path, which goes straight on, while the indistinct low path branches right to descend to the riverbank (and is used by Route 81b in *Central Highlands South*). You may pass the fork without noticing it. The two branches rejoin further up the glen. They may be shown incorrectly on the OS 1:50,000 map.

The high path continues towards still unseen Sgurr Choinnich Mor, hidden somewhere up on the left. It again contours across the hillside, passes a prominent right-angled bend on the Water of Nevis (NN 204688) and rises to another shoulder (NN 207691). A short distance further along it reaches the Allt Coire a' Bhuic (*Owlt Corra Voo-ichk*, Stream of the Corrie of the Roebuck, NN 208691,

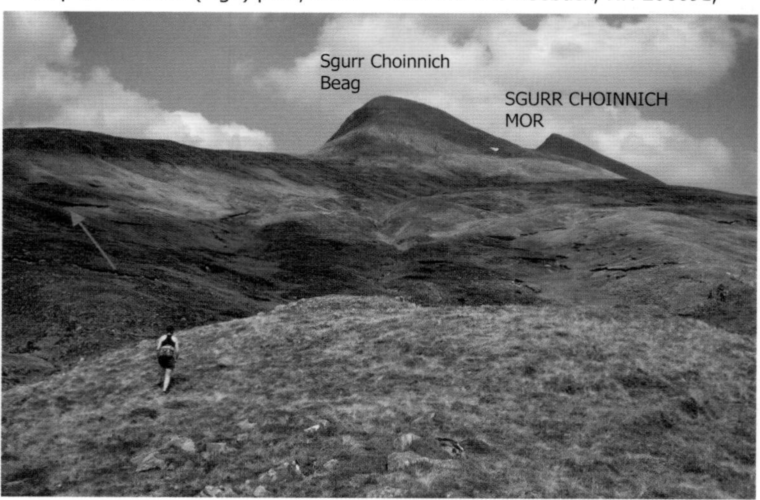

named only on OS 1:25,000 map), where it is left at last to follow the stream skywards.

N.B. Before reaching the stream an indistinct path takes a diagonal short cut to join it higher up. On approach to the bend on the Water of Nevis, three small burns cross the path. At the third, the short-cut path climbs away left. It's worth looking for. Note also that it is possible to make a higher diagonal short cut from further back along the main path but, if you're unfamiliar with the area, this could lead you onto hidden rocky ground.

An indistinct path climbs rough ground beside the Allt Coire a' Bhuic, on the left side at first then on the right, before disappearing. As height is gained, the twin peaks of stumpy Sgurr Choinnich Beag and pointy Sgurr Choinnich Mor finally come into view further right. It is difficult to decide which is the best way to approach them, as evidenced by the various traces of path that dot the hillside.

You could aim directly for the bealach between the two summits and climb Sgurr Choinnich Mor alone, but this involves a long, rough, rising traverse that could easily lead to Route Rage. Save that line for a possible descent route. We prefer to make directly for the skyline and, for the sake of an extra 70m/230ft of ascent,

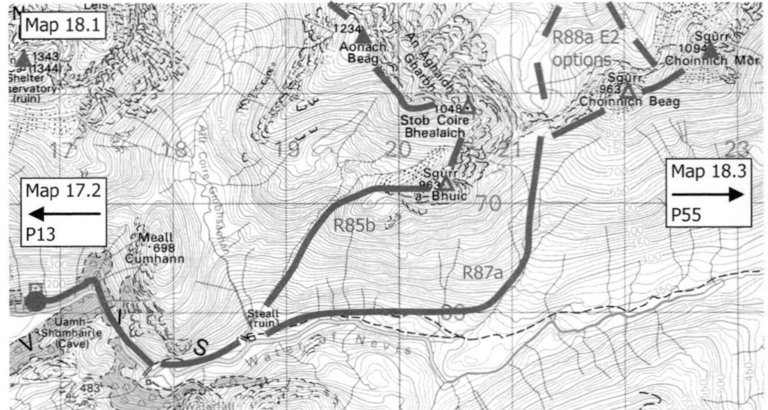

go over Sgurr Choinnich Beag. This leads to improved going in minimal time and opens up the views sooner, to say nothing of the bagging of an additional Top while indulging in a spot of Grey Corries ridge walking.

Stay with the Allt Coire a' Bhuic until, just below the skyline, it bears left into the crags of Sgurr a' Bhuic, Aonach Beag's satellite Top. Keep straight on and you'll soon reach the long, 731m/ 2398ft bealach at the foot of Sgurr Choinnich Beag's south-west ridge. Here the northern view opens up over the rocky expanses of the Back Basin to the great eastern faces of the Back Corries of the Aonachs.

Above the bealach, Sgurr Choinnich Beag's steep south-west ridge rises 232m/762ft to the grassy lump of a summit. The ascent is easier than it looks. With rough terrain replaced by turf underfoot, and with routefinding matters delegated to a ridge-top path, a steady ascent will soon get you up. You'll want to pause at the Δsummit to admire the soaring lines of Sgurr Choinnich Mor, newly revealed ahead in all its glory. The descent to the intervening bealach looks long and steep, and the re-ascent appears even stiffer, but neither is as demanding as it seems.

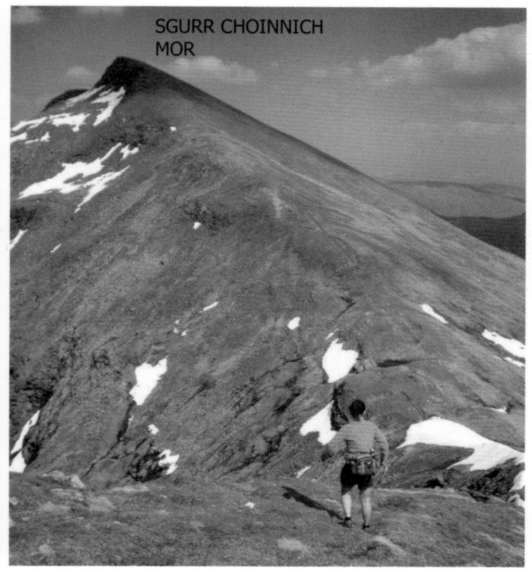

It is only 70m/230ft down to the bealach and, apart from some initial slight exposure, the path makes light work of it. The 200m/650ft re-ascent to the main peak has the advantage over other Grey Corries ascents of being devoid of underfoot quartzite. The ridge narrows between steep drops to give a feeling of great height, but the path climbs it without difficulty. The ▲summit itself is a roof-top eyrie with views that are, as the saying goes, 'worth any effort'.

On the return trip, you may be tempted to descend from the bealach between Sgurr Choinnich Mor and Sgurr Choinnich Beag. It's a rough short cut but it saves the climb back over the latter. Descend the rough hillside diagonally until you round its flanks and can see exactly where you are going, then rejoin the outward route beside the Allt Coire a' Bhuic.

F-Stop: Sgurr Choinnich Mor's sharp summit is a superb vantage point. The view to the east is dominated by the eastern Grey Corries, while to the west the enormous rock faces of the remote eastern corries of the Aonachs form one of the Highlands' great mountain walls (picture on Page 25).

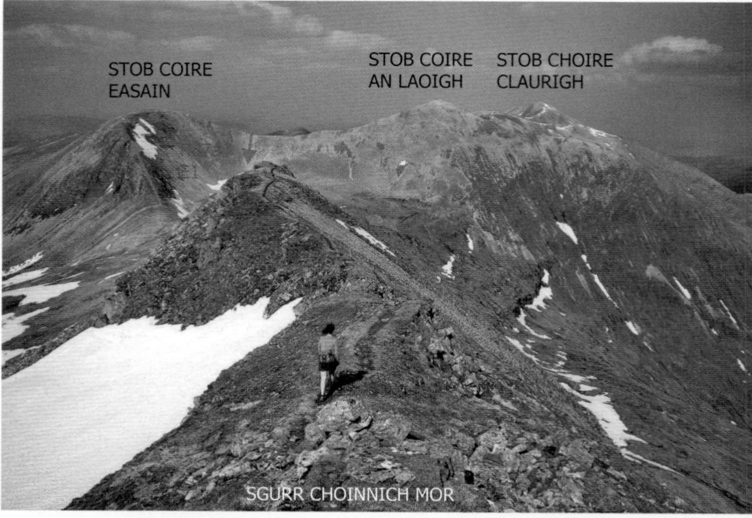

Torpedo: Add some interest to the return trip. Follow the Allt Coire a' Bhuic all the way down, crossing both the high path and the low path in upper Glen Nevis, to reach the Water of Nevis at its right-angled bend.

Just upriver from here, reached by a rough riverbank path, is a deep, water-scoured gorge that contains several water-falls. While it is not on the same scale as the celebrated Nevis Gorge downriver, it is a remote, wild, unexpected and striking sight, well worth making the effort to visit. N.B. Route 81b to Binnein Beag (in *Central Highlands South*) also passes this way.

Needlepoint: In cloud the only foolproof way of reaching the summit of Sgurr Choinnich Mor without routefinding problems is to follow the ascent route described, using the Allt Coire a' Bhuic as a guide. Do make sure that the stream *is* the Allt Coire a' Bhuic and not any of the smaller streams that flow across the Glen Nevis path from the cliffs of Sgurr a' Bhuic.

Once on the skyline, the path and the narrowness of the ridge make navigation straightforward. It would be prudent to descend the same way, rather than from the bealach between Mor and Beag.

Chilly Willy: Sgurr Choinnich Mor is an outstanding but tough winter objective. Apart from the long approach walk when snow lies on the ground, the very steep, exposed slopes of both Sgurr Choinnich Mor and Sgurr Choinnich Beag require great care when iced or snow-bound, especially on descent.

In some conditions a beautiful but potentially dangerous cornice adorns the Munro's roof-top summit. It is a magnificent winter peak that affords Alpine views, but only competent and experienced winter walkers should tackle it.

Route 87a Extension 1: Stob Coire an Laoigh

G4 **** Add-on: 3ml/5km, 250m/800ft M55

If you arrive at the summit of Sgurr Choinnich Mor with time and energy to spare, you may wish to consider extending the trip eastwards to ▲Stob Coire an Laoigh, which is normally reached from further east as part of an east-west Grey Corries Traverse. The extension adds considerable effort to the day and involves the negotiation of a steep scree slope, yet the ridge that connects the two Munros has a strong claim to being more exciting than anything on the Traverse itself.

The route is described fully in the reverse direction later in this section (Route 88a Extension 2 on Page 64). Briefly, in a west-east direction, first descend Sgurr Choinnich Mor's steep, narrow north-east ridge and climb the rock pavement of ΔStob Coire Easain's west ridge. Then cross the quartzite gap beyond to Stob Coire an Laoigh and retrace your steps to the gap.

You are now faced with a short but laborious descent southwards down a steep slope of quartzite rubble into Coire Easain (NN 235721). In the bowl of the corrie a smattering of tiny lochans provide welcome respite from the tough going.

Below the lochans, descend the hillside into lower Coire Rath, the Grey Corries' vast southern corrie. Curve south-west to avoid as much boggy streamside ground as possible and reach the Water of Nevis path west of Tom an Eite (see Page 82). All that remains then is the long walk out to Glen Nevis road-end car park.

For full details and pictures, see Pages 64-66.

▲88 Stob Coire an Laoigh 38 1116m/3661ft

(OS 41, NN 239725) *Stop Corran Leu-y*, Peak of the Corrie of the Calf
ΔStob Coire Easain 1080m/3543ft (OS 41, NN234727)
Stop Corra Essen, Peak of the Corrie of the Little Waterfall
(not to be confused with namesake ▲91)
ΔCaisteil 1106m/3629ft (OS 41, NN 246729) *Cashtyal*, Castle
ΔBeinn na Socaich 1007m/3304ft (OS 41, NN236734)
Ben na Sochkach, Peak of the Snout
ΔStob Coire Cath na Sine 1079m3540/ft (OS 41, NN 252730) *Stop Corra Ca na Sheena*, Peak of the Corrie of the Battle of the Elements

▲89 Stob Choire Claurigh 15 1177m/3861ft

(OS 41, NN 262738) *Stop Chorra Clowry*, meaning obscure; possibly Peak of the Corrie of Bellowing (of deer), from Gaelic *Clamhras*
ΔStob a' Choire Leith 1105m/ft (OS 41, NN256736)
Stop a Chorra Lyay, Peak of the Grey Corrie
ΔStob Coire na Ceannain 1123m/ft (OS 41, NN 267745)
Stop Corra na Kyownan, Peak of the Corrie of the Little Head
ΔStob Coire Gaibhre 958m/ft (OS 41, NN 261757)
Stop Corra Gyra, Peak of the Corrie of the Goat

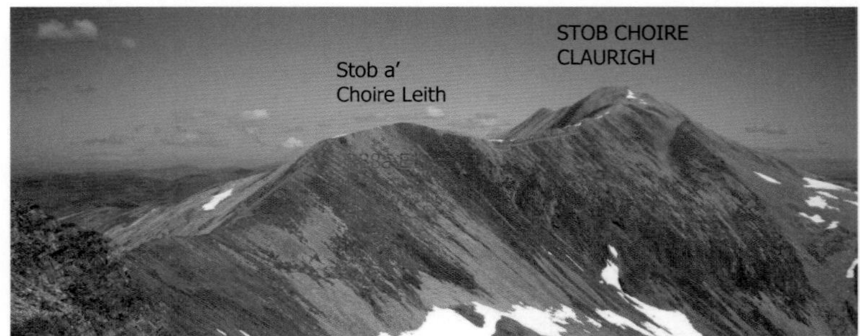

Peak Fitness: Beinn na Socaich was deleted from the Tables in 1921 but reinstated in 1981. Stob Choire Claurigh's North Top (NN 262744) suffered exactly the opposite fate, being introduced into the Tables as a Top in 1921 only to be deleted again in 1981. Stob Coire Cath na Sine was originally named Stob Coire Cath na *Sgine*, a subtle difference but one that changes its meaning to Peak of the Corrie of the Knife Fight.

The number of satellite Tops that cluster around the two central Grey Corries Munros indicates that what we have here is a true mountain range in miniature, one that faces the Mamores across upper Glen Nevis to provoke animated debate about their relative merits. With justification, both have their champions.

From most angles, central Grey Corries summits lack the shapely outlines of the Mamore peaks. This is not because they lack stature, as their Sgurr and Stob designations imply, but because many of them are no more than bumps on an undulating ridge. The two Munros are more significant than other highpoints only because they are slightly higher. Yet the reason for that lack of definition is what draws Grey Corries aficionados back again and again. Unlike in the Mamores, the ridge that connects the Munros and Tops is so consistently high-level that it smoothes out the skyline. There are no deep bealachs to cross here.

It has to be said that some of the Tops are so close together and separated by such shallow dips that they are very lucky indeed to find themselves basking in Top status. Stob a' Choire Leith, for instance, is a lowly bump on the ridge barely 600m from the summit of Stob Choire Claurigh. But that is part of the attraction.

The undulating 2ml/3km main ridge that connects the two Munros never once dips below 1040m/3400ft, while additional Tops beyond each end of it provide further ridge-walking opportunities. The terrain is mostly good, the gradients gentle, the ridge crest narrow without being too narrow, the scrambling very easy and the views sublime. It is less nerve-wracking than Aonach Eagach, less intimidating than the CMD Arête and less strenuous than the Mamores. While not challenging enough for the likes of Terminator, it tops many hill-walkers' lists as **The Best Ridge Walk in the Central Highlands**.

As might be expected, the rewards of high-level ridge walking in the remote country east of the Nevis Range don't come without effort. Because of the distances involved, Sgurr Choinnich Mor in the west and Stob Ban in the east are usually climbed separately. These two peripheral Munros are separated from the two central Munros by deeper

Sun and showers on the Grey Corries

bealachs and are more difficult to combine into a multi-bagging trip.

The two central Munros, at either end of the main ridge, can also be tackled separately. We describe individual routes up Stob Choire Claurigh (Routes 88a, 88b & 88c) and Stob Coire an Laoigh (88d). These explore some interesting side ridges that a combined ascent would bypass.

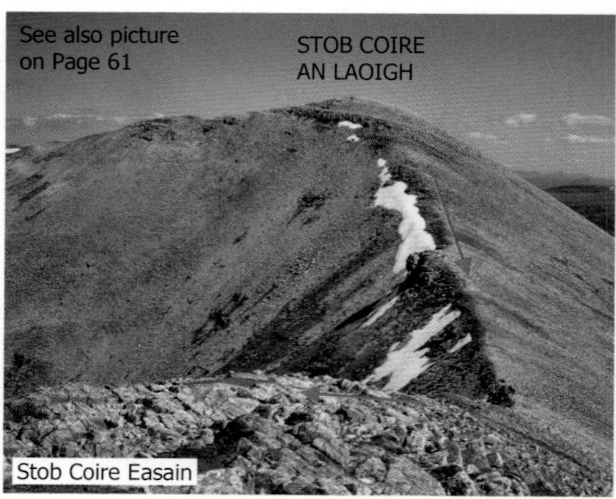

Nevertheless, as with Aonach Eagach in Glen Coe, the Grey Corries Traverse along the Munros' connecting ridge is the *pièce de résistance*, so they are usually climbed together (Route 88a Extension 1).

We recommend an east-west traverse, climbing Stob Choire Claurigh first, in order to keep the Aonachs and Ben Nevis in ever closer view ahead. Superfit hillwalkers could also climb Stob Ban *en route* to Stob Choire Claurigh (Route 90a Extension 1) and/or climb Sgurr Choinnich Mor after reaching Stob Coire an Laoigh (Route 88a Extension 2). The Grand Traverse of all four Munros is described as Route 90c.

Of the three routes to the summit of Stob Choire Claurigh, the most popular approaches via the north ridge from the satellite Top of Stob Coire Gaibhre. This is the shortest approach and has only one brief section of scrambling where the sensitive may feel uncomfortable (Route 88a). A more adventurous ascent route, offering some of the most dramatic scrambling in the range, approaches via the east ridge from the satellite Top of Stob Coire na Ceannain (Route 88b).

An ascent of Route 88b, followed by a descent of Route 88a, makes an exciting round for a shorter day on Stob Choire Claurigh alone. If you wish to avoid difficult ground altogether, the only hands-free route up Claurigh approaches via the south ridge from the Stob Ban bealach (Route 88c).

As a lone objective at the other end of the main ridge, Stob Coire an Laoigh is most easily reached via the satellite Top of Beinn na Socaich. This is the normal descent route from the main ridge. As an ascent route, it can be combined with a descent of the picturesque Back Basin (with or without the additional ascent of Sgurr Choinnich Mor) to give a rewarding round trip in its own right (Route 88d). As you can see, the complexity of the Grey Corries ridge system is such that route planning is essential before setting out.

Route 88a Stob Choire Claurigh from Coirechoille via Stob Coire Gaibhre

G3 (with G4/G5 options) Route Rage Alert **** NN 256788
(including return by route of ascent) 7ml/11km, 1020m/3350ft M53

> **!** The final section of this route crosses a narrow and exposed rock ridge. Although the easiest line requires little handwork, sensitive walkers may prefer to approach Claurigh via the Stob Ban bealach (Route 88c).

The route begins near Coirechoille Lodge, at the end of the 2½ml/4km minor road on the south side of the River Spean east of Spean Bridge. There are no parking places at the end of the paved road (NN 252807), but a rough Land Rover track on the right, open to the public and passable with care for most road vehicles, climbs past the lodge to give closer access to the mountains.

If you don't wish to drive the track you'll have to park a long way back and add considerable mileage to the route. Drive c.1½ml/2km up the track to a small car park just before a forestry plantation. On the right here is the LNGR line, which is used as a return route from the Grey Corries Traverse (see Page 63).

From the car park, walk 1ml/1½km along the continuing Land Rover track through the plantation to a gate at its upper end. From here, the track continues around the eastern foot of the Grey Corries through the ancient hill pass of the Lairig Leacach (and is used by Route 90a on Page 74). The range's two eastern Tops, Stob Coire Gaibhre and Stob Coire na Ceannain, flank the west side of the pass.

Leave the track at the gate and turn

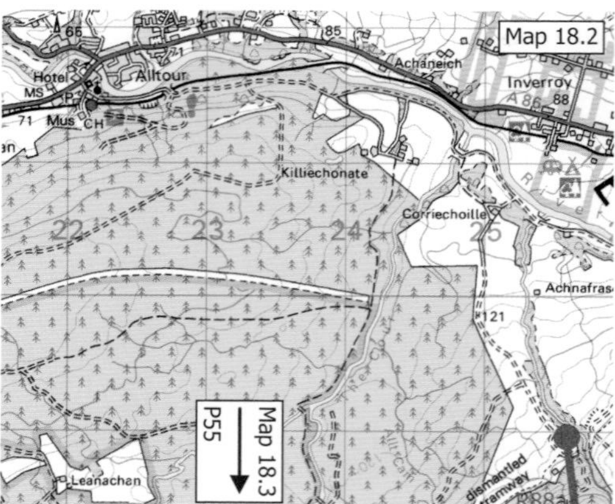

right to cross wet ground beside the trees. After crossing an old fence, take a curving line to the left, as steep or as gentle as you see fit, to make the long haul up the seemingly endless hillside of rough grass to Stob Coire Gaibhre.

The going improves higher up and there are also traces of path, but you'll be glad to top out on ΔStob Coire Gaibhre's grassy summit and doubly glad to hear that the newly revealed view of the Grey Corries' main ridge and the Nevis Range demands a halt.

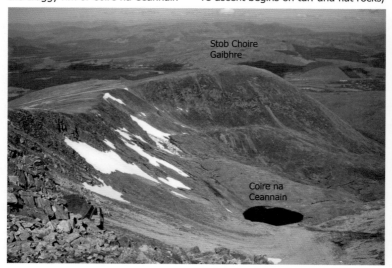

The continuation to Claurigh, around the craggy rim of Coire na Ceannain with its perfect circular lochan, begins with a gentle grassy stroll that descends a mere 24m/80ft to the low point between the two summits. The re-ascent begins on turf and flat rocks,

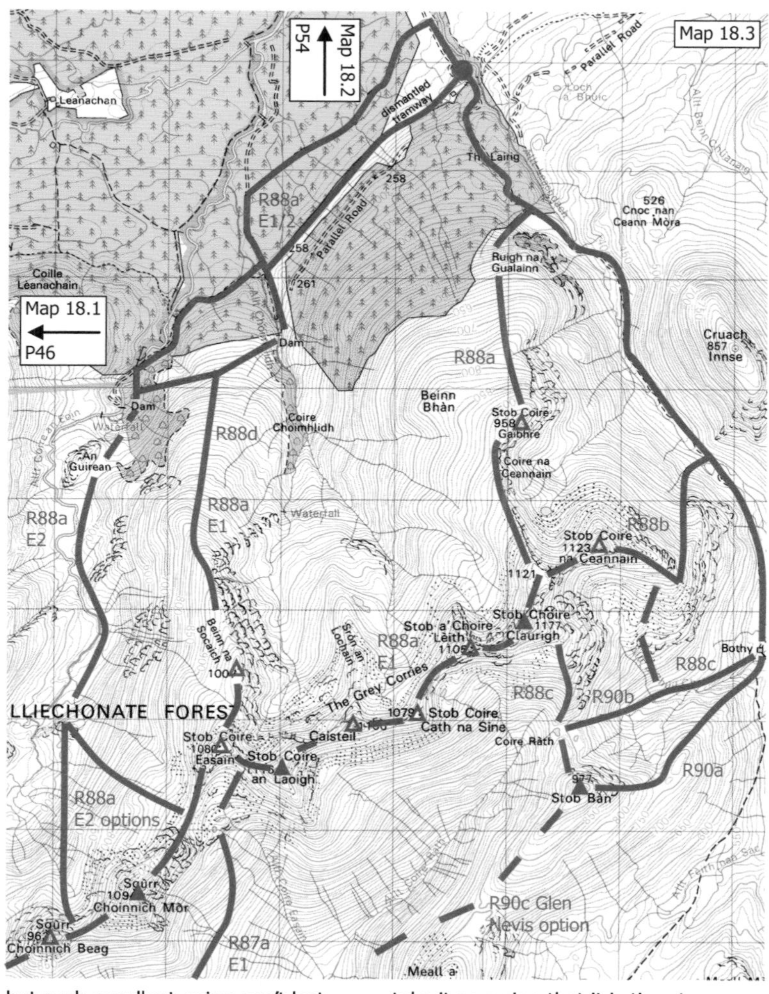

but such excellent going can't last forever... the Grey Corries *are* named for their quartzite, after all. When sharp rocks begin to appear underfoot, take it as a sign that it is time to knuckle down again.

A boulder-hop up a rockpile leads to a levelling where the terrain becomes

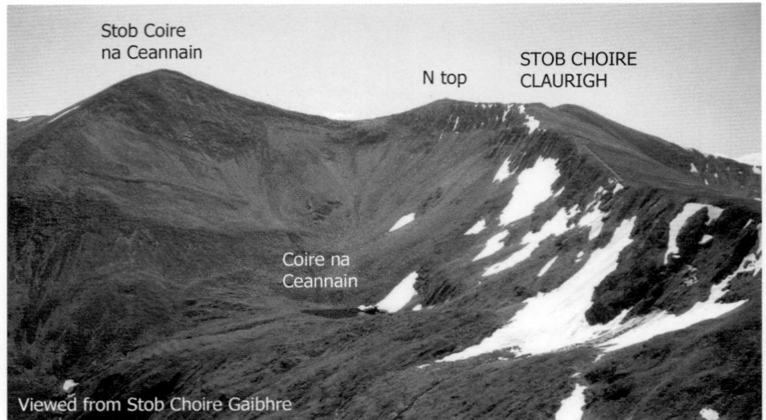

surprisingly complex. Claurigh's summit lies to the right across a curious saucer-like depression. The rockpile ridge carries straight on at an easy angle, left of the depression, to the Munro's north top, where it turns sharp right to continue to the summit.

The north top can be bypassed but it is close at hand and is worth visiting for the view left across the narrow connecting ridge to ΔStob Coire na Ceannain. We recommend the return trip to Ceannain to Top baggers and anyone who enjoys a ridge-top

scramble (return trip: exposed G4, 1ml/1½km, 120m/400ft; see Route 88b for description).

After turning right at the north top, the ridge climbs to another, cairned highpoint. The crest here is at least a G4/G5 scramble atop some very exposed knife-edge sections, but a path below right gives easier going.

A small dip follows, then the ridge crest continues in similar G4/G5 fashion. The path initially runs below it on the left and is quite exposed itself until it crosses to the right and regains the now stony crest to make the final short ascent to Stob Choire Claurigh's ▲summit.

Although little handwork is required if you stick to the path, the rocky terrain and the exposure give this last section of the ascent a serious air that may discomfort the sensitive. If in doubt, as noted earlier, use Route 88c (Page 71).

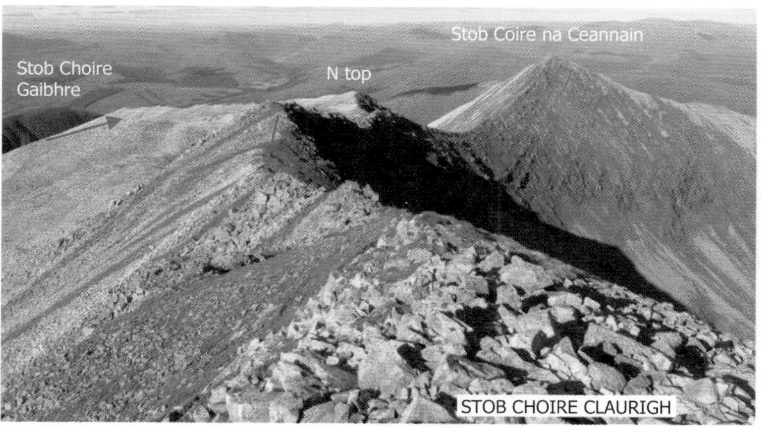

STOB CHOIRE CLAURIGH

Needlepoint: The slopes of Stob Coire Gaibhre will seem even more interminable in cloud, but the main navigational problems lie higher up, in the vicinity of Stob Choire Claurigh's north top. It is best here to stick to the ridge-crest. Any attempt to take a short cut across the adjacent depression described in the main text, in order to bypass the north top, will require careful navigation.

If descending from Stob Coire Gaibhre, avoid veering right too soon and ending up on cliffs above the Lairig Leacach. Instead, head north until you reach the edge of the forest, then follow the fence down to the approach track.

Chilly Willy: When the path is obliterated by snow, the knife-edge ridge between Stob Choire Claurigh's north top and summit is no place for walkers. The north top itself can be bypassed but the final stretch to the summit can't. In some conditions an exposed snow arête forms here. This has no technical difficulty but it would be unwise to cross it unless you are competent on such terrain.

Route 88a Extension 1: Stob Coire an Laoigh The Grey Corries Traverse

Total from Coirechoille (including ascent of Stob Choire Claurigh): G4 (with G5 options) ***** 10½ml/17km, 1290m/4250ft M55

We grade this route G4 more for its combination of seriousness, occasional exposure and G3 handwork than for the technical grade of its scrambling. Many would wish there were *more* scrambling involved.

Having reached the summit of Stob Choire Claurigh, normally by Route 88a but possibly by Route 88b or 88c, your reward awaits. And what a prize it is: a glorious 2ml/3km ridge walk along the spine of the Grey Corries to Stob Coire an Laoigh. Prepare for hillwalking at its most inspiring.

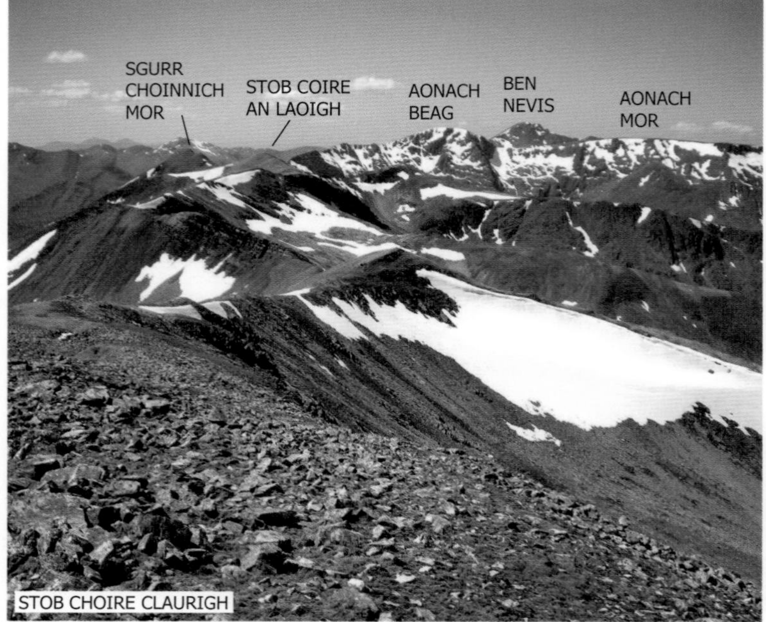

F-Stop: At the summit of Stob Choire Claurigh, the whole Grey Corries' main ridge lies before you, undulating and twisting its way westwards to the great rock faces of the Aonachs and Ben Nevis. That view will be with you all day and only become more awesome with every westward step.

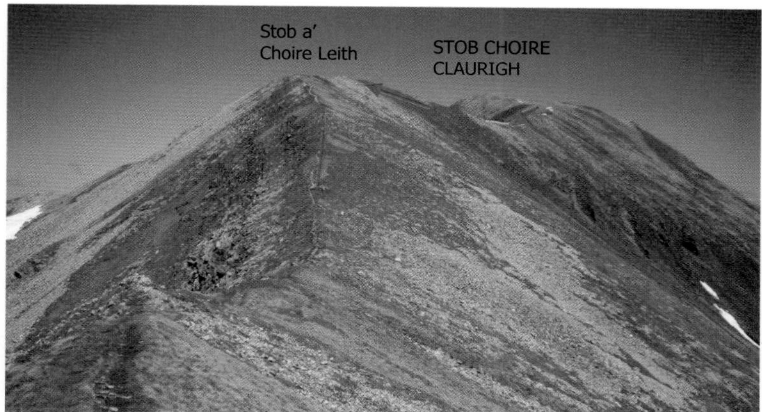

The Traverse begins with a leisurely descent of Claurigh's gentle, narrow south-west ridge, which affords time to admire the complex of mountain country ahead. Stob Coire Gaibhre, which took so much effort to reach, now looks like a minor grassy hillock amid such exalted company. Quartzite soon gives way to grass and a good path that bears left over a 15m/50ft rise and descends to a bealach, 80m/250ft down from Claurigh's summit. That small rise has, somewhat unbelievably, squeezed into the Tables as the Top of ΔStob a' Choire Leith.

Across the bealach, quartzite rubble returns as the ridge bears further left atop a sizeable crag. The crest is an exposed G4 scramble in places but the path finds an easier route below right. A highpoint is reached, then a dip is crossed to gain the summit of ΔStob

Viewed from Stob a' Choire Leith

Coire Cath na Sine. N.B. The scree slope that descends northwards from the dip gives a steep escape route down into Coire Choimhlidh (*Corra Choa-ily*, Door Corrie) and so back to your starting point.

At Stob Coire Cath na Sine the ridge swings right again across another dip and becomes slightly broader. There's still quartzite underfoot, but flat rocks, a gentle angle and a less than 50m/160ft rise contribute to an easy wander up ΔCaisteil. This Top's name may derive from the great crags that drop from it to the north, best seen from further along the ridge.

At Caisteil the ridge swings left again to give another blissful walk down a narrow section of quartzite pavement, with great flat flagstones to stride across (*carefully*, because of the drop on the right). Beyond the next bealach, the ridge swings right once more and ascends a brief steep section on rocky slopes. Another swing left brings easier ground above enormous cliffs, then you're at the summit of ▲Stob Coire an Laoigh. All too soon!

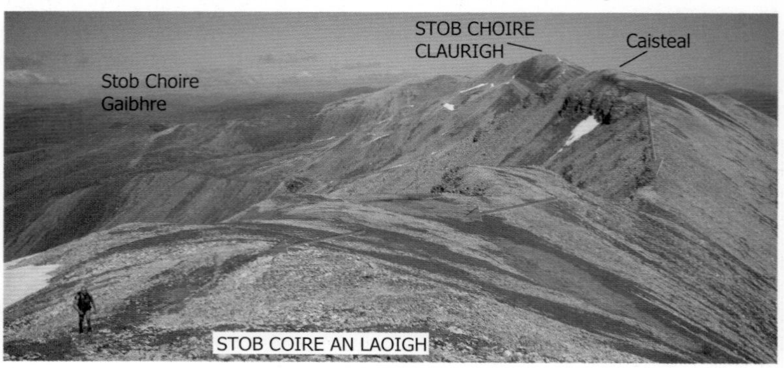

Descent from Stob Coire an Laoigh via Beinn na Socaich

At Stob Coire an Laoigh you have reached the second of the two Munros but not the end of the main ridge, which continues to one more Top: Stob Coire Easain. To reach it, the ridge turns sharp right and crosses a deeper gap, descending 100m/330ft and re-ascending 60m/200ft.

Much of the crossing is on a quartzite rockpile, steeper and looser than anything that has gone before, so take care on the ankle-twisting rocks. The ascent of the far side of the bealach is less awkward than the descent of the near side, with one brief, enjoyable respite when a more solid piece of rock demands a couple of unexposed G3 step-ups.

At Stob Coire Easain the main ridge turns sharp left to continue in a south-westerly direction to Sgurr Choinnich Mor (Extension 2), but the standard descent route goes northwards down a side ridge over the satellite Top of Beinn na Socaich.

N.B. The ascent of Sgurr Choinnich Mor is an exciting option, and the descent from there via the Back Basin, although it adds considerable effort to the day, is the supreme return route. Even if you omit Sgurr Choinnich Mor, a return via the Back Basin is still worthy of consideration. See Extension 2 for details.

The descent from Stob Coire Easain towards Beinn na Socaich begins steeply on quartzite rubble but, with a height loss of less than 100m/350ft to the intervening saddle, grass and turf are soon underfoot. From there, the ascent to the lowly summit of ΔBeinn na Socaich is less than 30m/100ft.

The broad ridge leads onwards along the craggy rim of Coire a'

See also picture on Page 52

STOB COIRE AN LAOIGH

Not recommended: Stob Coire Easain bypass route

From Stob Coire an Laoigh, it is possible to bypass Stob Coire Easain by traversing from the Laoigh-Easain gap to the Easain-Socaich saddle. The narrow, unstable, treacherous little 'path' crosses steep, loose quartzite and earth slopes below Stob Coire Easain's summit crags and above sizeable drops falling to Coire a' Mhadaidh (*Corra Vatty*, Fox Corrie).

The hardest section, on which you are likely to use as many points of contact as you can muster, is the initial steep descent from the Laoigh-Easain gap. If you can manage that, you should manage the rest, but it can hardly be recommended. For the sake of a mere 60m/200ft of ascent, it is safer and much more enjoyable to go over Stob Coire Easain.

Mhadaidh and gives a pleasurable descent on rock-strewn turf at a gentle angle. The corrie debouches into the great catchment area of Coire Choimhlidh, where the Allt Choimhlidh is dammed at the forest edge (NN 239765). That dam is your goal. By ascending over Stob Coire Gaibhre and descending over Beinn na Socaich, you'll have completed the skyline circuit of this great north-facing corrie.

As you descend, keep to the crest of the ridge, away from the corrie rim, to pick up an ATV track that eases the remainder of the descent. It zigzags down the ridge until the flanking crags peter out, then it veers right to descend the broad, grassy north-east hillside. Follow it down until just above the forest, where it turns sharp left to join the ATV track in the Back Basin (see Page 66). Leave it at this point to bear right and descend a steeper streamside slope to the Allt Choimhlidh. Aim for a point c.100m before the dam, at the foot of a gorge, where a watersplash will get you across to the far (right) bank.

At the dam on the Allt Choimhlidh you reach the network of hydro and

Not recommended: Descent of Coire a' Mhadaidh

A glance at the map may tempt you into descending directly from the Laoigh-Easain gap into Coire a' Mhadaidh and so to the Allt Choimhlidh dam, but the route is less straightforward than it appears and is best left for another day's exploration.

It is *possible* to descend slopes of scree, boulders and grass into the round bowl of the upper corrie (NN 238228) from the Laoigh-Easain gap, from the Stob Coire Easain bypass route or (much more easily) from the Easain-Socaich saddle. Once down, it is *possible* to make a way down beside the stream to the dam.

A clear path in places is testament to a number of previous descents, but it eventually leads nowhere. There are some considerable waterfalls to see on the way, but the steep, rocky ground they inhabit does not make for easy going. On descent to lower Coire Choimhlidh, deep rocky gorges on both the main stream and right-hand tributaries are likely to force you left onto the north-east slopes of Beinn an Socaich, leaving you to rue your decision not to return over that Top.

GiGi: The 19ml/30km Lochaber Narrow Gauge Railway (LNGR) was built in the 1920s to aid construction of a pipeline carrying water from Loch Treig to the aluminium works at Fort William. It was gradually replaced by dirt roads and formally closed in 1971. Since then much of it has become overgrown and its many bridges have fallen into ruin. Sections nevertheless remain passable on foot or bicycle, especially where the flat bed has been re-utilised for the construction of hydro and forest tracks. Its presence will become familiar on any approach to the mountains between Fort William and Fersit (see also Route 91a on Page 91).

forest tracks that ease the final stretch of a long trip. A track runs down the right bank for c.600m to a more substantial track at NN 238771. At a Z-bend 120m before the junction, the track crosses the LNGR line. On the right-hand bend, note the ruined bridge on the left. On the following left-hand bend, look on the right for the path that heads back along the line to your starting point.

Return along either the LNGR path or the forest track. The shortest route (1½ml/2½km) follows the LNGR path directly back to the car park. The forest track (c.½ml/1km longer) bears left, branches right at a T-junction and emerges from the forest on the Land Rover track below the car park for a short end-of-day uphill finish.

As the LNGR line is level and undrained, it holds water admirably and is best avoided after rain. The path along it has to detour around downed bridges and is much churned up in places. It also has stretches that give excellent walking. Overall it is harder work than the forest track but, as it is more interesting and less undulating, it can seem less tiring.

Both forest track and LNGR path involve something of a forced march at the end of a long day, but be assured that the effort will soon be forgotten, eclipsed by indelible memories of the main ridge.

Needlepoint: The narrowness of the Grey Corries main ridge, together with the path along it, make foul-weather routefinding generally straightforward as long as you maintain concentration. But there is ample opportunity for error, especially when the path disappears on quartzite rubble.

The ridge's numerous undulations and twists can prove disconcerting, so try to keep track of exactly which highpoint you are on. Take especial care to avoid side ridges that jut north from Stob a' Choire Leith and Caisteal, and make sure you quit Stob Coire Easain in the right direction.

Chilly Willy: The Grey Corries peaks rival the Mamores for winter 'ridge walking' and should be taken just as seriously. Depending on conditions, knife-edge arêtes can form in more places than one and there are no easy escape routes between the two Munros. The initial ascent of Stob Choire Claurigh will give some indication of conditions ahead and enable you to gauge your capabilities.

For experienced campaigners, the Grey Corries Traverse presents a lengthy and exhilarating winter challenge to rival anything in the Central Highlands, but it is no place to practise winter skills. The easiest winter ascent routes of the two Munros, as in summer, avoid the main ridge (Routes 88c & 88d).

Route 88a Extension 2: Sgurr Choinnich Mor G4 **** M55

Add-on to Route 88a Extension 1: 2ml/3km, 160m/500ft
Total from Coirechoille car park (including Grey Corries Traverse)
by Stob Gaibhre: 12½ml/20km, 1450m/4750ft
by Stob Coire na Ceannain: 14ml/22km, 1480m/4850ft

For those happy few who still have the energy at the summit of Stob Coire Easain, it is possible to continue along the spine of the Grey Corries to ▲Sgurr Choinnich Mor, and from there descend the beautiful valley of the Cour river system. Extending the Traverse in this way adds considerable effort to an already long day but rewards with arguably the most exciting and picturesque terrain in the whole Grey Corries.

At the summit of Stob Coire Easain, the main ridge turns left to descend 90m/300ft to the bealach below Sgurr Choinnich Mor (named Bealach Coire Easain on OS 1:25,000 map). After the sharp rocks encountered on the ascent of Stob Coire Easain from Stob Coire an Laoigh, the quartzite on descent now exhibits a flatter surface that makes for improved going.

At one point, rock pavement leads down to a sudden narrowing of the ridge, where a short rock wall descends into a gap. The easy G4 descent requires no more than a couple of steps down big ledges, perhaps in a seated position. It is less exposed than it appears at first sight,

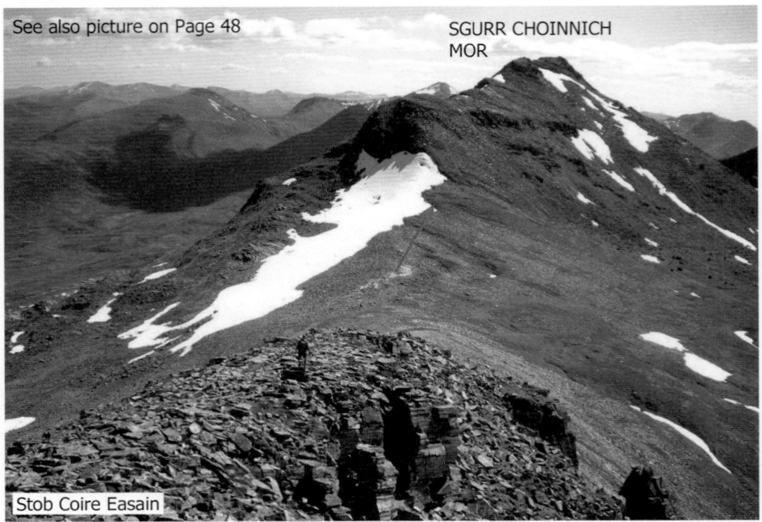

but beside it there has nevertheless developed a rubbly bypass route that is more trouble than it is worth.

The rocky terrain continues all the way to the bealach. You'll use hands for balance occasionally, but there is no exposure and the going is easy (as long as you don't trip, that is).

Across the bealach, Sgurr Choinnich Mor's north-east ridge cleaves the sky like a shark's fin. The 160m/500ft

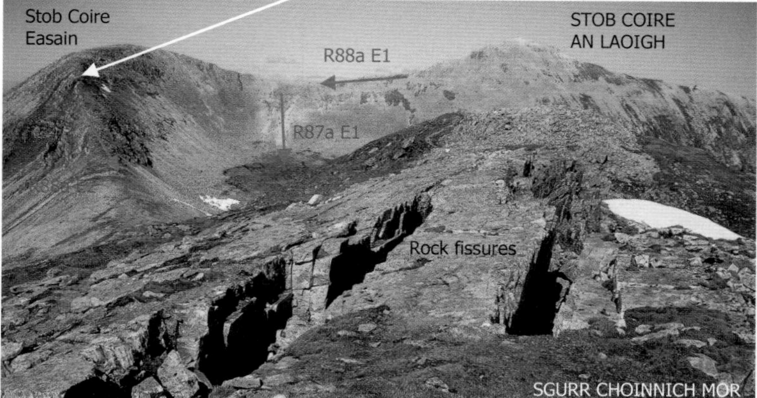

ascent begins up a slope of grass and rubble that is steeper than anything you have come across on the main ridge so far. The main path goes far to the left and is very exposed above crags. You may feel more comfortable further right, where traces of path indicate you would not be the first. As the amount of rubble increases, hands may well come in useful again.

You emerge onto an easy but complex section of ridge that, with a good path underfoot again, undulates up to the foot of steeper rocks. At the start of this section, just over the rise of the initial steepening, the ridge is cut by some **extraordinary rock fissures**, deep enough to swallow a person.

At the end of the undulating section, a steeper section of broken rocks climbs onto Sgurr Choinnich Mor's roof-like summit ridge. With some exposure, minor scrambling is required as the path finds the easiest way up. The ridge then becomes so narrow that in places there is room only for the path, and handwork is again required in a couple of places before you arrive at the eyrie of a ▲summit.

Needlepoint: In either direction, linking Stob Coire Easain to Sgurr Choinnich Mor in cloud demands as much concentration as reaching the summit of either in the first place, especially when the steep, rocky terrain is wet. And make sure you don't step into a fissure.

Chilly Willy: As in cloud, so in winter. Linking the two Munros in either direction poses a whole new set of problems. Stob Coire Easain's west ridge can seem surprisingly steeper and more exposed under snow, especially in the vicinity of the rock wall, while Sgurr Choinnich Mor's north-east ridge is an even more formidable winter challenge.

The lower section becomes a very steep snow slope when the rocks are covered, while the narrow upper section can become a corniced snow arête. Iced rock adds to difficulties and a further, unique danger is posed by the rock fissures, which form hidden 'crevasses' under the snow.

Descent of the Back Basin

The return route from Sgurr Choinnich Mor descends the great rocky Back Basin to the north. Streams from numerous high corries on the north side of the Grey Corries and the east side of the Aonachs join in this basin to force a way northwards to Glen Spean, becoming the Allt Coire an Eoin then the River Cour.

Once down into the basin, the huge rock faces of the Back Corries of the Aonachs dwarf surroundings, making one feel very small indeed. It is **one of those supreme mountain sanctuaries** that fills even the hardest of hearts with humility. If only it weren't so awkward to reach... but then it is that very remoteness that enhances its power to move.

To reach the Back Basin from Sgurr Choinnich Mor, descend from one of the bealachs on the ridge. There are three options. (1) Continue down Sgurr Choinnich Mor's steep but easy south-west ridge to the bealach below Sgurr Choinnich Beag (see Route 87a for description). (2) Continue over Sgurr Choinnich Beag to the bealach beyond, bagging the final Grey Corries Top *en route* (add-on: 1ml/2km, 60m/200ft). (3) Reverse the route of ascent, down Sgurr Choinnich Mor's north-east ridge to the bealach below Stob Coire Easain.

Although there is a great deal of ice-smoothed rock around, it is possible with judicious routefinding to descend into the corrie from any of these three bealachs. Anyone who has managed to make it thus far should have little problem finding a way down. Which route to choose? It is tempting to complete the ridge walk by continuing across Sgurr Choinnich Beag, but the

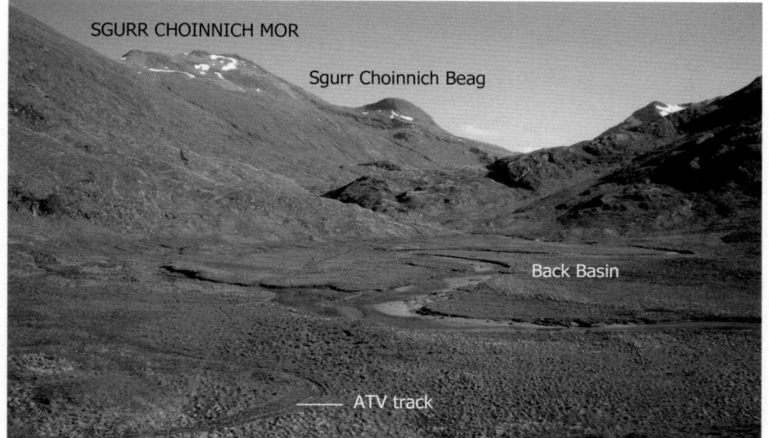

quickest and easiest way down begins with a return down from Sgurr Choinnich Mor's north-east ridge.

Once down into the Back Basin, tramp down the right bank of the river, past innumerable waterfalls and pools. Progress is slowed by the rocky riverside bluffs that cause those waterfalls and by the need to keep peering back at the growing panorama of skyline peaks. An intermittently useful path develops along the bank, used more by sheep than humans, but you'll want to take short cuts across meanders.

Back Basin waterfall and pool

The going improves dramatically once you reach the grassy haughs before the rocky riverside hillock that goes by the appealing name of An Guirean (*An Gooren*, The Pimple). On the right of the plain, around NN 221745, you'll pick up an ATV track that will take you out of the wilderness and back to civilisation.

The river cuts a way down left of An Guirean and becomes difficult to follow on awkward ground. Rather than follow the riverbank, stick to the track, which improves to make a short 15m/50ft climb over the shallow saddle *right* of An Guirean. Once over the saddle, the track descends to rejoin the river lower down.

Back Basin scenery

Having circumvented An Guirean, the steeply descending river boasts a formidable stretch of water that remains unknown to all but the few privileged hillwalkers who pass this way. The track affords a bird's eye view of a series of waterfalls: twin upper falls and a staircase of lower falls above a hydro dam.

From the dam, hydro and forest tracks will take you back to your starting point. N.B. You don't need to leave the track and cross the river to reach the dam and hydro track. The ATV track joins the hydro track *below* the dam, at the point where the latter crosses from the river's left bank to its right (NN 227762).

The hydro/forest track continues down into the extensive Leanachan Forest. Note the right-hand bend where a ruined bridge on the left indicates it has joined the line of the LNGR (NN 230766).

Waterfall above dam

Further along, at the bridge over the Allt Choimhlidh, there is one last choice to be made between two ways back to the car park: the track or the path along the LNGR line, as described on Page 63. To find the LNGR path, turn right at the track junction just beyond the Allt Choimhlidh bridge and walk 120m to a right-hand bend. The path begins here on the left.

Route 88b Stob Choire Claurigh from Coirechoille via Stob Coire na Ceannain

G4 (with G5 options) **** NN 256788 M55
Stob Choire Claurigh alone (ascent via Stob Coire na Ceannain, descent via Stob Coire Gaibhre): 8½ml/14km, 1080m/3550ft
Add-on to Route 88a: 1½ml/2km, 30m/100ft
(Total Grey Corries Traverse from Coirechoille: 12ml/19km, 1320ft/4350ft)

Stob Coire na Ceannain, the highest of Stob Choire Claurigh's three subsidiary Tops, is connected to the main peak's north top by a narrow, rocky, dramatic-looking arête that drops 60m/200ft to a gap, climbs 60m/200ft back up the far side and looks much deeper than it really is. The traverse involves some exposed, easy scrambling that will delight some and give nightmares to others. For Top baggers, the return trip from Claurigh's north top is 1ml/1½km, 120m/400ft, while scramblers may wish to begin the Grey Corries Traverse by climbing Stob Coire na Ceannain rather than Stob Coire Gaibhre.

On its complex east side, Ceannain drops a ridge that runs south-east then north-east to end at a craggy spur above the highpoint of the Lairig Leacach. This ridge gives rougher going than Stob Coire Gaibhre's north ridge but is the key to the ascent. To reach it from the car park above Coirechoille, first follow the Land Rover track for 3ml/5km to the 500m/1650ft highpoint of the Lairig Leacach at NN 278753, just before the spur.

Leave the track here to tackle steep slopes of grass and heather right of the crags at the foot of the spur. A

stream that descends the hillside can be used as a guide. Once above the crags, bear left to reach the skyline at the foot of the now well-defined south-east ridge, around 300m/1000ft below the summit. The ascent continues up very steep grass slopes left of scattered crags and then on increasing amounts of quartzite. The pyramid ∆summit is the most striking in the Grey Corries.

N.B. For a less steep, if more roundabout, route to the upper ridge, follow the track to the Lairig Leacach bothy and continue up the Allt a' Chuil Choirean path towards the Giant's Staircase, as per Route 90b. Keep to the stream when it turns right, climb beside its picturesque waterfalls and bear right to climb less steep grass slopes to gain the ridge crest.

On the traverse to Stob Choire Claurigh, the easiest ground will unfailingly be found on the north side. A stony, often exposed path, and one that is not devoid of handwork itself, takes the line of least resistance. Initial summit rocks are bypassed on the north, then easier ground leads down to and across the gap.

On ascent to Claurigh, the ground again steepens with height. The quartzite blocks on the crest give good holds but many are loose and require care. The rough path again moves to the north side before rejoining the crest and reaching Stob Choire Claurigh's north top. The ▲summit lies not far beyond, as described in Route 88a (Page 57).

Needlepoint: If cloud hangs low over the Lairig Leacach, a safe route up Stob Coire na Ceannain may be hard to find. Once on the south-east ridge, however, and on the narrow crossing to Stob Choire Claurigh, the line will be difficult to miss.

Chilly Willy: In hard winter conditions, the snow arête that forms between Ceannain and Claurigh is a thing of beauty. Its traverse is of Alpine quality and difficulty.

Route 88c Stob Choire Claurigh from Coirechoille via Stob Ban bealach M55

Ascent and descent of Stob Choire Claurigh alone via the Giant's Staircase:
G2 (with G3/G4/G5 options) **** NN 256788 12ml/19km, 1050m/3450ft

This is a roundabout route up Stob Choire Claurigh but it is the only one that has no exposure and requires handwork only for balance on quartzite rubble. From Coirechoille car park it follows the Lairig Leacach track to the south side of the mountain and approaches via the Stob Ban-Claurigh bealach (see Route 90b).

The ascent can be combined with that of Stob Ban, although the steep slope of broken quartzite rocks that separates Stob Ban's summit from the bealach is not recommended to anyone who is seeking to avoid difficult ground.

Follow Route 90b up beside the Giant's Staircase to the bealach, taking the bypass path to avoid scrambling, as described on Page 80. Above here, despite patches of quartzite rubble that may require putting hand to rock for balance (Grade 2½?), unexposed slopes climb to Claurigh's ▲summit. See Route 90a + Extension 1 for full description.

Route 88d Stob Coire an Laoigh from Coirechoille via Beinn na Socaich

Ascent and descent of Stob Coire an Laoigh alone:
G3 **** NN 256788, 10ml/16km, 1120m/3650ft M55
Add-on descent of Back Basin: 1ml/2km
Add-on Sgurr Choinnich Mor and descent of Back Basin: 2ml/3km, 160m/500ft

The Grey Corries Traverse descent route from Stob Coire an Laoigh over Stob Coire Easain and Beinn na Socaich can also be used to make a direct ascent of Laoigh as a lone objective. In terms of distance from Coirechoille car park, the route is almost as long as an approach over Stob Choire Claurigh, so it is normally used only by those wishing to avoid the Traverse. More interestingly, it can be combined with an ascent of Sgurr Choinnich Mor and/or a descent via the Back Basin to make a superb round trip.

The route is described on descent in Route 88a Extension 1, but we make a few notes here about using it for ascent. Your first objective is the dam on the Allt Choimhlidh at NN 239765, 1½ml/2½km away along the LNGR path opposite the car park or c.½ml/1km further away using the better-surfaced forest track that begins at the T-junction below the car park.

Using the forest approach, follow the track into the woods, turn left at another T-junction and reach the bridge over the Allt Choimhlidh. At a fork just before here, take the left branch up to the dam. The LNGR path joins this side track at the first Z-bend.

Above the dam it is necessary to cross the stream, which here runs through a deep V-shaped dell. Walk along the left-hand bank for c.100m to the foot of a small gorge, where a watersplash that can normally be crossed dryshod gives access to the right-hand bank. A steep climb on grass then takes you away from the streamside onto more open terrain at an easier angle.

As you ascend, bear right to pick up the ATV track that climbs to the skyline. As crags begin to build on the left above Coire a' Mhadaidh, the track zigzags up the crest of Beinn na Socaich's north ridge and ends.

The watersplash

Good going continues over ΔBeinn na Socaich to ΔStob Coire Easain, where a short stretch of quartzite ridge separates you from the ▲summit of Stob Coire an Laoigh.

N.B. In this direction, the Stob Coire Easain bypass route described on Page 61 looks easy to begin with but becomes progressively more difficult and is not recommended.

See also picture on Page 62

Needlepoint: On ascent of Beinn na Socaich's north-east hillside in cloud, take care not to veer left onto the craggy ground that flanks Coire a' Mhadaidh. The ATV track is a useful aid if you can find it. Following the broad ridge that traverses Beinn na Socaich's summit is made easier by the craggy corrie rim. Once you have reached Stob Coire Easain, crossing the gap to Stob Coire an Laoigh should be easy if you keep to the ridge-crest, although the quartzite will be more awkward when wet.

Chilly Willy: This is a relatively easy winter route as far as Stob Coire Easain. Above there, conditions dictate all. The steeper quartzite slopes encountered on the climb over Stob Coire Easain to Stob Coire an Laoigh will seem more exposed when the rocks are under snow. When they are incompletely covered, they present even more ankle-twisting opportunities than in summer.

▲90 Stob Ban 178 977m/3205ft (OS 41, NN 266723)

Stop Baan, White Mountain, named for its quartzite cap (not to be confused with namesake ▲74 in the Mamores)

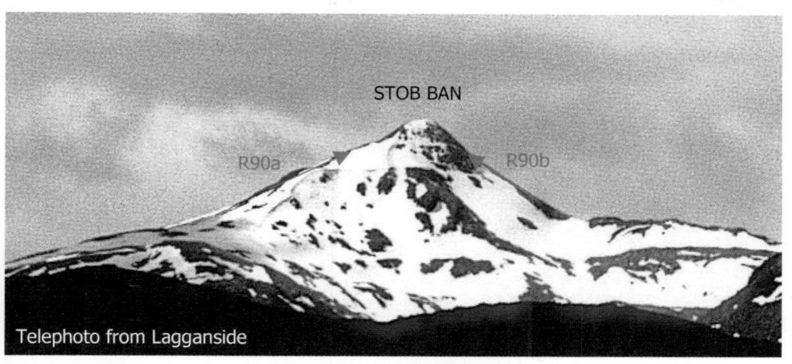

Telephoto from Lagganside

Peak Fitness: No change since 1891 Tables.

Stob Ban is an idiosyncratic Munro with multiple personalities. While the three highest Grey Corries Munros sit atop the main spine of the range, Stob Ban stands detached to the south across an 800m/2600ft bealach. Viewed from Lagganside, its summit cone dominates its surroundings, making it one of the most recognisable peaks in the Central Highlands. On the other hand, it is 200m/656ft lower than its neighbour Stob Choire Claurigh and, when viewed from there, appears somewhat dumpy.

Closer inspection provides no help in pinning down its true nature. The northern flanks harbour the Giant's Staircase, which aspires to be the best scramble in the Grey Corries. On the other hand, that summit cone, like that of its Mamores namesake, is one big heap of quartzite rubble.

The GoTH view? We like Stob Ban. It is a quirky peak that constantly surprises. Tackle it on its own, either by the normal route up the easy east/north-east ridge (Route 90a) or by the scramblers' route up the Giant's Staircase (Route 90b), or by a round trip using both routes, and it rewards with a multifarious ascent to a commanding viewpoint. For a taste of Grey Corries ridge walking, combine it with an ascent of Stob Choire Claurigh (Route 90a Extension 1). Tag it on to a traverse of the Main Ridge and you'll join an elite minority (Route 90c).

N.B. This section concentrates on the northern approaches to Stob Ban, but it can also be approached by a very long walk-in from Glen Nevis to the west (see Route 90c for details).

Route 90a Stob Ban from Coirechoille

Ascent and descent by East/North-east Ridge:
G2 **** NN 256788 11ml/17km, 850m/2800ft M55

The approach is as for Route 88a. From Coirechoille car park, follow the Land Rover track up through the forestry plantation and along the deep trench of the Lairig Leacach. On the right are the Grey Corries' two most easterly Tops (Stob Coire na Ceannain and Stob Coire Gaibhre), while on the left are the twin rocky lumps of Cruach Innse (*Croo-ach Eensha*, Island Mound) and Sgurr Innse, the nearest thing Scotland has to a butte.

It is 4ml/6km to the foot of the mountain and the same distance back at the end of the day, but it is an easy, scenic walk that takes you to the heart of remote country. Relax and savour. Above the upper forest boundary, the track crosses the river and rises very gently to the summit of the lairig, gaining only 140m/450ft in 2ml/3km. The pass is so gentle that you'll have difficulty spotting its highpoint.

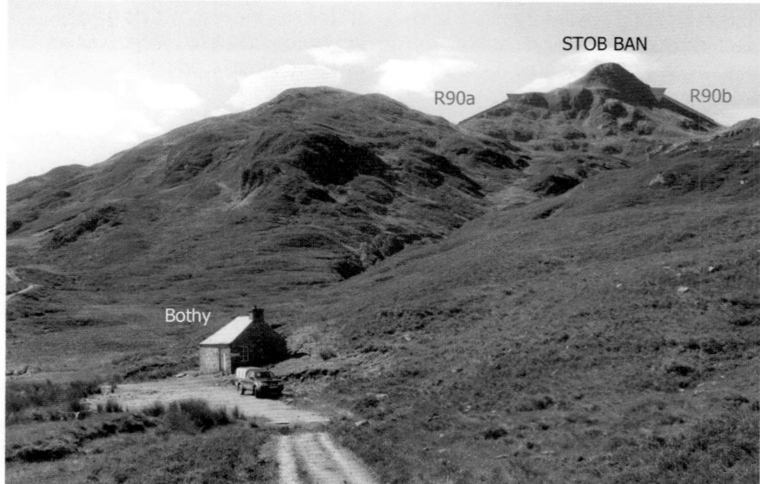

GiGi: The Lairig Leacach (*Lahrik Lyech-kach*, Slabby or Granite Pass) was once used by rustlers along the Thieves' Road (see Page 100). The broad trench, hemmed in by steep mountainsides, made it one of the easier routes for cattle control.

In earlier times, it contained a glacially dammed loch that drained away at the end of the last Ice Age. Look for signs of the ancient shoreline at the 260m contour, in the forest above the car park, marked on the OS map as a Parallel Road.

Over the summit, the track descends slightly into a broad green valley. A corner is rounded and Stob Ban bursts into view at last. It's hard to believe that the soaring, conical summit is only 500m/1650ft above. A little further along, the track rounds another corner and reaches an open bothy, superbly sited at the foot of the mountain's north-east ridge.

Behind the bothy, a path starts up beside the Allt a' Chuil Choirean (*Owlt a Choo-il Corran*, Stream of the Back Corrie), heading for the Giant's Staircase (Route 90b). The easier normal route crosses the stream (stepping stones or bridge just upstream) and follows the continuing path through the Lairig Leacach. After a couple of hundred metres the path splits at a Y-fork. Take the right branch to climb the north-east ridge.

Incorrigibly, the path goes straight up the rocky hump seen ahead before continuing less steeply up a shallow depression right of the skyline (this latter section can become quite boggy after rain). At the top of the depression the path emerges onto a shoulder, from where there are great views both of the summit and the Giant's Staircase in the corrie below.

The path now follows the ridge left, traversing the hillside below (right of) the crest to bypass a minor rise and reach the saddle beyond. The ridge then veers right and rears steeply upwards. The path climbs grassy slopes to a small levelling, beyond which you are faced with the final

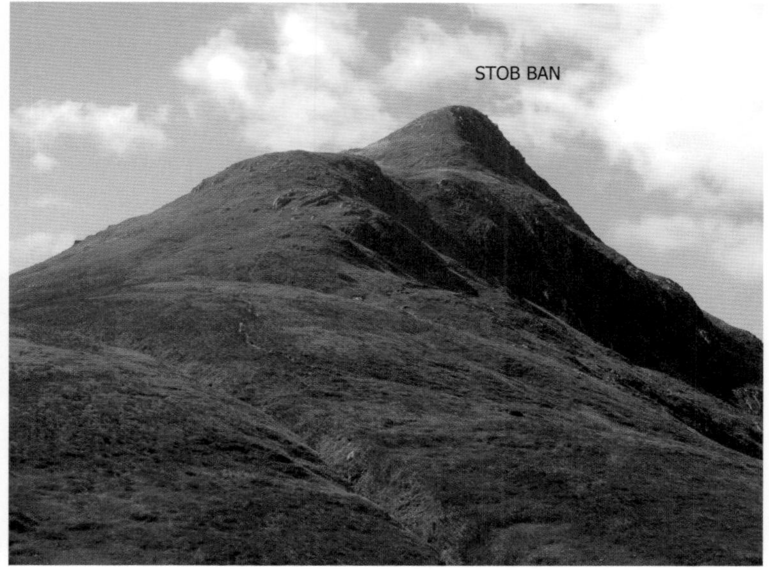

150m/500ft summit pyramid of quartzite shale. Fortunately, the going isn't as tiresome as it looks. The stony path zigzags up without causing too many retrograde steps and you'll soon be at the ▲summit admiring the view.

F-Stop: Stob Ban's separation from the spine of the Grey Corries gives it panoramic views. To the west are the major Grey Corries summits, to the south-west are the Mamores, to the east are the wall-like Easains and to their south is a long corridor that leads into the wilderness, past Corrour, as far as the eye can see.

Needlepoint: The path makes a foul-weather ascent straightforward, but the quartzite is ankle-twistingly slippery when wet. More careful navigation and attention to footing is required to descend the north ridge safely (Extension 1).

Chilly Willy: Stob Ban's 150m/500ft summit cone is not to be taken lightly in winter. When path and rocks are under snow, very steep and exposed slopes guard the summit on nearly all sides. Of the three ridges that meet at the summit (east, north and south-west), only the gentle south-west ridge gives a straightforward winter ascent (see Route 90c).

The ascent of Stob Coire Claurigh from the intervening bealach (Extension 1) is more straightforward, and you can reach the bealach by Route 90b to avoid going over Stob Ban. Nevertheless, the ground steepens higher up, so this is not a beginner's route.

Route 90a Extension 1: Stob Choire Claurigh

With descent via Stob Gaibhre (R88a): G3 (with G4/G5 options) ****
extra mileage: zero; extra ascent: 380m/1250ft M55
With descent via Giant's Staircase (R90b): G3 (with G4/G5 options) ***
extra mileage: 2ml/3km; extra ascent: 380m/1250ft M55

Fresh from your escapades on Stob Ban's summit rockpile, a return trip via Stob Choire Claurigh may well tempt. Reaching the summit involves a 380m/1250ft ascent from the intervening bealach, but the going is easier than on Stob Ban and there's no extra mileage because, from the summit, you can descend over Stob Coire Gaibhre (reversing Route 88a).

The main problem is reaching the intervening bealach in the first place, as this requires the descent of the loose quartzite chippings on Stob Ban's very steep north ridge. Take a look over the edge and you'll soon know whether you want to tackle it or not. The main scree run goes right, dangerously close to the cliff edge. It is safer to descend further left, using traces of stony path wherever possible. You'll use many parts of the anatomy on the way down, and not always intentionally.

Across the bealach, a broad ridge, mostly grassy at first, climbs more easily to a small levelling. It then bears left, becoming steeper and more rock-strewn as it climbs to a larger levelling. Finally it bears left again and becomes encrusted in more of those quartzite chippings. The terrain is never as awkward as on Stob Ban, but you'll probably need to use hands here and there to pick your way up the loose rocks (Grade 2½?).

STOB COIRE CLAURIGH

As noted earlier, this is the easiest route up ▲Stob Choire Claurigh. If you wish to climb Claurigh alone and avoid Stob Ban's north ridge, reach the intervening bealach by the easy path up beside the Giant's Staircase (Route 90b).

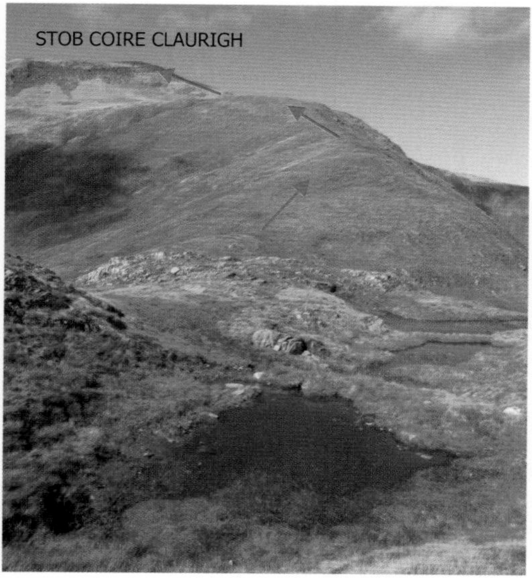

Route 90b Stob Ban from Coirechoille: The Giant's Staircase

G2 or G3/G4/G5 ***** NN 256788, 11ml/17km, 850m/2800ft M55
(including descent by Route 90a (east/north-east ridge)

Stob Ban towers over the bothy at its foot but its best-kept secret is hidden from there. At the back of Coire Claurigh above the bothy, tier upon tier of beautifully clean quartzite slabs rise to the bealach at the foot of the north ridge, between Stob Ban and Stob Choire Claurigh. They form a series of rock steps known as the Giant's Staircase. Quartzite on Scottish mountains, as at the summit of Stob Ban itself, usually means horrendous going on sharp cuttings, but the Giant's Staircase shows how exhilarating the stuff can be when it puts its mind to it.

N.B. A path beside the Staircase avoids all scrambling, but anyone not confident on rock will find the ensuing rockpile of the north ridge nerve-wracking. We'll describe the path for those who wish to use it to find an easy way up Stob Choire Claurigh, as described on the previous page, but otherwise this is a scramblers' route *par excellence*.

To reach the foot of the stairs, take the path that starts behind the bothy and climbs the right-hand side of the gorge of the Allt a' Chuil Choirean. The path is patience-testingly boggy but it does the job and it's not far to the Staircase. It runs to a confluence where the main stream, complete with picturesque waterfalls, turns right to climb into the upper reaches of Cul Choirean beneath Claurigh.

Continue straight on at the confluence, following a less convincing path along the left-hand side of the smaller stream, to reach a grassy bowl. At the back of this the Staircase erupts from the greenery.

Now... which way up?

The slabs are scattered across the mountainside and separated by the grassy terraces that turn them into a staircase for giants. A direct ascent is at least a hard G5 scramble, but there are innumerable easy G4 routes, working back and forth up lines of weakness. You can always take to the grass if necessary, to outflank a particular outcrop here and there but, once you grasp the solid gleaming rock, you'll find it very more-ish.

Viewed overall, the Staircase is divided into three tiers. The first tier consists of a maze of small slabs, giving a choice of routes up to a little terrace that harbours a few tiny lochans. Above here, the more daunting second tier can be tackled by a long rib that rises in a fine situation on its right-hand side. This leads to a larger terrace with more tiny lochans.

Above here rises the even more daunting third tier, a great buttress of rock that reaches up to the skyline. Like the second tier, it is easier than it looks. On its right-hand side is a grassy

gully whose left-hand edge gives excellent scrambling on big rock steps with loads of handholds. If you go all the way up, you'll emerge on the north ridge just above the bealach.

If you are unsure about committing to the rock, you can dabble along the edge of the Staircase by climbing steep but easy grass slopes between the lower slabs and a deep rock-filled gully further left. You'll find traces of path that take you up to the grassy terrace below the third tier. From here, an indistinct path traverses right across the terrace to the bealach, where there is an attractive lochan with a small island.

If, having arrived at the foot of the Staircase, you wish to avoid the rocks altogether, simply stay on the path. Indistinct for a while, it crosses the foot of the rocky gully and climbs the grassy spur to its left. Higher up, it re-crosses the gully and continues across the terrace between second and third tiers, as noted above.

Stob Ban's summit towers 170m/550ft over the bealach. It doesn't sound like much, but it certainly looks like much. Trust your eyes – that steep pile of sharp quartzite cuttings does not make for an equilibrious ascent. If your fingers are too delicate to wrap around the stuff, you've come to the wrong place.

A path tries its best but eventually gives up the ghost. The main scree run stays left and aims directly for the summit, but you may well decide it is too loose and close to the north-east face for comfort. You'll find safer ground and easier going further right, where the rocks are eventually stabilised by grass slopes bordering the easy south-west ridge. Knuckle down, remind yourself that it is the 170m/550ft of ascent that makes the mountain a Munro, and work your way as steadily as possible to the ▲summit.

To descend, follow the normal route down the east/north-east ridge to the bothy... unless, of course, you decide to return over Stob Choire Claurigh (Route 90a Extension 1).

Knuckling down on Stob Ban

Needlepoint: An ascent of Stob Ban via the Giant's Staircase is a more awkward foul-weather proposition than the normal route. Not only do the slabs complicate routefinding on ascent to the bealach, but trying to find a way up the steep wet rubble of the north ridge above there may lead you onto difficult ground.

Chilly Willy: The Giant's Staircase is a scrambler's playground best enjoyed when glinting in summer sun. In winter, the ascent of the north ridge is an even steeper steep snow climb than the normal route up the north-east ridge. It is still more awkward if iced rocks protrude.

The only viable reason to come this way in winter is to find the easiest route up Stob Choire Claurigh (Route 96 Extension 1). Reach the bealach by following the line of the summer path left of the slabs. If you feel uncomfortable on the snow slope here, it would be wise to go no higher.

Route 90c The Grey Corries Grand Traverse from Coirechoille or Glen Nevis

G4 (with G5 options) ***** M46/M55
From Coirechoille: NN 256788, 19ml/30km, 1750m/5750ft
From Glen Nevis: NN 168691, 17ml/27km, 1860m/6100ft

Given sufficient fitness, bagging all four Grey Corries Munros from Glen Nevis or Coirechoille in a single trip is a tempting challenge. A Glen Nevis start makes for a shorter round, but the initial 7½ml/12km walk to Stob Ban is longer, rougher, involves 110m/350ft more ascent and seems to take forever.

Ideally, the Grand Traverse would be done in linear fashion but, for the benefit of those who don't have the luxury of transport at both ends, we describe the route as a round trip from each starting point in turn.

(1) From Coirechoille. Climb ▲Stob Ban (Route 90a or 90b) and ▲Stob Choire Claurigh (Route 90a Extension 1), then cross the main ridge to ▲Stob Coire an Laoigh (Route

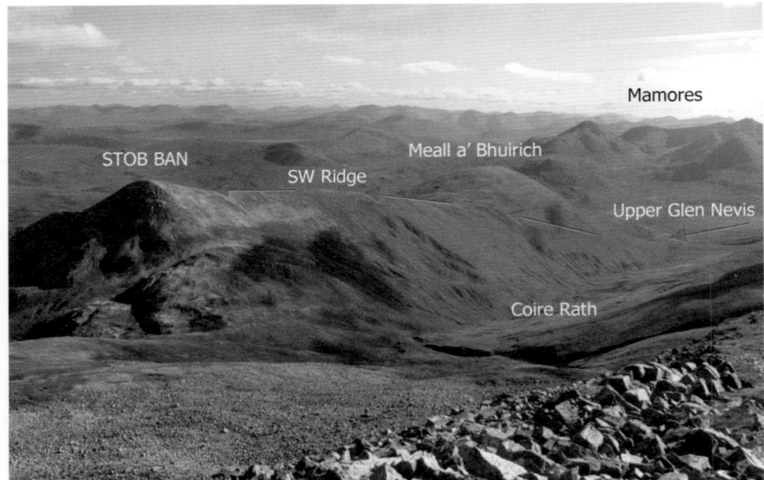

88a). Continue to ▲Sgurr Choinnich Mor (and ΔSgurr Choinnich Beag for an extra 1ml/2km, 60m/ 200ft) and return to Coirechoille via the Back Basin (Route 88a Extension 1).

(2) From Glen Nevis road-end. Take the path through the Nevis Gorge and past Steall Waterfall (Route 87a). Leaving Sgurr Choinnich Mor for later, follow the rough, boggy path along upper Glen Nevis to the mouth of Coire Rath beyond the moorland lump of Tom an Eite (*Tome an Aitya*, Knoll of the Ear of Corn). From here, the round of all four Grey Corries Munros amounts to a skyline circuit of that long, wild corrie. Rath (*Ra*) means Good Fortune... and we hope you have some.

You are now faced with the 2½ml/4km climb up Stob Ban's south-west ridge. This is guarded by the great round lump of Meall a' Bhuirich, (*Myowl a Voorich*, Hill of Rutting or Roaring – of deer), which forms the ridge's end point at the corrie mouth. To avoid the steep, rocky ground that a full-frontal assault would entail, to say nothing of the 90m/300ft descent to the saddle beyond it, walk up Coire Rath until you can take an easier diagonal line up the hillside directly to the saddle.

Beyond the saddle, the ridge narrows and climbs easily to Stob Ban's summit. As a way of climbing Stob Ban alone, this approach makes an epic return trip for anyone seeking a *really* off-the-beaten path route (G3 *** 15ml/24km, 930m/3050ft). To continue the Grand Traverse, cross the main ridge to Sgurr Choinnich Mor (and Beag?) as described above, then re-descend to Glen Nevis (Route 87a).

And if that's not enough, try the next route.

Route 90d The Eightsome Reel: The Grey Corries and The Nevis Range from Coirechoille to Glen Nevis

G4 or G5 ***** NN 256788 to NN 128718, 19ml/31km, 3330m/11,000ft

Having bagged the four Munros of the Grey Corries, why not tack on the four Munros of the Nevis Range to complete the traverse of all eight Munros on the north Glen Nevis skyline? We're joking, right? Only acolytes of Torpedo need read on.

A round trip would involve a leg-numbing end-of-day march back to the starting point, so it is ideally done end-to-end, starting at Coirechoille and finishing in Glen Nevis.

From Coirechoille, first complete the Grand Traverse of the Grey Corries over ▲Stob Ban, ▲Stob Choire Claurigh, ▲Stob Coire an Laoigh and ▲Sgurr Choinnich Mor, as per Route 90c. Separating the two quartets of Munros is the 731m/2398ft bealach west of Sgurr Choinnich Mor and Sgurr Choinnich Beag. Across the bealach, the great eastern wall of Aonach Beag towers intimidatingly, seeming to offer no easy way up to either of its two satellite Tops. On the skyline immediately above the bealach is ΔStob Coire Bhealaich, with ΔSgurr a' Bhuic to its south (left) around the craggy rim of Coire a' Bhuic.

Rising to Stob Coire Bhealaich, a steepening spur becomes a rock rib that is a no-go area without a rope. Amazingly, however, it is possible to make a way up to its left, where a steep, loose, very exposed 'path' finds a zigzagging G3 route up through the cliffs. The line tops out on the skyline at a corner (cairn) just below Stob Coire Bhealaich's summit.

Although this route barely rates a scramble in technical terms, it will be too nerve-wracking for many. Unless you are as sure-footed as a mountain goat and thrill to exciting situations on awkward ground above big drops, we advise you to avoid it.

Fortunately for most hillwalkers, there's an easier if less well-known way up – a G2 grassy gully that requires no rockwork at all. From the bealach, go left across a broad, grassy shelf to the foot of Sgurr a' Bhuic, then bear right up the obvious gully. Lack of a path at the time of writing shows that few people pass this way, but the gully climbs without incident all the way to the skyline, which it reaches at the lowest point between Sgurr a' Bhuic and Stob Coire Bhealaich, close under Sgurr a' Bhuic's summit.

The gully is quite steep near the top but, with developing traces of path, should remain easy to all but the most sensitive of souls. The fact that the rock rib route is more popular says more about the kind of mountain athletes who tackle the Eightsome Reel than it says about the relative ease of the two ascent options.

Once up, all that remains is the simple matter of continuing over ▲Aonach Beag, ▲Aonach Mor, ▲Carn Mor Dearg and ▲Ben Nevis, as per Route 85a Extension 1, and descending the Mountain Track to Glen Nevis (Route 83a).

Torpedo: And if *that's* not enough, add the Mamores as well. First completed by Philip Tranter in 1964, *Tranter's Round* of 18 Munros involves upwards of 36ml/58km and 6300m/20,600ft of ascent. The record stands at under 13 hours.

And if that's *still* not enough, add the five Munros around Loch Treig (Section 19), as Charlie Ramsay did in 1978. *Ramsay's Round* was devised to climb 24 Munros (now 23 + Sgurr an Iubhair, demoted to Top status in 1997) in 24 hours. It involves some 60ml/96km and 8500m/28,000ft of ascent. Good luck!

Sgurr a' Bhuic

Stob Coire Bhealaich

Difficult route

Easy route

Needlepoint: Trying to find, let alone climb, the rock rib route in cloud, when wet rock is likely to add to difficulties, is not a leisure pursuit we recommend. As for the grassy gully, it remains navigationally straightforward once you're in it... but are you really sure you're starting up the hillside in the right place?

Chilly Willy: Both the rock rib and grassy gully routes are difficult winter propositions that demand winter mountaineering skills. The rock rib is a mixed rock and ice route for experts only, while even the grassy gully becomes a steep and exposed snow climb whose exit may well be corniced.

As a complete route, the Eightsome Reel is a huge winter's day (and night?!) There are easier routes in the Alps.

19 CORROUR

At a height of 410m/1307ft, Corrour Station on the West Highland Railway lies in the middle of a 50ml/80km-wide expanse of roadless land that stretches from the west coast to the Cairngorms. Rarely can such remote country be reached for so little effort. If you can step aboard a train, you can get there.

On some routes in this book you may suffer from vertigo. The main hazard at Corrour is agoraphobia. Despite the railway, estate tracks and sporadic buildings, it feels like wilderness. When the train departs and leaves you stranded on the platform, you may experience a frisson of misgiving over what you have let yourself in for.

To the north and east are seven varied Munros, split into three groups by fjord-like Loch Treig (*Loch Trake*, Forsaken Loch) and Loch Ossian. Some of them can be tackled more easily from roadside starting points, but the presence of the station allows intrepid walkers to take the morning train to Corrour and spend the day walking back out over the mountains, point-to-point style.

The western group of two Munros, Stob Coire Easain and Stob a' Choire Mheadhoin, collectively known as the Easains, are usually climbed from the hamlet of Fersit to the north, off the A86 in Glen Spean (Route 91a), but for a real walk on the wild side consider a Corrour-to-Fersit traverse (Route 91b). The central group of two Munros, Chno Dearg and Stob Coire Sgriodain, can similarly be climbed from Fersit (Route 93a) or more memorably by a point-to-point trip from Corrour to Fersit (Route 93b).

Separated from Chno Dearg by a deep glen is Beinn na Lap, an isolated mountain that is the closest Munro to Corrour. It is awkward to reach from anywhere else without a very long walk-in and is usually climbed from the station between trains (Route 95a).

Further east again, the two Munros of Sgor Gaibhre and Carn Dearg can be climbed by a between-trains round trip from Corrour (Route 96a), from near Rannoch station in the south (Route 96b), or by a station-to-station traverse that begins at Corrour and ends at Rannoch (Route 96c).

Arranging a climbing trip around a railway timetable requires more pre-planning than usual, but such is the pull of Corrour that a single visit is never going to be enough.

The relief of Corrour
NB The bridge no longer exists

For information on access restrictions during the stalking season, contact Corrour Estate. Website: www.corrour.co.uk. Tel: 01397-732200.

GiGi: Some point-to-point routes in this section begin at Corrour (reached from Tulloch Station on the A86) and end at Fersit. Without transport at Fersit, you then have a 3½ml/6km end-of-day road walk back to Tulloch.

The road passes the Inverlair kettle holes, formed by giant chunks of glacial ice that became partially covered by sediment before melting to leave deep depressions. The largest one, right by the roadside, is known as The Robber's Pit (NN 337801).

By rail it is only 1½ml/2½km from Fersit to Tulloch, but there is no right of way along the line and, at the time of writing, no path runs all the way beside it.

Making the most of Corrour

The train runs between Glasgow and Fort William and carries bicycles. From the east, drive to Crianlarich, Tyndrum or Bridge of Orchy and board it there. From the north, board it at Tulloch in Glen Spean.

From Monday to Saturday the timetable normally allows around seven hours between trains to and from Corrour (c.11.30 to c.18.30 from the south, c.8.30 to c.15.30 from the north). There are other trains at more unsociable hours. On Sundays there are no useful trains for day trips. For up-to-date timetable information, visit www.scotrail.co.uk or call 0845-6015929.

In order to spend more time at Corrour and go a-baggin' to your heart's content, plan an overnight stay. The Scottish Youth Hostels Association runs two hostels in the area: the long-standing (1931) former boathouse on the shore of Loch Ossian, 1ml/1½km from the station, and Corrour Station House itself. The latter, leased from Corrour estate in 2010, also serves refreshments. For up-to-date information on opening times and winter closures, call direct (01397-732-236) or contact SYHA (website: www.syha.org.uk, tel: 0845-2937373).

To solve all access problems, rent a cottage at Loch Ossian and obtain a gate code for the estate track that runs to the loch from the A86 (NN 432830). For further information, visit www.corrour.co.uk.

Torpedo: Some Culra Munros can also be reached from Corrour (see Pages 130 & 148).

The Easains:

▲91 Stob Coire Easain 39 1115m/3658ft (OS 41, NN 308730) *Stop Corra Essan*, Peak of the Corrie of the Little Waterfall

▲92 Stob a' Choire Mheadhoin 46 1105m/3625ft (OS 41, NN 316736) *Stop a Chorra Vey-an*, Peak of the Middle Corrie

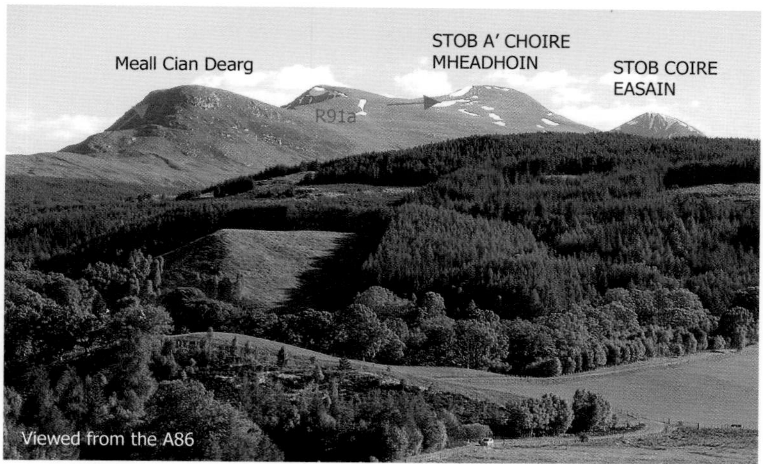

Peak Fitness: No change since 1891 Tables, although the two peaks were originally named Stob Coire Easain Mhoir and Stob a' Choire Mheadhoinaiche. Easain Mhoir means Big Little Waterfall.

These two shapely peaks form a huge mountain wall on the west side of Loch Treig, which occupies a deep glacial trench north of Corrour. The two summits are the high points on a long ridge that runs the entire length of the lochside.

With Tulloch Station near the north end of the loch and Corrour Station near the south, you can make a challenging one-way trip along the ridge by taking the morning train from Tulloch to Corrour and walking back to Fersit (Route 91b). However, as the additional road walk from Fersit back to Tulloch acts as a deterrent, the most popular way of bagging the summits is by a round trip that begins and ends at Fersit road-end (Route 91a). Whichever way you climb the pair, their complex mountainsides make for 'interesting' routefinding.

Route 91a Stob Coire Easain and Stob a' Choire Mheadhoin round trip from Fersit

G3 *** NN 350782 Return via Coire Laire: 10ml/16km, 1040m/3400ft M89
Return via outward route: save 1½ml/2½km, add 140m/450ft

! This is the normal route up the Easains, but anyone who feels nervous on steep, rocky ground may prefer to avoid the ascent of Meall Cian Dearg and reach the two Munros by walking up Coire Laire and climbing to the bealach between them (described below as a descent route).

Begin at Fersit car park, at the end of the public road near the head of Loch Treig, 3½ml/6km from the A86. Your first task is to reach the craggy nose of Meall Cian Dearg (*Myowl Chee-an Jerrak*, Bare Red-headed Hill) on Stob a' Choire Mheadhoin's north-west ridge. A prominent 3m/10ft stone pyramid at the foot of the nose (actually a hydro survey pillar) makes a useful landmark (NN 337767). The hillside above the car park is complex and beset with crags, making the approach to the pillar less than straightforward. Two routes lead to it, presenting you with an immediate choice.

The first route follows a path that starts at the left-hand corner of the car park. It contours to a stile in a fence, crosses the flat bed of the LNGR line (see Page 91) and makes a shallow rising traverse across the hillside. It is, in parts, rough, boggy and difficult to follow. It even surmounts a 3m/10ft rock outcrop at one point. If you lose it, which is quite likely, you'll have to make your own way across the hill-side. It is no accident that most of the footprints in the mud point downhill, as it is easier to deduce where the path is going on descent.

The second route is less popular because it is less direct, but it is easier to follow and more pleasant to walk. It begins with a 1ml/1½km stroll along a hydro track that begins at the end of the car park. Stay right at a first fork and left at a second to reach a pleasant section beside Loch Treig.

Meall Cian Dearg

hydro pillar

The track leaves the lochside to round a hillock and reach a left-hand bend beside a small stream (NN 343765). Two side tracks branch sharp right here. Take the second, rougher one, which crosses the stream and climbs the hillside beside an even smaller stream, which it crosses in turn to reach some old sheep fanks. When it ends immediately above the sheep fanks, a path continues straight up the hillside. This eventually re-crosses the stream and makes a rising traverse to the pillar, which isn't seen on this approach until you are almost upon it.

The two approach paths join just beyond the pillar for a combined assault on craggy Meall Cian Dearg itself. The now single path stays well left until it reaches the upper rocks, where incorrigibly it veers right to pick a way straight up the nose. The path is steep and stony, requires occasional handwork and is briefly exposed. You may prefer an easier path that curves up to the right, although even here you'll still find hands useful for balance.

You emerge onto the flat top of Meall Cian Dearg for a stroll along a broad, almost level ridge, whose lawn-like terrain makes a path superfluous. When the ridge steepens onto a shoulder, revealing the dark waters of Loch Treig below, the path becomes more distinct again. Atop the shoulder, another level section and another rise around the rim of craggy Coire Meadhon (for which the Munro is named) lead to the flat, rocky ▲summit of Stob a' Choire Mheadhoin.

Ahead, across the bowl of Coire Easain Beag (*Bake*, Little), lies the steep, stony pyramid of Stob Coire Easain, sporting some impressively contorted folds of rock beneath its summit. A stony path among loose rocks descends around the corrie rim to the bealach between the two Munros. Note the cairn on the near (north) side

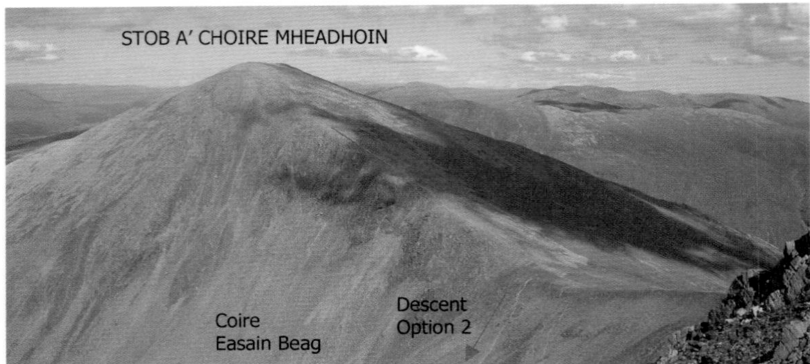

of the bealach, which marks the start of a path down into the corrie. The re-ascent to Stob Coire Easain is equally rough and even steeper (and certainly feels it). The quartzite boulder ▲summit occupies a commanding position at the apex of three ridges and has views to spare.

Now you have another decision to make: which way to return to Fersit. Although it seems unlikely, the quickest way back is to reverse the outward route over Stob a' Choire Mheadhoin. The alternative is to return via Coire Laire (*Corra Lahra*, Low Corrie), the deep trench to the west. This option is more interesting and makes a round trip possible, but it can end up feeling like a route march if you're not in the mood.

You should have guessed by now that there are two ways down into the corrie, each of which begins with a path that peters out far too soon. One way down (Option 1) descends Stob Coire Easain's stony north-west ridge around the rim of Coire Easain Beag. Once past the corrie's flanking crags,

bear right down steep grass slopes.

The other way down (Option 2) takes the path noted above which descends from the bealach between the two Munros. Coire Easain Beag's scree-and-rock headwall immediately below the bealach is very steep, but the path takes a diagonal line down to make amazingly light work of it. Once into the bowl of the corrie, stay close to the stream until you reach Coire Laire, avoiding the temptation to take a short cut right, which leads onto unseen steep ground.

We find it hard to recommend one descent route over the other, so you decide. Both routes eventually involve a traipse down clingy moor to reach the grassy flats of Coire Laire. Once down, you'll pick up a good path on the right bank of the Allt Laire, which leads to a confusing network of paths and tracks at the edge of forestry plantations west of Fersit. Stay on the right bank to reach the path along the LNGR line, which provides a genteel stroll back to your starting point. On reaching the first trees at Fersit, just before a ruined bridge, a path descends to the car park.

GiGi: For information on the LNGR and the Lochaber hydro-power scheme, see Page 61. The Coire Lair intake, which captures the waters of the Allt Laire, was renowned for its whisky still, which kept construction workers happy at their task.

Needlepoint: The ascent of Stob a' Choire Mheadhoin remains fairly straightforward in cloud, but continuing to Stob Coire Easain requires more concentration. If you lose the indistinct path on descent to the intervening bealach, there is a danger of straying too far right onto the crags of Coire Easain Beag. On return from Stob Coire Easain, the safest route is a descent from the bealach into Coire Laire.

Chilly Willy: In winter, steep snow may be encountered in several places. Meall Cian Dearg, especially, can present a formidable obstacle. On the corrie rim walk around Coire Easain Beag between the two Munros, the exposure is considerable and care is required when the rocks are iced. When the descent path into the corrie is obliterated by snow, descend instead by Stob Coire Easain's north-west ridge.

Route 91b The Easains Traverse: Stob Coire Easain and Stob a' Choire Mheadhoin one-way trip from Corrour to Fersit

G3 **** NN 356664 to NN 350782, 12ml/19km, 1130m/3700ft M93

This is a rugged route that will challenge both stamina and route-finding ability. From Corrour Station, your first goal is Creaguaineach Lodge at the south end of Loch Treig. From here the route climbs Stob Coire Easain's south ridge and continues over Stob a' Choire Mheadhoin, reversing Route 91a along the whole length of Loch Treig's western wall to Fersit.

The 4ml/6km walk down to the lodge is an adventure in itself. For the first 1½ml/2km, as far as the Allt Luib Ruairidh (*Owlt Loo-ib Roo-airy*, Stream of Rory's Bay), it follows a path that begins on the west side of the station, just north of the platform, and runs parallel to the railway line. The path is wondrously boggy in parts, but then it *is* crossing the edge of the watery wilderness that is Rannoch Moor. In general, it is drier than it has any right to be, and you can at least practise your tightrope-walking skills on railway sleepers that attempt to float over the deepest mires (picture on Page 86).

Beyond the Allt Luib Ruairidh a rough track takes you the remainder of the way to the lodge. It descends to the head of Loch Treig, leaves the railway line behind and feels very remote indeed as it rounds wave-lapped beaches to reach the now forlorn and boarded-up lodge.

GiGi: On the short but scenic rail journey along the shore of Loch Treig from Tulloch to Corrour, look across the water for the Easain Mor (*Essan Moar*, Big Waterfall, NN 318715), from which Stob Coire Easain derives its name.

Here the character of the route changes completely. Beyond the lodge, keep to the near bank of the Allt na Lairige (*Owlt na Lahrike*, Stream of the Pass) to pick up a path to a fence, at the foot of which you'll find a bridge over the river (NN 308693).

On the far side, a path continues to the Easan Dubh (*Essan Doo*, Black Waterfall) in a deep gorge. To surmount the gorge's flanking crags, the path climbs right then back left, much churned up by trail bikes.

The path continues across the hillside well above the river beneath the crags of Creagan a' Chaise (*Craikan a Chasha*, Steep Rocky Hillock). Once beyond the crags, make a rising traverse into an ill-defined corrie. Your goal is the corrie's far skyline, which is the south-west ridge of Point 916 (Stob Coire Easain's south top).

Once you have worked your way onto this ridge, all routefinding difficulties are over. On the climb to Point 916, the ridge takes more shape, the going improves and you reach an entertaining section among (or over) sharply upturned folds of rock. The ridge then broadens and levels over Point 916 to reveal the two Munros ahead (at last!).

From the shallow dip beyond Point 916, the final 214m/703ft climb to Stob Coire Easain follows the curving south-west ridge around the rim of deep Coire Easain Mor (*Voar*, Big) above Loch Treig. Traces of path appear underfoot to verify that you're not the first to pass this way. Approaching the ▲summit, the rim narrows, with turf and rocks underfoot, to provide a perfect finish. The narrow section rejoices in the name Irlick Chaoile (*Cheula*, Narrow).

From the summit, reverse Route 91a, making the steep descent and re-ascent around the rim of Coire Easain Beag to ▲Stob a' Choire Mheadhoin, then descending northwards over Meall Cian Dearg to Fersit.

Needlepoint: The rising traverse onto the SW ridge of Point 916 crosses complex ground that will be very difficult to navigate in cloud. Not that I've tried. Or intend to.

Chilly Willy: Stob Coire Easain's SW ridge is the best winter ascent route on the Easains. In the right snow conditions, the Irlick Chaoile becomes a beautiful snow arête.

▲93 Chno Dearg 86 1046m/3432ft (OS 41, NN 377741)

Craw Jerrak, Red Nut, but more likely to be a misprint for Cnoc Dearg (*Crochk Jerrak*, Red Hill), which was the mountain's name in the original 1891 Tables before it was changed in 1921

△Meall Garbh 976m/3203ft (OS 41, NN 371727)
Myowl Garrav, Rough Hill

▲94 Stob Coire Sgriodain 174 979m/3212ft

(OS 41, NN 356743) *Stop Corra Screejan*, Peak of the Corrie of Scree

△South Top 958m/3144ft (OS 41, NN 359739)

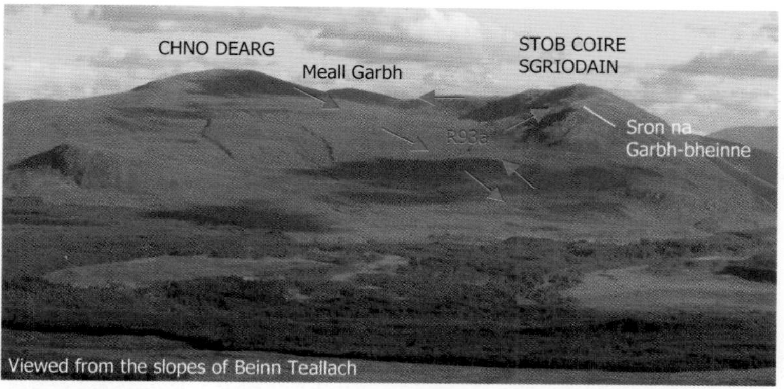

Viewed from the slopes of Beinn Teallach

Peak Fitness: Following re-measurement, the summit of Meall Garbh was moved from its north top to its south top in 1981.

As the Easains tower over the west side of Loch Treig, Stob Coire Sgriodain dominates the east side, its rugged ridges mirroring those of its neighbours across the water. Further east, around the rim of Coire an Lochain, lies Chno Dearg, a contrasting lump of a Munro about which it is more difficult to enthuse.

Both Munros are in plain sight of the A86 Glen Spean road to the north and are usually climbed from this direction (Route 93a). For a more memorable outing, as with the Easains, they can be tackled by taking the morning train to Corrour and walking back over them to Fersit. This point-to-point route is much easier than the equivalent Easains traverse (Route 91b) and passes a number of interesting features on the long south-west ridge of Chno Dearg. It also gives you the option of bagging Beinn na Lap along the way (Route 95a Extension 1).

Route 93a Chno Dearg and Stob Coire Sgriodain: round trip from Fersit

G1 *** (or, if you fail to find the paths: ** Route Rage Alert)
NN 350782, 8ml/13km, 950m/3100ft M97

We suggest tackling Stob Coire Sgriodain first because route-finding on its craggy slopes is easier on ascent than descent. Long miles of clingy moor cover the lower slopes of both mountains, so finding the path up and the ATV track down will make the difference between equanimity and route rage. There are short cuts to the start of the path but follow these directions if you want to make absolutely sure of finding it.

Beginning at Fersit, as for Route 91a, take the Land Rover track eastwards past the houses to a bridge over a stream at a hairpin bend (NN 358779). From here, take an old right-of-way that leaves the track to round Chno Dearg and head for Corrour. Leave this in turn no more than 20m from the bridge at a minor stream confluence. Follow the banks of the right-hand stream, initially beside a fence. It looks unpromising but

eventually a reasonable path appears on the left-hand bank.

When the two streams rejoin higher up at NN 362760, the path crosses to the right-hand bank and continues up into the shallow wasteland of Coire an Lochain. The path peters out before it reaches the lochan in the bowl of the corrie (imaginatively named Lochan Coire an Lochain), but you'll need to leave it before then anyway.

On your right, as you ascend beside the stream, is the craggy nose of Sron na Garbh-bheinne (*Strawn na Garrav-venya*, Nose of the Rough Mountain), an outpost at the end of Stob Coire

Sgriodain's north ridge. Scramblers can happily be left to their own devices here. To avoid any scrambling, stick with the path until you have passed the main crags and can climb easy grass slopes to gain the skyline.

Once on the north ridge, which is broad and knobbly and littered with broken rocks, traces of path lead easily to the ▲summit, a cliff-top eyrie above Loch Treig. The steep corrie that drops to the lochside is the Coire Sgriodain that gives the mountain its name. The view is considerable, although most of the mountains are too distant to make an impact. The overriding sensation is one of space.

Beyond the summit, steep grass slopes descend into a little dip called the Glac Bhan (*Glachk Vahn*, White Defile, named only on OS 1:25,000 map), then bouldery slopes re-ascend to the plateau summit of the ΔSouth Top. Broken rock continues to characterise the terrain as you follow the ridge around the skyline of Coire an Lochain, descending over and around knolls to the broad, grassy 890m/2900ft bealach between the two

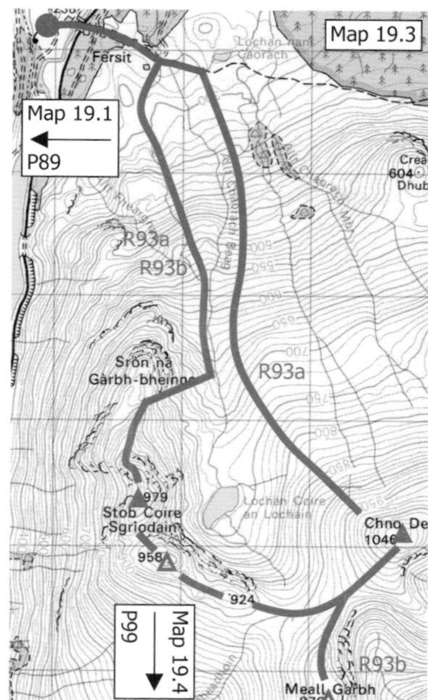

STOB COIRE SGRIODAIN
See also picture on Page 94

Descending from Stob Coire Sgriodain S Top

Munros, where there are a few small lochans. Top baggers note that a short distance further along on the right, and only c.30m/100ft higher, is the bealach that separates Chno Dearg from ΔMeall Garbh.

On gentle slopes of heath, climb easily to Chno Dearg's flat, bouldery ▲summit, an unremarkable spot but one that does open up the view eastwards to the Loch Laggan hills.

The key to an equable descent of the surrounding moor is an ATV track that climbs to the bealach between the two Munros. Such tracks are not to be encouraged in mountainous country, of course, because one accepts that wild land should stay wild, but one might as well use a track if it's there, mightn't one? Begrudgingly, of course.

To find the best going, it climbs to around 900m on Chno Dearg's western flank before traversing south to the bealach. Its surface consists mostly of squelchy grass and tyre tracks, but that's infinitely more appealing than the terrain to either side.

To find the track from the summit of Chno Dearg, descend bouldery slopes to the west, in the direction of Lochan Coire an Lochain, until you intersect the track as it crosses the hillside in a north–south direction. Stay watchful – it is indistinct in parts at this height. If you find yourself lower than the dip on the skyline opposite, you've missed it.

The track curves down the hillside to follow the line of the Allt Chaorach Beag (*Owlt Cheurach Bake*, Little Stream of the Rowan Berries) at varying distances from the stream. Don't worry about variations – they all rejoin lower down. The track reaches the Fersit–Corrour path a few hundred metres from the hairpin bend on the Land Rover track back to Fersit.

Needlepoint: With two adjacent bealachs at different heights, the triangle of land enclosed by Meall Garbh, Chno Dearg and Stob Coire Sgriodain can be a very confusing place in cloud. The fact that the paths over Stob Coire Sgriodain's rocky ground and Chno Dearg's featureless heath are patchy adds to routefinding difficulty.

Chilly Willy: Provided that steep ground is avoided on Sgriodain, this is a good introductory winter round. Chno Dearg's northern slopes under snow give one of the easiest winter ascents of any Munro, to say nothing of the long yomp of a descent.

Route 93b The Treig Traverse: Chno Dearg and Stob Coire Sgriodain one-way trip from Corrour to Fersit

G2 **** NN 356664 to NN 350782, 11ml/17km, 900m/2950ft M97/99

By turning the ascent of Chno Dearg and Stob Coire Sgriodain into a point-to-point traverse from Corrour to Fersit, it is surprising how much more interesting (and challenging) the two Munros become.

The route begins as for the Easains (Route 91b), on the path to Loch Treig. N.B. If adding Beinn na Lap to the route (Route 95a Extension 1), see Page 102 for alternative start.

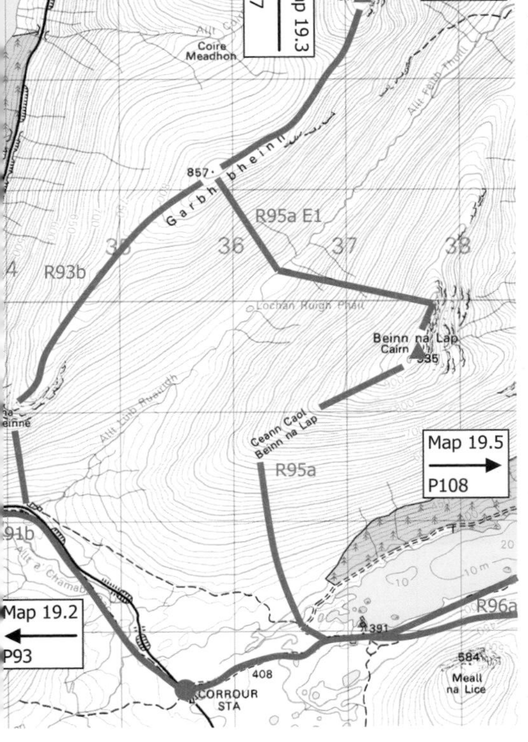

When you reach the Allt Luib Ruairidh, leave the track to Loch Treig, go under the railway bridge and climb the hillside in front of you to Sron na Garbh-bheinne, a less craggy twin of its namesake at the north end of Stob Coire Sgriodain. The going is quite steep and rough, with long grass at first and increasing amounts of rock higher up, but it is only c.250m/800ft to the top.

Once up, you find yourself on a fine tramping ridge above Loch Treig. On good terrain, at a gentle angle and with excellent views and curious erratic boulders to investigate, this is a very fine walk indeed. Rising little more than 200m/650ft in 3ml/5km, the ridge crosses the minor top of Garbh-bheinn and reaches the bouldery twin summits of ΔMeall Garbh.

See also pictures on Page 104

A shallow grassy bealach is then all that separates you from Chno Dearg. Note the red screes on the mountain's steep south side, which may give it its name. On ascent to the summit, pause to look back at Meall Garbh's east face, which boasts an unexpectedly considerable crag, adventurous climbers for the benefit of.

After reaching ▲Chno Dearg, reverse Route 93a around the head of Coire an Lochain to cross ▲Stob Coire Sgriodain and descend to the streamside path to Fersit. N.B. Unless you wish to scramble off the end of Stob Coire Sgriodain's north ridge, make sure you descend easy grass slopes to the streamside before then.

GiGi: The route from Corrour to Loch Treig is part of the former Thieves Road, a 100ml/160km route across Scotland used by clansmen of the west to plunder the fertile lands of the east. From east of the Cairngorms it ran via Loch Ericht, Culra, the Bealach Dubh and Corrour into either the Lairig Leacach or Glen Nevis.

▲95 Beinn na Lap 241 935m/3068ft (OS 41, NN 376695)

Ben na Laap, Dappled Mountain

Peak Fitness: No change since 1891 Tables.

This isolated mountain is the high-point on a ridge that runs the whole length of Loch Ossian's north-west shore, parallelling Chno Dearg's south-west ridge across the next glen to the north-west. As the furthest Munro from any road, it is the only one in the Highlands that, unless you're superfit or have a mountain bike, requires a train journey to its foot. Other Munros around Corrour can easily be reached in a day from other starting points. Not Beinn na Lap.

In shape it resembles an enormous unrepentant pimple with two of its sides squeezed together. From Corrour the whole ascent route is in view – a prolonged tramp up uniform slopes from lochside to summit, with zero features of interest.

Fortunately, the mountain's supreme location generates a tremendous sense of being at the heart of wilderness and gives plenty of reason to pause and ponder the nature of existence. Just hope there isn't a rail strike while you're up there.

The usual way to bag Beinn na Lap is as a round trip from Corrour between trains (Route 95a). Those in search of something more adventurous can continue across the bealach to the north-west and so add Beinn na Lap to the Corrour-to-Fersit crossing of Chno Dearg and Stob Coire Sgriodain (Route 95a Extension 1).

Torpedo: From Laggan Dam on the A86 (NN 372809) it is possible to use forest and estate tracks to cycle to the foot of Beinn na Lap's north-north-east ridge (NN 398730). The 8½ml/14km each-way ride involves appreciable ascents. From the bridge over the stream at the foot of the ridge, the walk to the summit is as easy as the normal route (return trip: G2 *** 5½ml/9km, 520m/1700ft).

Route 95a Beinn na Lap: round trip from Corrour

G2 *** NN 356664, 6ml/10km, 550m/1800ft M99

From Corrour Station, take the Land Rover track to Loch Ossian. When the track forks to encircle the loch, go left for a few hundred metres to another fork (NN 366671). Walk up the left branch, signposted 'Loch Treig Road to the Isles', for c.50m, to the first left-hand bend.

The obvious boot-worn path up Beinn na Lap begins here and makes a beeline up the hillside to the skyline of the south-west ridge. It is boggy (of course) and steepens higher up, making it necessary to maintain a cheerful disposition if you hope to complete the ascent with a minimum of route rage.

Once on the south-west ridge, which is optimistically named Ceann Caol (*Kyann Keul*, Narrow Head) on the map, the going and the views improve dramatically. The ridge rises at a gentle angle, surfaced by grass and broken rocks on which a developing path is trying to gain purchase. The ascent tops out on a small, gently sloping summit plateau, with a small rise at the near end, beyond which a tiny lochan separates you from the ▲summit.

Ascent to the SW Ridge

On the SW Ridge

F-Stop: What Beinn na Lap lacks in character it makes up for in views. The summit panorama encompasses a swathe of wonderfully remote country unknown to the vast majority of visitors to Scotland.

Walk a short distance beyond the cairn to the edge of the deep north-east corrie (Coire na Lap), for views over the mouth of Loch Ossian to the 'back sides' of the Culra Munros (Section 20).

summit plateau and lochan

Needlepoint: In cloud, keep climbing and, as long as you don't succumb to apathy, you *will* reach the summit plateau. Just remember not to stop at the rise at the near end but to keep going past the lochan to reach the summit cairn.

Chilly Willy: In summer it's a plod. In winter it's a snow plod. But Munro bagging at Corrour on a crisp winter's day is something you'll never forget.

Baffies: For a scenic wilderness taster, try a between-trains stroll around Loch Ossian, which lies just east of Corrour Station (9ml/14km, on a Land Rover track all the way).

Spring and autumn at Loch Ossian are exceptionally colourful. Go a-wanderin' in spring to catch the rhododendrons in full bloom, or in autumn to see the sycamores blaze with colour.

Route 95a Extension 1: To Fersit via Chno Dearg and Stob Coire Sgriodain

G2 *** Add-on to Route 93b: ½ml/1km, 430m/1400ft, considerable effort (N.B. This is a one-way route that ends at Fersit, not Corrour) M99

Beinn na Lap is separated from the Garbh-bheinn on Chno Dearg's south-west ridge by a deep glen whose highpoint is a 529m/1736ft bealach. By crossing the bealach, fit walkers can join Route 93b and continue over Chno Dearg and Stob Coire Sgriodain to Fersit.

The slopes leading down to the bealach and back up the other side are as uniform and featureless as you have become accustomed to on Beinn na Lap, with the added ingredient of roughness. Higher up, lots of rocks lurk in the grass; lower down lies a tangle of heather and peat. The crossing of the bealach is nowhere difficult, but you're going to need more than a modicum of determination if you intend to enjoy it.

A diagonal line down the hillside from Beinn na Lap's summit, aiming directly for the lochan on the bealach, crosses the roughest ground. To find easier going, continue beyond the summit for a few hundred metres, to the top of a rise from where you can see down the north-north-east ridge.

Descend east from here, straight down the hillside to an oasis of green that can be seen right of the peat hags, directly beneath Garbh-bheinn. Climb straight up similar slopes to join Route 93b at the top of Garbh-bheinn. The ascent looks tough but is neither as steep nor as long as it appears.

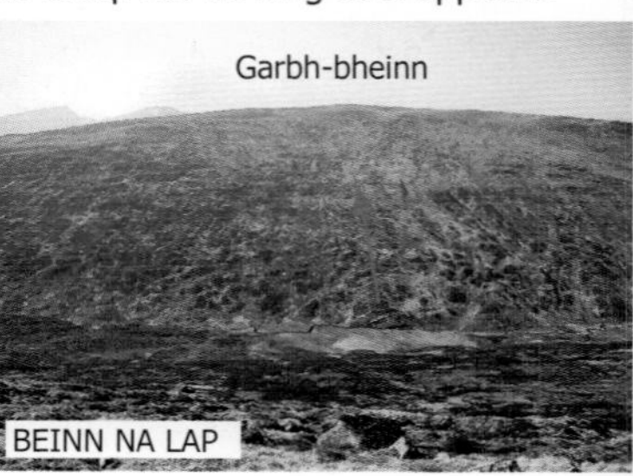

▲96 Carn Dearg 231 941m/3087ft (OS 42, NN 417661)

Carn Jerrak, Red Cairn
(not to be confused with namesakes ▲103 and ▲117)

▲97 Sgor Gaibhre 208 955m/3133ft (OS 42, NN 444674)

Skorr Gyra, Goat Peak
△Sgor Choinnich 929m/3049ft (OS 42, NN 443683)
Skor Chawnyich, Mossy Peak

Peak Fitness: Sgor Choinnich was a Munro from 1891 to 1921.

In an area as scenic as Corrour, these two nondescript Munros would never win prizes for pulchritude. Add to that the fact that they are far from any road and surrounded by boggy moorland, and it is no wonder that they are among the least known and least appreciated of all Munros. On the plus side, they do give a good old tramp with expansive views over some secret corners of the Central Highlands, and this is enough to make them worthy objectives.

There are three ways to bag the pair. The best way, whether viewed in terms of terrain or scenery, is on a round trip from Corrour to the west (Route 96a). From near Rannoch Station to the south, an excellent path makes a round trip from this direction equally easy (Route 96b). A third option is to take the morning train from Rannoch to Corrour and make a one-way trip back over the summits (Route 96c).

All three routes are of similar length and each has something to offer but, if you can manage the logistics, we'd opt for a round trip from Corrour to make the most of the scenery.

Torpedo: The nearest starting point for an ascent of Sgor Gaibhre is Benalder Cottage to the east, but the route involves a rough moorland crossing and a steep finish to the north of the summit cone... and first you have to get to the cottage (see Page 132).

Route 96a Carn Dearg and Sgor Gaibhre: round trip from Corrour

G1 *** NN 356664, 13ml/21km, 820m/2700ft M99/108

Map note: Both Munros are on OS 42 but the route begins on OS 41.

Much of this walk is on good tracks and paths but, to complete it in the seven hours or so between morning and evening trains, you'll have to maintain a 'steady' pace. We suggest an anti-clockwise route, climbing Carn Dearg first, to make the best of the going.

From Corrour Station, take the Land Rover track to Loch Ossian. At the junction at the head of the loch, keep right along the south-east shore and pass a first access track to the Youth Hostel. When a second access track crosses the main track, turn right then fork immediately left on a less salubrious ATV track that was formerly known as the 'Road to the Isles'.

Follow the ATV track across the moor beneath the crag-rimmed summit of Meall na Lice (*Myowl na Leeka*, Hill of the Slabs), making a beeline for the hidden summit of Carn Dearg directly ahead. Apart from a few boggy wallows to be leapt over, this part of the route is a stroll in the park. As you gain height, pause occasionally to look back at the expanding western view over the array of massive mountains flanking upper Glen Nevis.

The track eventually bears right to reach Peter's Rock at a junction with another path that comes up from Loch Ossian. This spot, 2½ml/4km from Corrour but a mere 100m/350ft above it, gets its name from a boulder with a memorial plaque. The path-cum-track continues across the flanks of Carn Dearg to Rannoch, but it is now time to leave it.

From Peter's Rock, head straight up the hillside ahead to Carn Dearg's

north-west ridge. The going looks rough from below, but patches of heath and an increasingly gentle angle make the ascent more congenial than it could be in these parts. Once on the ridge the going improves further, with spacious views of Loch Ossian and its surrounding mountains.

Eventually you'll reach turf-like terrain and an indistinct ATV track that runs almost all the way to Carn Dearg's surprisingly rock-strewn ▲summit, whose reddish granite gives the mountain its name. It is tempting to loiter here to admire the extensive view, which now also extends south and east to the pyramid of Schiehallion (▲46). However, you may have a train to catch.

If Carn Dearg's summit is retiring to the point of timidity, Sgor Gaibhre's soars over the moors like a giant cone. Separating the two Munros is the gentle Mam Ban (*Maam Baan*, White Pass), a 720m/2350ft saddle at the head of an enormous south-east corrie (Coire Eigheach, C*orra Aighach*, Noisy Corrie, named for its stream). A

GiGi: Carn Dearg's one claim to fame is that, by some measurements, it is the most central Munro in the Central Highlands and hence in the whole of Scotland.

developing path links the two peaks.

The descent from Carn Dearg's summit is initially stony but soon improves again. The peaty bealach can be a nuisance when wet but is soon passed. The path makes a beeline for Sgor Gaibhre's summit with little need for deviation. Although the ascent requires a steady pull, the turf higher up is a joy to tread. The ▲summit cairn stands at the rim of another great eastern corrie, across whose lochan are revealed close-up views of the 'back sides' of the Culra Munros (Section 20).

The return trip begins with a descent to the mouth of Loch Ossian to pick up the lochside Land Rover track back to Corrour. The shortest way down descends east into Coire Creagach (*Corra Craikach*, Craggy Corrie) but, thanks to the rough terrain there, it is neither the quickest nor the friendliest. Instead, descend northwards, following a gritty path down steeper slopes to the Bealach nan Sgor (*Byalach nan Skorr*, Pass of the Peak), which lies between Sgor Gaibhre and its equally conical satellite ΔSgor Choinnich.

Top baggers will want to make the 127m/418ft ascent of Sgor Choinnich, especially given its former Munro status. Others may be content to bypass the summit by making a shallow rising traverse across the grassy hillside to the north-east ridge.

From the end of the broad ridge, alarmingly called Meall Nathrach Mor (*Myowl Narach Moar*, Hill of the Big Snake), gentle slopes descend to the mouth of Loch Ossian. Aim west-north-west to the point where the Allt a' Choire Chreagaich enters the

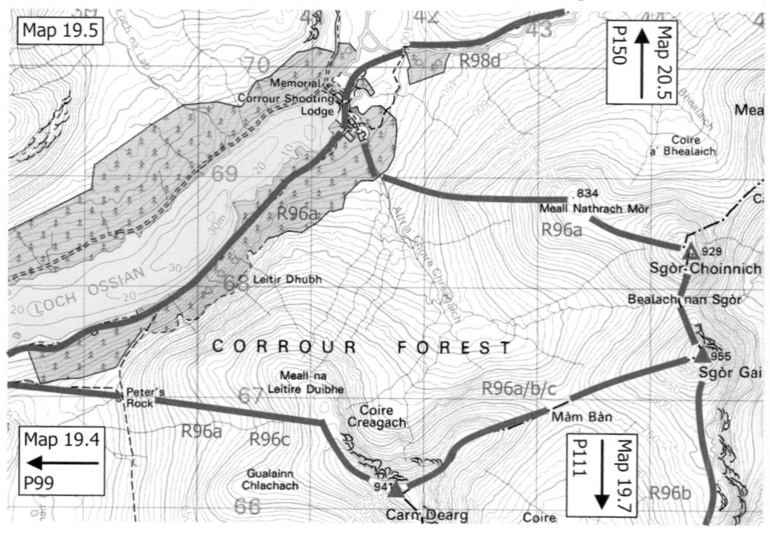

F-Stop: In winter and spring, one of the great sights of the Central Highlands is the view from Carn Dearg of the mighty summit of Ben Nevis, which resembles nothing less than a giant ice-cream cone.

Needlepoint: The two Munros are not unduly difficult to navigate in cloud, as long as you make sure you come off each summit in the correct direction. Be advised that in wet weather the track to Peter's Rock and the Mam Ban become sodden.

Chilly Willy: Excellent paths, good terrain and gentle angles make any one of the three routes described a rewarding winter tramp for suitably equipped beginners. The main challenge is trip length, so it may be prudent to opt for Route 96b or 96c, which end at the roadside near Rannoch station, rather than Route 96a, which could leave you stranded in the wilderness at Corrour on a parky night.

Viewed from the slopes of Carn Dearg

lochside woods (NN 416690). Here you'll find a small dam that can be crossed to reach a forest track on its far side. This descends through the trees to Loch Ossian cottages and the shore of the loch, hopefully sparkling in the afternoon sun. Now it's a mere 4½ml/7km back to Corrour along the south-east side of the loch (or slightly longer along the north-west side).

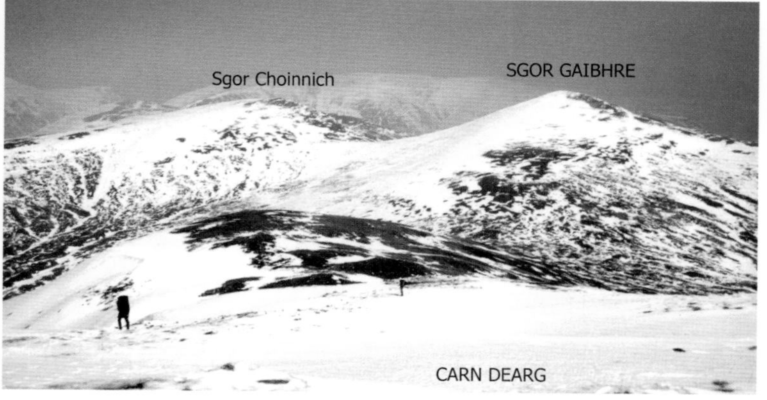

Route 96b Carn Dearg and Sgor Gaibhre: round trip from Rannoch

G1 *** NN 446579, 15ml/24km, 1010m/3300ft M110/111

On their south sides, both Munros throw out long ridges around the vast hollow of Coire Eigheach, such that a round of the corrie skyline has a distinct aesthetic appeal. Compared to Route 96a, a southern approach lacks the ambience and omnipresent views afforded by an ascent from Corrour to the west, but there are compensations. You *will* get those views at the summits, approach paths are equally excellent and you can dawdle to your heart's content without worrying about being abandoned on a station platform in the wilderness.

Begin on the B846 opposite Loch Eigheach, 1½ml/2½km from the road end at Rannoch Station, on a gritty Land Rover track signposted Public Footpath to Ft William by Corrour. The track runs north-west then north across the moor, contouring around a rise into the glen of the Allt Eigheach. From here, the view up Coire Eigheach to the two Munros is blocked by the corrie's elevated mouth, although the summit of Sgor Gaibhre can just be seen on the skyline. The track fords the river but a footbridge just before the ford saves a wetting.

Several hundred metres further along, the track leaves the riverside to curve left around a forestry plantation. A side path continues up the corrie and will form the return route, but for now keep to the track. Becoming more overgrown, yet still in excellent condition, this former 'Road to the Isles' makes a rising traverse across the western flanks of Carn Dearg to Loch Ossian and Corrour.

Follow it until it begins to level out around 1½ml/2km south of Corrour Old Lodge, then climb 300m/1000ft up the hillside to Sron Leachd a' Chaorainn (*Strawn Lechk a Heurin*, Slabby Nose of the Rowan). This hill

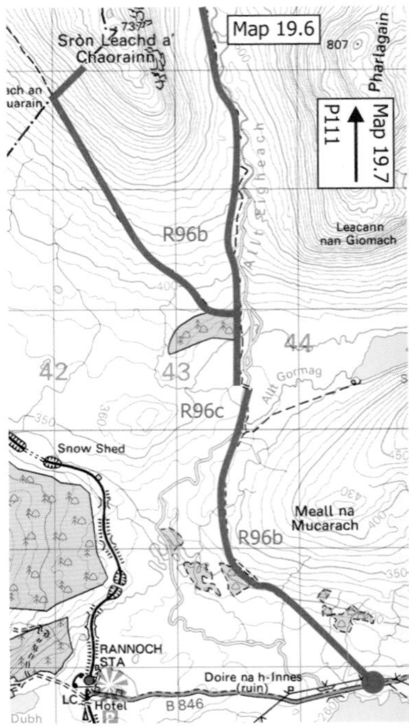

top marks the start of the broad ridge that forms the western arm of Coire Eigheach. With expanding westward views becoming ever more insistent, follow the ridge northwards, on good terrain and over several minor tops, to the ▲summit of Carn Dearg.

With Loch Ossian now in view below, cross the Mam Ban at the head of Coire Eigheach, as per Route 96a, to ▲Sgor Gaibhre, then turn south to complete the round of the corrie skyline by descending its eastern arm. From the summit, broad, gentle slopes undulate down over a couple of rises to a saddle. For the best views, keep to the left, where the hillside drops away steeply towards Loch Ericht.

Quit the ridge at the saddle to descend yet more gentle slopes into Coire Eigheach, aiming for a stalkers' path on the far bank of the stream. As you'll have noticed on the outward journey, the Allt Eigheach carries a considerable volume of water lower down, so cross it as soon as possible.

In its upper reaches, the path has disappeared beneath an ATV track; when this veers away from the river, the path continues along the bank. Both path and track give a pleasant riverside walk down to the mouth of the corrie to join the outward track.

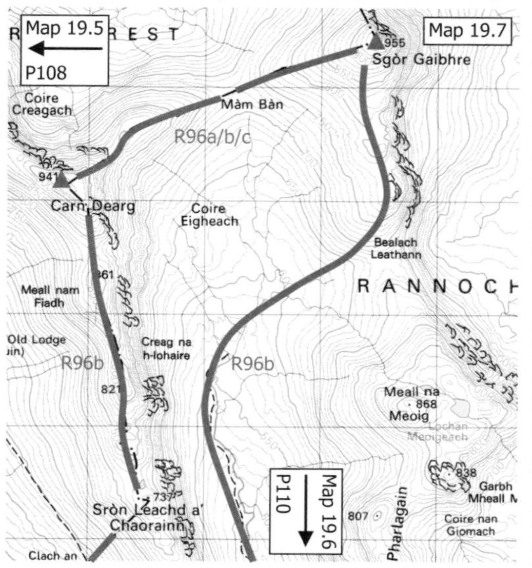

GiGi: The 'Road to the Isles' was a long-distance drove road used by farmers from the north and west to reach the great cattle market at Falkirk. From Peter's Rock it crosses the flanks of Carn Dearg and, after 2ml/3km, passes Corrour Old Lodge. Situated at a height of 523m/1723ft, the lodge was built for deer stalkers in the early nineteenth century and for a time was the highest inhabited residence in Britain.

After the opening of the West Highland Railway in 1894, Sir John Stirling Maxwell, director of the railway, built a new lodge down at Loch Ossian. The gardens he established still flourish and surround the new lodge, completed in 2003.

The old lodge later became an isolation hospital. Now the ruins could be mistaken on a misty day for an ancient Druid monument. The open corrie behind them is Coire Odhar Mor (*Corr-Oa-ar Mor*, Big Dun-coloured Corrie), for which the lodge and station are named. If you're tempted to visit the ruins, be advised that the ascent of Carn Dearg from there is steeper and rougher than the normal route.

Route 96c Carn Dearg and Sgor Gaibhre: one-way trip from Corrour to Rannoch

G1 *** NN 356664 to NN 446579, 13½ml/22km, 800m/2600ft M110/111

Map note: Both Munros are on OS 42 but the route begins on OS 41.

This route combines the outward part of Route 96a from Corrour Station with the return part of Route 96b from Rannoch Station, thereby enabling you to experience the unique landscapes of Corrour without having to rush for a return train.

First take the morning train from Rannoch to Corrour. From here, as per Route 96a, climb ▲Carn Dearg and continue across the Mam Ban to ▲Sgor Gaibhre. From here, as per Route 96b, descend via Coire Eigheach to pick up the path/track to the B846 Rannoch road, which is reached 1½ml/2½km from Rannoch Station.

! At the bridge over the Allt Eigheach (NN 436603), it is tempting to leave the track and take a shortcut across country to Rannoch Station, thereby saving 1½ml/2½km. This would be a mistake because the terrain is horrendously boggy and even dangerous in parts. This *is* Rannoch Moor.

20 CULRA

North-east of Corrour, in the triangle of land bordered by Loch Ossian, Loch Laggan and Loch Ericht, lies a great tract of mountainous country that has no road or railway access. At its core is an immense secret basin where Loch Pattack floats on the moor and Culra bothy stands at the foot of soaring rock ridges.

In character the mountains are big and bold, having much in common with the Nevis Range, except that they are much more remote. Above Culra, the great plateau summits are indented by craggy corries whose dividing ridges make superb approach routes. Their tempting lines, easily reached by excellent stalkers' paths, beckon across the moor, while the swathes of heath, turf and moss that clothe the summits are a joy to hike.

Even if you think you know the Highlands well, you won't fail to be surprised and inspired by what you'll find far from the roadside in the hidden mountain sanctuary of Culra. Not only does hillwalking here merit superlatives in its own right, but nowhere in the Central Highlands, Corrour included, will bring you as close to **a genuine wilderness hillwalking experience**.

There are six Munros, divided into groups of two and four by the defile of the Bealach Dubh (*Byalach Doo*, Black Pass). The prime draw, south of the pass, is Ben Alder, a peak that has the stature of Ben Nevis in everything but height. Owing to the logistics involved in reaching it, its satellite Munro Beinn Bheoil is often bagged on the same trip (Routes 98a-98e).

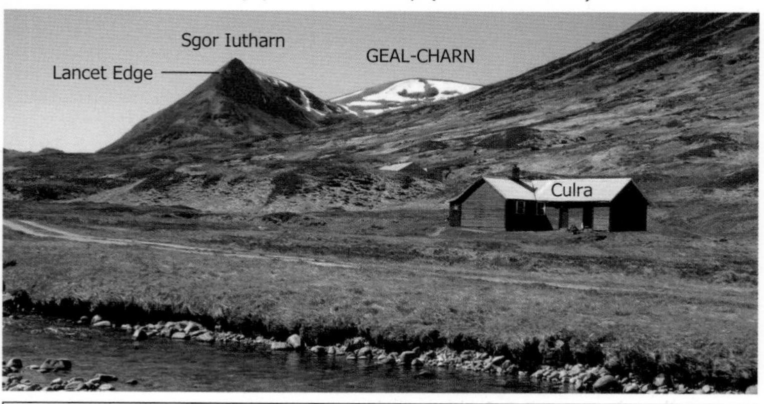

For Monday-Saturday access restrictions during the stalking season, contact Loch Ericht Estate, Dalwhinnie PH19 1AE (01540-672000).

North of the Bealach Dubh, the four Munros of the Geal-Charn Group stand in line high above Culra. The complete traverse gives a memorable ridge walk of exceptional contrasts, but such a long route in remote country won't be within the capability of all (Routes 100a-100d). This is even more true if you feel uneasy on rock, as the shortest lines up both Ben Alder and Geal-Charn involve exposed scrambling.

To give you some idea of the distances involved, it is 10ml/16km to the summit of Ben Alder from the west (Corrour station), 11ml/18km from the south (Loch Rannoch on the B8456), 13ml/21km from the east (Dalwhinnie on the A9), and 14ml/23km from the north (Kinloch Laggan on the A86).

The two shortest routes, from Corrour and Loch Rannoch, do not approach via Culra, which is on the north side of the mountains, but the shortest route isn't always the best, the quickest or the easiest. And from Dalwhinnie and Kinloch Laggan Culra can be reached by mountain bike. It would be a crime not to go there at some point on your Munro round.

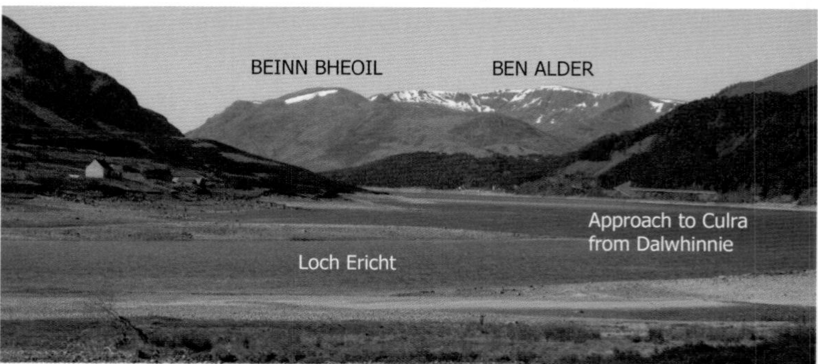

Getting to Culra (NN 523762)

From Dalwhinnie: NN 634846, 9½ml/15km, *out* 150m/500ft *back* 50m/150ft
From Kinloch Laggan: NN 554898, 10ml/16km, *out* 200m/650ft *back* negligible

It's a long way in to Culra, but its remoteness is part of what makes it special. The bothy is situated near the foot of the mountains, 2½ml/4km south of a point we'll call Culra Junction, where an old shed used to stand (NN 548787). Here, the two approach tracks from Dalwhinnie to the north-east and Kinloch Laggan to the north meet (actually they form one long continuous Land Rover track that does a U-turn at the junction). From here, a stalkers' path leaves the track to cross the moor to Culra.

The Dalwhinnie track begins at the station and undulates south along Loch Erichtside to Ben Alder Lodge, where it turns west to climb onto the moor and reach Culra Junction. The best starting point for the Kinloch

Laggan track is at the second bridge a mile or so east of Loch Laggan on the A86. From here, the track climbs south along the glen of the River Pattack to Loch Pattack, where it turns east to climb onto the moor and reach Culra Junction.

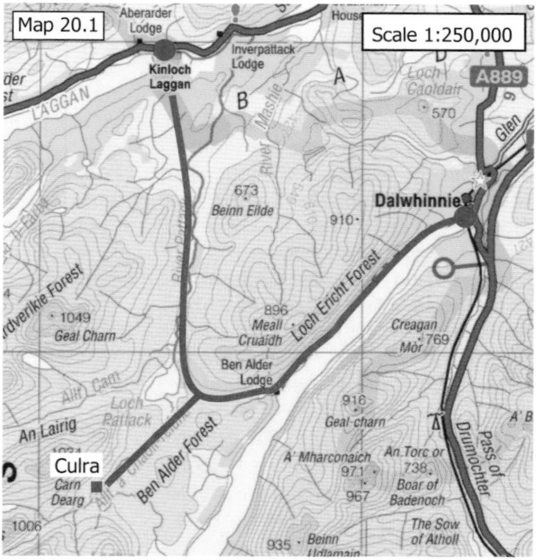

Map 20.1 Scale 1:250,000

The Dalwhinnie track is the traditional approach route. At one time it was possible to drive to Culra Junction. When estate ownership changed it was still permissible for many years to drive part of the way. Under current ownership the estate runs a strict policy of no unauthorised vehicle access. For the latest position contact Loch Ericht Estate, Dalwhinnie, Perthshire PH19 1AE (01540-672-002). Website: www.lochericht.co.uk.

Despite increased access problems, we still prefer the Dalwhinnie approach to the Kinloch Laggan approach. The latter passes some fine waterfalls in a scenic glen, but the track is 1ml/2km longer, starts at a lower elevation and is less well surfaced.

The Dalwhinnie track is so well surfaced that the Culra Munros can be put within day reach by using a mountain bike. Even beyond Culra Junction, the paths are so good that you can cycle them all the way to Culra bothy and beyond, in fact as far as you need to go before tackling the hills (providing you are blessed with the necessary power and technique).

From Culra Junction, there are two ways to reach Culra bothy, which stands a further 2½ml/4km south on the far (west) side of the Allt a' Chaoil-reidhe (*Owlt a Ceul-Ree-a*, Stream of the Level Narrows; *Culra* is the anglicised pronunciation). A few hundred metres beyond the junction, a side Land Rover track leaves the main track at Loch Pattack, fords the stream (there's an adjacent footbridge) and undulates along the foot of Carn Dearg to the bothy. Unfortunately, this track

GiGi: The flow of water out of Loch Ericht has reversed since the loch was dammed at both ends during the construction boom following the Second World War. Water now flows south into the Tummel hydro-electric power scheme.

is circuitous, rough, undulating and tiring to walk or cycle.

More preferable is the beautifully engineered and well-drained stalkers' path that leaves the track at Culra Junction and crosses the flat floor of the basin south of Loch Pattack. With soaring ridges (the Long Leachas and the Lancet Edge) on each side of the Bealach Dubh to draw you onwards, this is **one of the most uplifting approach routes in the Central Highlands**.

At the stream bend just before the bothy, a side path leads to a bridge (NN 525764) that gives access to the bothy on the west bank. The bridge has been destroyed by floods before but, even if it is downed again in the future, the stream crossing remains an easy paddle in normal conditions.

There is nothing at Culra except the renovated bothy, open to all-comers, and a wooden building that has replaced old Culra Lodge. The bothy has three separate rooms with wooden bunks, yet you may still find it full at popular times of the year. Unless you need no more than a roof over your head, a floor to sleep on and strangers for sleeping companions, it would be wise to take a tent. From the bothy it is still at least 3½ml/6km by scrambling routes to the summits of Ben Alder and Geal-Charn.

If you can't cycle in, and don't wish to stay at the bothy or camp, it might be worth considering an approach to the six Munros from other points of the compass. However, not only would this mean missing Culra, but these alternative approaches also have their own logistical problems. We detail the possibilities in the following pages.

After considering the options, you may decide to break down the groups and approach different Munros from different starting points.

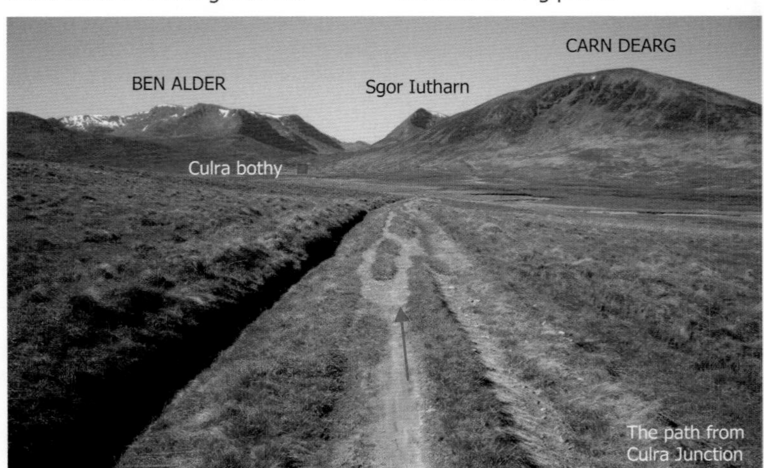

The path from Culra Junction

▲98 Ben Alder 25 1148m/3766ft (OS 42, NN 496718)

in Gaelic Beinn Eallar, *Ben Yallar*, possibly Mountain of Rock and Water, from the archaic words *Ail* and *Dobhar*

▲99 Beinn Bheoil 112 1019m/3343ft (OS 42, NN 516717)

Beinn Vyawil, Mountain of the Mouth (of Loch a' Bhealaich Bheithe?)

△Sron Coire na h-Iolaire 955m/3135ft (OS 42, NN 513704)

Strawn Corra na Hill-yera, Nose of the Corrie of the Eagle

Peak Fitness: No change since 1891 Tables.

It is difficult to describe Ben Alder without using clichés like *majestic* and *magnificent* . It may have no single feature that isn't bettered elsewhere, but there's something about its site and situation, its picture-postcard framing, its combination of vast summit plateau, gaping corries, soaring ridges... You get the picture. It's a big mountain that stands in big country. We like it.

Facing Ben Alder across Loch a' Bhealaich Bheithe (*Loch a Vyalich Vay-ha*, Loch of the Birch Pass) is humble Beinn Bheoil, whose summit is little more than the highest point on a long ridge. Although it possesses few features of interest to distract attention from its imposing neighbour, that long, lazy ridge occupies a commanding position between Loch a' Bhealaich Bheithe and Loch Ericht, and that means there are great views to be had from it in both directions.

Alder's 400-acre summit plateau, **an island in the sky**, dominates the flatlands of Culra and throws out two perfectly positioned narrow ridges that give scenic scrambles: the Long Leachas and the Short Leachas.

A combination of both is the classic round on Ben Alder (Route 98a) but necessitates leaving Beinn Bheoil for another day (Route 98c). More likely, you'll prefer to bag both Munros together, approaching either by a scramble up the Long Leachas (Route 98b) or a non-scrambling route up Alder's north-west slopes (Route 98b Alternative Ascent). It is also possible to reach the Munros from Corrour station or Loch Rannoch (Routes 98d & 98e), although these routes entail more arduous approaches that miss out Culra.

1990 storm damage above Culra

Trouble brewing on Ben Alder summit plateau

Needlepoint: The scrambles on the Long and Short Leachas (Route 98a) are of course best avoided in foul weather. In fact, when cloud envelops Ben Alder's summit, trying to cross the featureless summit plateau by *any* route requires precision navigation. Congratulations if you manage to locate the summit cairn. A sturdy if roofless stone shelter just below the cairn is a good place to ruminate.

A direct ascent of Beinn Bheoil from Culra (Route 98c) is the only route in this section that should give little problem on a driech day.

Chilly Willy: In winter, the only easy ascent route on Ben Alder climbs the north-west slopes above the Bealach Dubh (Route 98a Alternative Ascent). When snowbound, the Long and Short Leachas (Route 98a) are no place for walkers, while steep snow slopes above the Bealach Breabag and Bealach Cumhann complicate ascents from Benalder Cottage (Route 98e) and Corrour (Route 98d). Beinn Bheoil is easier to climb, either from Culra (Route 98c) or Benalder Cottage (Route 98e).

If you do manage to get up Ben Alder, the summit environment is spectacular. Garbh Choire, the southernmost of three great east-facing corries, ranks alongside Coire Ardour of Creag Meagaidh as one of the Central Highlands' great winter corries.

The massive walls of rock are too broken to offer classic summer climbs but they boast remote winter routes on an Alpine scale. Giant cornices last late into the year. A good time to visit is late spring, when the melting ice assumes fantastic shapes.

Route 98a Ben Alder alone from Culra: The Long and Short Leachas

G4 ***** NN 523762, 7ml/11km, 730m/2400ft M123

South of Culra, the three deep corries that indent Alder's east face tower over hidden Loch a' Bhealaich Bheithe. Facing you on approach are the two bounding ridges of the northernmost corrie, Coire na Lethchois (anglicised to *Leachas*, Half-foot). The left-hand ridge is known as the Short Leachas and the right-hand ridge is known as the Long Leachas.

In their upper reaches, both ridges sport easy scrambling. The Long Leachas is the more interesting and scenic, especially on ascent, so it is normal to go up the Long and down the Short. This is both the shortest route on Ben Alder and the classic round on the mountain.

The approach is by the excellent path along the east bank of the Allt a' Chaoil-reidhe, which was rebuilt to 'motorway' standard after the floods of 1990 washed sections of it away. If approaching from Culra Junction, stay on the east bank past Culra bothy. If starting from the bothy, cross the bridge to gain the east-bank path.

In due course the path bears left, away from the stream, to climb to Loch a' Bhealaich Bheithe. Several hundred metres further along, at a sharp left-hand bend, a white boulder marks the start of a traverse path to the foot of the Long Leachas.

It feels good to be heading 'off-piste' at last, even if that feeling, along with one's boots, is soon dampened by a rough moor with boggy tendencies. Still, it's not far to the Allt Bhealaich Bheithe (the stream that descends from the loch), and this can usually be crossed dryshod on large boulders.

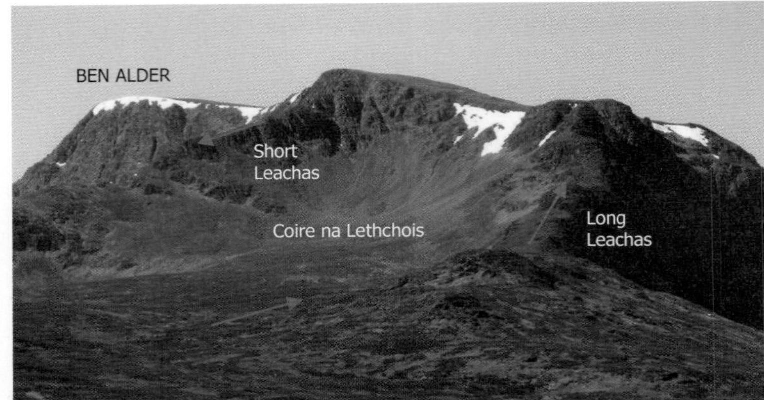

On the far side of the stream, when the path becomes lost, keep heading up slopes of grass and heather to a hump at the foot of the Long Leachas. This can be climbed over or bypassed on the left to avoid the minor descent on the far side. After a second small hump, the ridge proper rears up steeply in a series of steps. A more distinct path appears to ease the going

Loch Ericht

Pinnacles of the Long Leachas

and there are now some short stretches of very easy scrambling, more G3 than G4.

Eventually you reach a levelling above which another steep slope of grass and heather rises to a rockband. This looks intimidating from below but turns out to be less so. The path wends its way up lines of least resistance, finishing up a stony gully where a degree of exposure may well produce the first adrenaline rush of the day. Alternatively, you can go straight up the rocky crest of the ridge on good holds.

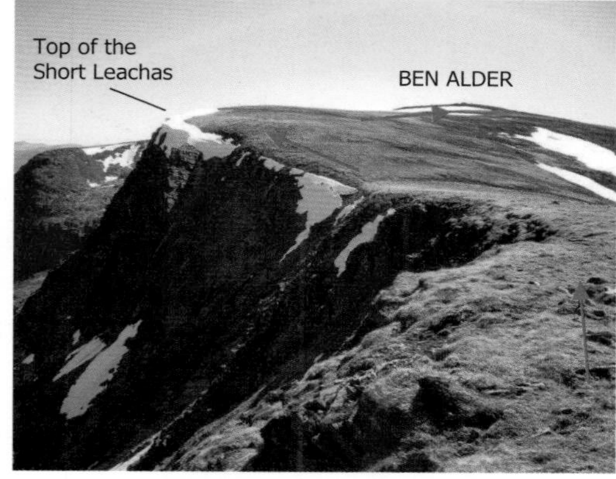

At the top of this section, the angle of ascent lessens and the ridge breaks out in a succession of pinnacles that block the way to Ben Alder's summit plateau. Again, it's easier than it looks. In a superb situation above the Culra flatlands, the path weaves among the pinnacles in a way that makes the scrambling, though occasionally exposed, nowhere difficult.

Once off the ridge onto the plateau, the character of the route changes completely. Keeping to the rim of Coire na Lethchois for the views, head up broad bouldery slopes to the top of the Short Leachas. Note the cairn at the top of this ridge for the return trip.

The Short Leachas separates Coire na Lethchois from the central of Alder's three east-facing corries, Garbh-choire Beag (*Garrav Corra Bake*, Little Rough Corrie). Stay back from the convex rim (you'll get better views later) and continue across the plateau, which becomes ever broader and mossier as it climbs to Ben Alder's ▲summit. The cairn lies a couple of hundred metres from the cliff edge.

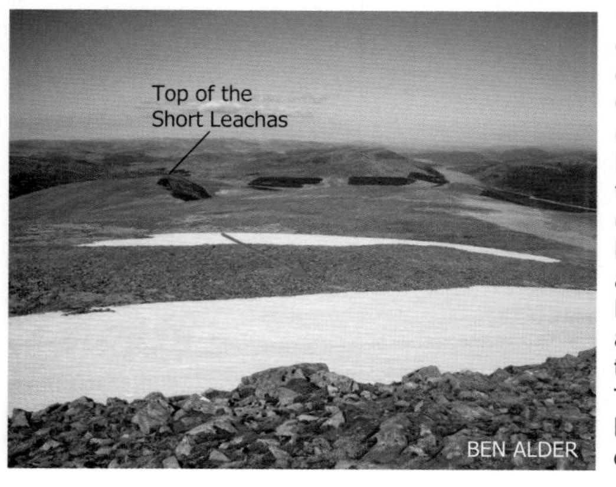

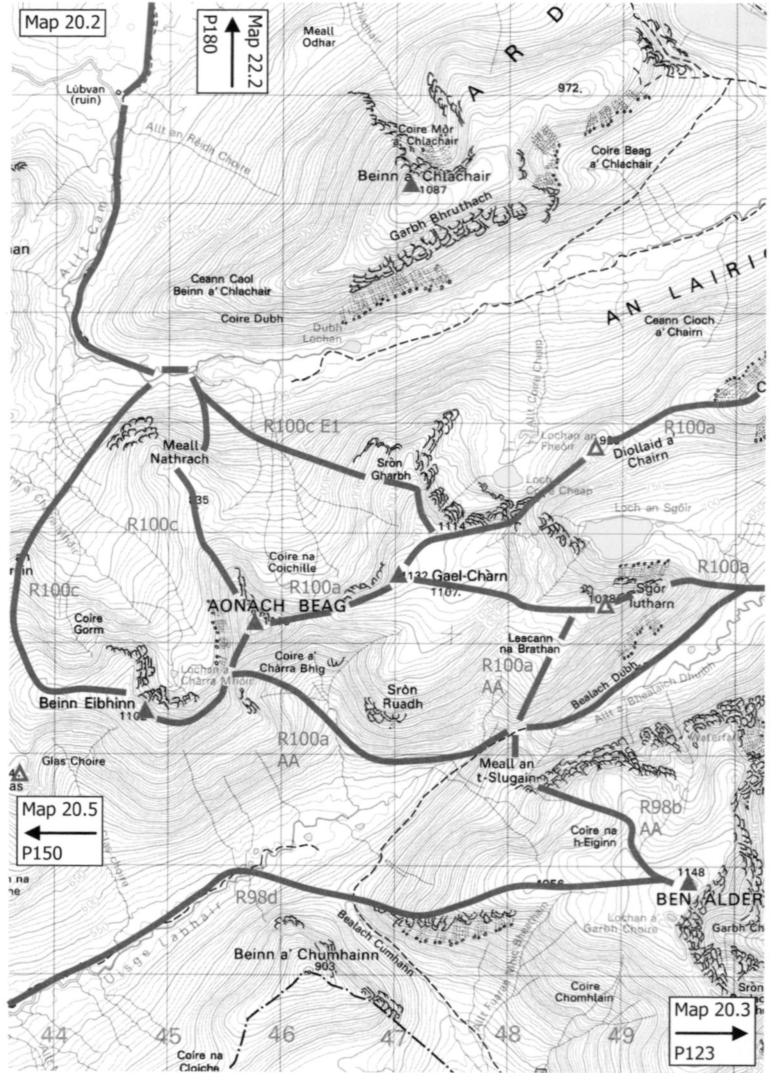

Map 20.2
Map 22.2
P180
Map 20.5
P150
Map 20.3
P123
Meall Odhar
Lùbvan (ruin)
Allt an Rèidh Choire
Coire Mòr a' Chlachair
Beinn a' Chlachair
1087
972
Coire Beag a' Chlachair
Garbh Bhruthach
Ceann Caol Beinn a' Chlachair
Coire Dubh
Dubh Lochan
AN LAIRIG
Ceann Cioch a' Chairn
R100c E1
Meall Nathrach
835
Sròn Gharbh
Lochan an Fheòir
Diollaid a' Chairn
R100a
Loch Coire Cheap
Loch an Sgòir
1114
R100c
Coire na Coichille
1132 Gael-Chàrn
1107
AONACH BEAG
Sgòr Iutharn
Coire Gorm
Leacann na Brathan
Coire a' Chàrra Bhig
Lochan a' Chàrra Mhòir
R100a AA
Sròn Ruadh
Bealach Dubh
Allt a' Bhealaich Dhuibh
Beinn Eibhinn
Glas Choire
Meall an t-Slugain
R98b AA
Coire na h-Eiginn
1148
BEN ALDER
Lochan a' Garbh Choire
R98d
Bealach Cumhann
Beinn a' Chumhainn
903
Coire Chomhlain
Uisge Labhair
Coire na Cloiche
44
45
46
47
48
49

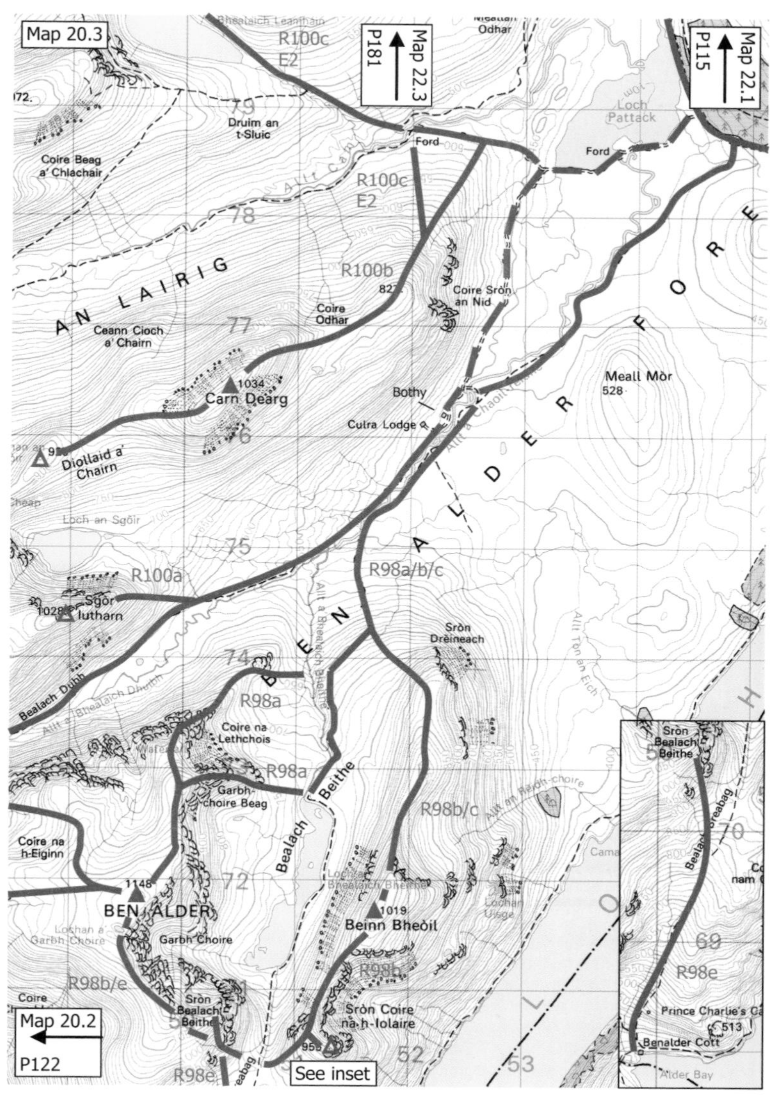
Map 20.3
Map 22.3
P181
Map 22.1
P115
R100c
E2
Druim an t-Sluic
Coire Beag a' Chlachair
Ford
Loch Pattack
AN LAIRIG
R100b
Coire Sròn an Nid
Coire Odhar
Ceann Cioch a' Chairn
Carn Dearg
1034
Bothy
Culra Lodge
Diollaid a' Chairn
Meall Mòr
528
BEN ALDER FOREST
Loch an Sgòir
R100a
Sgòr Iutharn
1028
R98a/b/c
Allt a' Bhealaich Bheithe
Sròn Dreineach
Allt Tòn an Eich
Bealach Dubh
R98a
Coire na Lethchois
Garbh-choire Beag
Bealach Beithe
R98b/c
Allt an Fhèidh-choire
Coire na h-Eiginn
1148
BEN ALDER
Lochan a' Garbh Choire
Garbh Choire
Beinn Bheòil
1019
R98b/e
R98b
Sròn Bealach Beithe
Sròn Coire na h-Iolaire
953
R98e
Map 20.2
P122
See inset
Bealach Breabag
R98e
Prince Charlie's Cave
513
Benalder Cott
Alder Bay

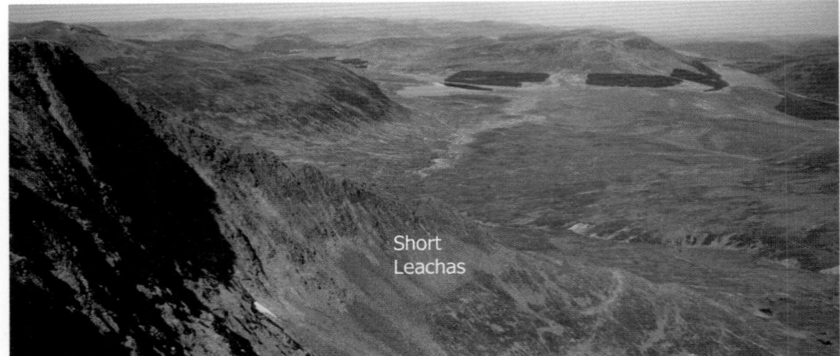

To return to Culra, retrace steps across the plateau and descend the Short Leachas. The initial steep descent off the plateau is not as hard as it appears. In general the ridge is less exposed, less sustained and less interesting than its cousin.

Although tackled on descent, the scrambling is soon over and should cause few problems for anyone who has already managed the Long Leachas. To avoid the rocky nose at the foot of the ridge, bear right down the heathery hillside to regain the path to Culra near the mouth of Loch a' Bhealaich Bheithe.

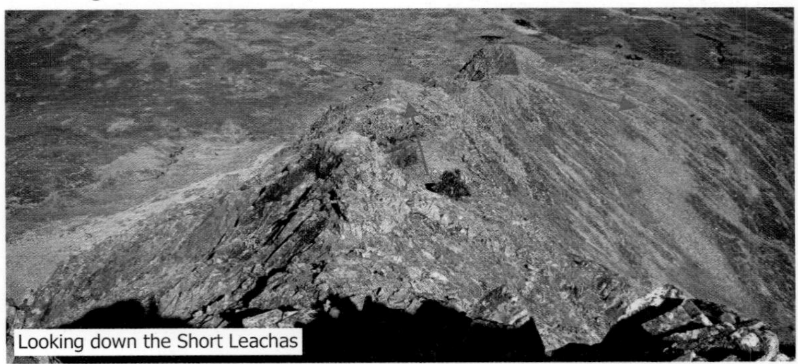
Looking down the Short Leachas

F-Stop: Ben Alder's summit commands a mighty all-round view but most mountain groups are too distant to make a big impression. Below the summit a steep spur separates Garbh-choire Beag from the more spectacular Garbh Choire. Wander beyond the summit to obtain dramatic views, but stay back from the cliff edge if there are still cornices around.

It's worth going a few hundred metres along the corrie rim to see an unusual plateau-top lochan (Lochan a' Garbh Choire) that is the highest of its kind in the Central Highlands.

Route 98b Ben Alder and Beinn Bheoil from Culra: The Long Leachas

G4 ***** NN 523762, 9½ml/15km, 990m/3250ft M123

After you've climbed Ben Alder via the Long Leachas (Route 98a), Ben Bheoil is temptingly close. Its ascent is something of an anti-climax after Alder, especially as it requires a fair amount of effort (more than you'd think for an extra 2½ml/4km and 250m/800ft). Yet there are superb views to be had and the summit is certainly a much-prized tick on the list.

First climb ▲Ben Alder. If you wish to avoid the Long Leachas, you'll find a non-scrambling route up the north-west slopes above the Bealach Dubh (Alternative Ascent on Page 128).

Heading south from the summit, the route hugs the rim of massive Garbh Choire. On traces of path among the moss and boulders, follow the cliff edge as it describes a scenic arc above the gaping depths.

After crossing a low point the rim walk reaches the south-east top above the Bealach Breabag (*Byalach Brepak*, Pass of the Cleft). This is the pass that separates Alder from Sron Coire na h-Iolaire, Beinn Bheoil's satellite Top. The hillside that descends to the bealach

from here is steep and broken. You *could* go straight down it, but it is easier to continue around the corrie rim to its scenic end point above Loch a' Bhealaich Bheithe. From here, a diagonal descent back right will find easier ground, mostly on grass rakes among the boulders.

Once on the mossy bealach, a more distinct path climbs easier grass slopes to Sron Coire na h-Iolaire. The Δsummit lies a couple of hundred metres off-route across a small stony plateau, but it is worth visiting if only for the view. Continuing to Beinn Bheoil, heath and turf are the order

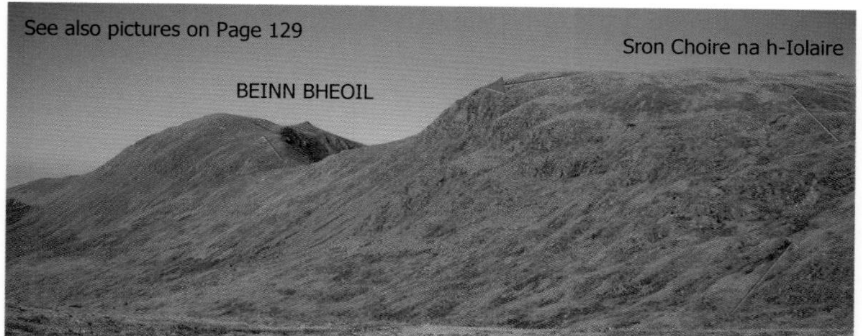

of the day as a path heads northwards along the connecting ridge. There's an unwelcome 70m/250ft descent to an intervening bealach, then the good going continues all the way up to Bheoil's bouldery ▲summit.

Beyond the summit cairn, the short summit plateau soon gives way to a continuing ridge that makes a gentle descent to a dip. There's a lot of broken rock among the grass but the path manages to maintain good going. To the west are pause-worthy views across Loch a' Bhealaich Bheithe to the narrow ridges and broad summits of Ben Alder and the Geal-Charn Group.

At the dip, if you're heading back to Dalwhinnie rather than Culra, it is tempting to descend the grassy hillside on the right (east) to pick up a good path, becoming a track beside Loch Ericht to Ben Alder Lodge. However, it takes twice as much effort to reach that path, in both distance and height, than it does to reach the Culra path.

Beyond the dip, a short rise leads to a level section that gives a great little ridge walk high above the scenery. This is followed by another descent to another level section, where it is sadly time to leave the ridge, descend the hillside on the left (west) and cross rough moorland to regain the path to Culra. Although it seems a fair way down, the path lies a mere 180m/600ft or so below the north end of the ridge.

F-Stop: The summit of Sron Coire na h-Iolaire protrudes over Loch Ericht and offers immense views up and down the 15ml/24km-long loch. The vista also forces a reappraisal of much maligned Beinn Bheoil, whose craggy western hillside, falling straight to the lochside, gives it a surprisingly imposing demeanour.

Viewed from Sron Choire na h-Iolaire

Route 98b Alternative Ascent: Ben Alder North-west Slopes

G2 **** Add-on: 1ml/1½km, zero extra ascent M122/123

To avoid all scrambling on Ben Alder, climb it by its easier north-west slopes above the Bealach Dubh. An excellent 3½ml/6km stalkers' path connects Culra to the bealach, making light work of the extra mileage.

While the path to the Long Leachas runs along the *east* side of the Allt a' Chaoil-reidhe, the path to the Bealach Dubh runs along the *west* side. It begins just beyond the bothy, where the track from Loch Pattack bears right to the (private) wooden building that has replaced old Culra Lodge. Follow the path past the Lancet Edge (Route 100a) and through the increasingly steep-sided trench between Ben Alder and Geal-Charn. There's barely any ascent at all until the final climb to the bealach, where the path finally outflanks Alder's northern crags.

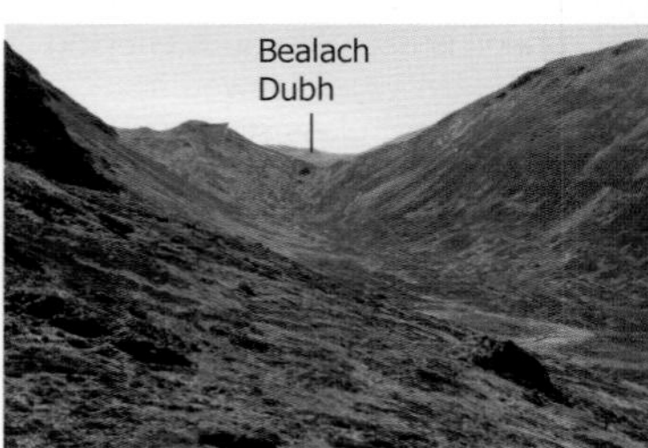

Over the bealach, the path continues around the mountain to Benalder Cottage (see Route 98e), but it is now time to leave it. Climb over the hillock (Meall an t-Slugain, *Myowl an Slookan*, Hill of the Gullet) on the south side of the Bealach Dubh, then bear left above the last of the northern crags into Coire na h-Eiginn (*Corra na Haygin*, Corrie of Violence or Distress). On grass among rocks, climb out the head of the corrie on increasingly gentle slopes that merge into Ben Alder's summit plateau, then bear right to the ▲summit.

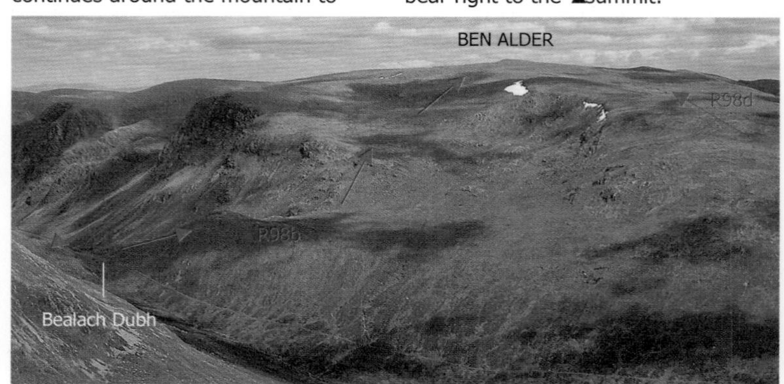

Route 98c Beinn Bheoil alone from Culra

G2 *** NN 523762, 7ml/11km, 580m/1900ft M123

As a separate objective, Beinn Bheoil is decidedly less enticing than Ben Alder when viewed from Culra, with featureless slopes of moor and scree that rise to an unseen summit. However, as already noted, summit views are sublime and the stalkers' path to Loch a' Bhealaich Bheithe climbs to within 180m/600ft of the summit ridge, making access easy.

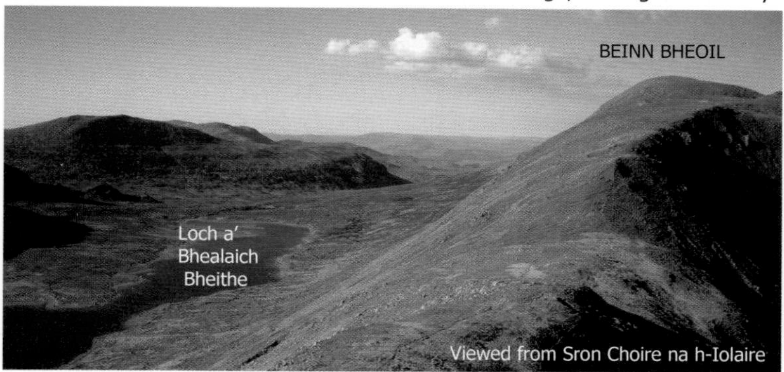

Viewed from Sron Choire na h-Iolaire

From Culra, reverse the last section of Route 98b. Follow the stalkers' path onto the flanks of Beinn Bheoil until it makes a sharp right turn at the 630m contour, then climb rough moor to gain the north end of the long summit ridge and reach the ▲summit.

To make a longer day of it, you could follow the stalkers' path all the way up to the Bealach Breabag and join Route 98a to bag an extra Top (ΔSron Coire na h-Iolaire) and traverse Beinn Bheoil's whole summit ridge from south to north. The path is excellent all the way to Loch a' Bhealaich Bheithe, becomes boggy around the shoreline then improves again as it climbs towards the Bealach Breabag. It ends short of the bealach, but by then the going is easy. (Total mileage/ ascent from Culra: 9ml/14km, 710m/2350ft)

BEINN BHEOIL

Route 98d Ben Alder from Corrour: The Balderdash

G2 *** Route Rage Alert NN 356664, 20ml/32km, 800m/2600ft M122

Via Loch Ossian and the glen of the Uisge Labhair (*Ooshka Lah-ir*, Loud Water) Ben Alder is 3ml/5km closer to Corrour than it is to Dalwhinnie. Even so, it is still a 10ml/16km walk to the summit and the return trip would certainly be a forced march if attempted between trains. Torpedo calls it *The Balderdash* (B-Alder-dash). You can reduce the effort by cycling around Loch Ossian.

For the logistics of getting to Corrour station, see Page 86. From there, follow either of the Land Rover tracks around Loch Ossian. The south-east shoreline track is slightly shorter, while the north-west shoreline track is better surfaced (and used by road vehicles). A rougher track runs from the bridge at the loch's outlet (NN 413696) to a bridge over the Uisge Labhair at NN 418701. You can cycle to this point.

A path continues up the glen of the Uisge Labhair. For the first mile or so it runs along an embankment and is fairly dry, but beyond the Allt Feith a' Mheallain it deteriorates notoriously. It's a 3ml/5km walk up the dreary glen from the bridge and it seems a good deal longer. Be prepared.

After passing the north-west nose of Beinn a' Chumhainn, leave the glen and head diagonally up the hillside to the Bealach Cumhann (*Byalach Coo-an*, Narrow Pass) between Beinn a' Chumhainn and Ben Alder. Above the bealach, make a beeline for Ben Alder's summit. Rough, steepish slopes ease with height as the angle of ascent lessens towards the ▲summit plateau and cairn.

And remember: trains don't wait.

Route 98e Ben Alder and/or Beinn Bheoil from Loch Rannoch via Benalder Cottage

From Loch Rannoch (NN 506577) to Benalder Cottage (NN 498680):
8½ml/14km *each way*, 280m/900ft *out*, 130m/400ft *back*
From Benalder Cottage: G2 **** M123
Ben Alder + Beinn Bheoil: 9ml/15km, 1140m/3750ft
Ben Alder alone: 6ml/10km, 820m/2700ft
Beinn Bheoil alone: 6/ml/10km,740m/2400ft

Culra, on the north side of Ben Alder, isn't the only open bothy in the area. On the south side of the mountain, picturesquely sited by the shore of Loch Ericht at Alder Bay, stands equally remote Benalder Cottage. Return trips from here to the summits of Ben Alder and Beinn Bheoil are shorter than from any other base. Excellent approach paths also put the Geal-Charn Group within range, and it is additionally worth noting that Sgor Gaibhre (▲97) is closer to the cottage than from any other starting point.

However... you just knew there had to be a however... first you have to get to Benalder Cottage, and that involves an arduous 8½ml/14km walk from the B846 Loch Rannoch road. It follows that, for a day trip up Ben Alder on foot from the roadside, only the extremely fit need apply. Use of a mountain bike shortens the approach by 6ml/10km each way.

The normal option is to backpack in, although, as with Culra, it would be unwise to assume that you'll have the three-roomed bothy to yourself. It may be remote, but that is part of its attraction.

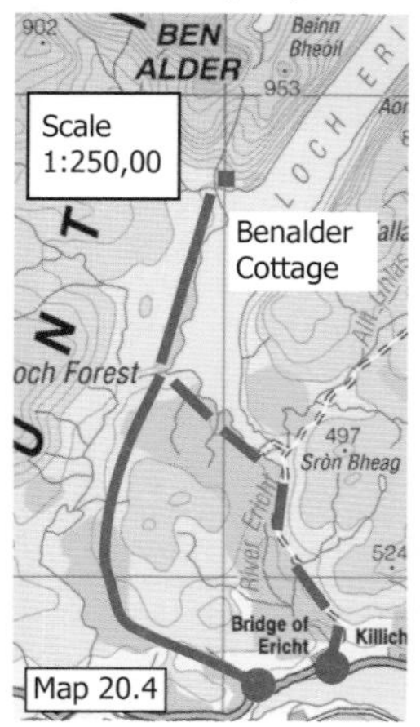

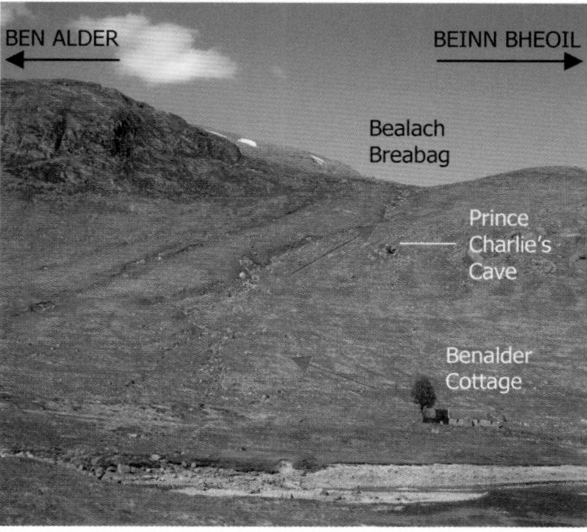

Getting to Benalder Cottage (NN 498680)

Two approach routes meet at the south-west corner of Loch Ericht for the final stretch along the lochside.

1. The first approach route begins on a Land Rover track at the west end of Loch Rannoch. After you have passed the access road to Rannoch Lodge on the B846, the track is the second on the right, just around a bend. There are parking spaces at the start of the track. It climbs 240m/800ft through forestry plantations before descending 90m/300ft across moor to reach the private building at the south-west corner of Loch Ericht, 5½ml/9km from the roadside (NN 488640).

At the start of the second forestry plantation reached (NN 488588), a short side track on the right leads to a gate and a path that takes a short cut around the trees to the track's highpoint (NN 481610). The path is overgrown and boggy in places and, as it saves a distance of only c.400m, takes longer to climb than the track. Optionally, use it on the return trip, on descent, to break the forced march back to the roadside.

The long and winding road

2. The second approach route to the south-west corner of Loch Ericht is the same length as the track and involves *no* loss of height. It begins on the east side of the River Ericht in Bridge of Ericht (NN 522582), a mile or so east of the Land Rover track. From here, a 3½ml/6km paved hydro road climbs 150m/500ft to the dam at the south-east corner of the loch. So far, so good, but the 2ml/3km shoreline route from there to the south-west corner crosses rough, boggy ground much churned up by ATV tracks.

GiGi: Alder Bay wasn't always as wild a spot as it is now. Before Loch Ericht was dammed and the waters raised 8m/26ft, there used to be a small township here.

At one time the cottage was home to the local gamekeeper, named McCook. Legend has it that he hanged himself from the rafters and that his ghost haunts the place. In reality, he retired to Newtonmore and the legend was spread by later deer poachers anxious to keep intruders away. But the legend persists and adds a certain frisson to dark bothy nichts spent sheltering from the howling wind.

Which route to choose? With a long way still to go to Benalder Cottage from the south-west corner of Loch Ericht, the effort involved in following the ATV tracks of the second approach route, except in very dry conditions, is dispiriting. Despite the 90m/300ft extra ascent, the first approach route is normally the preferred option. As an added incentive, it gives much better views, especially westwards across Rannoch Moor and northwards to looming Ben Alder.

Having reached the building at the loch's south-west corner, the toughest 3ml/5km of the walk-in is still to come. The Land Rover track turns west, crosses the stream called the Cam Chriochan (*Cam Cree-achan*, Crooked Boundary) and ends at another forestry plantation (NN 486642). The 6ml/10km to this point can be cycled.

A grassier track continues along the lochside between the forest fence and the shoreline. It deteriorates as it progresses and becomes very boggy after rain. You may prefer to take to the sandy shore in places. The track bridges the stream that enters the loch at NN 494662 and continues to another small stream at NN 496670, on the near side of a final promontory that separates you from the still unseen bothy.

Following a line of posts, leave the shoreline to climb 40m/150ft over boggy ground, bearing left then right to reach a stand of pine trees atop the promontory. A better path then descends the far side to a footbridge over the Alder Burn and, at last, Benalder Cottage itself. We trust you arrive with energy intact and spirit uplifted.

Climbing Ben Alder from Benalder Cottage

Despite the fine setting of Alder Bay, Ben Alder itself looks bulky and disappointing, like Ben Nevis from Glen Nevis, with massive southern slopes rising to a hidden summit. To climb it, first reach the Bealach Breabag between Ben Alder and Beinn Bheoil. A rugged little path runs up the right-hand side of the stream that comes down from the bealach, giving a straightforward route up an otherwise tough hillside of tussocky grass, heather and rocks.

The path begins at the tree behind the bothy. Don't confuse it with the better path that goes right along the lochside to Ben Alder Lodge, or with another, better path that goes left from the cottage to Culra bothy via the Bealach Dubh. The Bealach Breabag path is less distinct at first. It rises diagonally across the hillside to reach the stream and climb beside it.

On the map, it looks tempting to leave the streamside early and make a beeline for the summit of Ben Alder, but the off-path going is horrendous. It is less tiring to stay on the path until it peters out just before the bealach, where the main stream veers left (north-west) up the hillside towards the south-east top.

Follow the stream initially then keep going in a north-west direction, using grassy rakes on rough ground among craglets and boulders, to reach the skyline in the vicinity of the south-east top. From there, follow the cliff edge of Garbh Choire to the ▲summit, reversing the route described on Page 126 (Route 98b, which also covers the ascent of Beinn Bheoil).

GiGi: While on the run from government troops following his defeat at the Battle of Culloden in 1746, Bonny Prince Charlie hid in a cave formed by rocks on the hillside above the cottage, marked on the OS map at NN 499684. The cave lies 90m/300ft in height above Benalder Cottage and c.100m in distance to the right of the stream that descends from the Bealach Breabag. A lone rowan tree, not present in Charlie's day, marks the spot and makes it easy to find.

It is not so much a cave as a couple of cramped rock shelters, one above the other. On the flat roof Charlie's supporters built a wooden structure in which he lived for a while with Cluny MacPherson and three others. It became known as Cluny's Cage. Five servants had to bed down elsewhere. The accommodation may not have been up to normally acceptable royal standards, but if you're on the run from the Redcoats...

Torpedo: Culra bothy and Benalder Cottage are linked by an excellent, well-drained 8ml/13km path that, starting at Culra, follows the west bank of the Allt a' Chaoil-reidhe to the Bealach Dubh, climbs around the western slopes of Ben Alder to the Bealach Cumhann, then descends to Alder Bay. A shorter, rougher 6ml/10km link between the bothies, pathless in parts, crosses the Bealach Breabag.

For those who revel in idiosyncratic accomplishments, a combination of the two routes enables a complete 'girdle traverse' of Ben Alder to be made. Yet another good path runs along Loch Erichtside from Benalder Cottage to Ben Alder Lodge. If you're into wilderness backpacking, there's a lot to do around these parts.

The Geal-Charn Group:

▲100 Geal-Charn 26 1132m/3714ft (OS 42, NN 469746)

Gyal Charn, White Cairn
(not to be confused with namesakes ▲107, ▲111 and ▲116)
ΔSgor Iutharn 1028m/3373ft (OS 42, NN 489743)
Skorr Yoo-arn, literally Hell Peak but also possibly Knife-edge Peak (from aspirated Gaelic Faobhar + Roinn)

▲101 Aonach Beag 37 1116m/3661ft (OS 42, NN 457741)

Ernach Bake, Little Ridge (not to be confused with namesake ▲85)

▲102 Beinn Eibhinn 48 1102m/3615ft (OS 42, NN 449733)

Ben Ayvin, Odd or Happy (in fact Ecstatic) Mountain
ΔMeall Glas Choire 924m/3032ft (OS 42, NN 436727)
Myowl Glass Corra, Hill of the Grey Corrie
ΔMullach Coire nan Nead 922m/3025ft (OS 42, NN 430734)
Moolach Corra nan Ned, Summit of the Corrie of Nests

▲103 Carn Dearg 98 1034m/3392ft (OS 42, NN 504764)

Carn Jerrak, Red Cairn
(not to be confused with namesakes ▲96 and ▲117)
ΔDiollaid a' Chairn 922m/3025ft (OS 42, NN 488758)
Jee-alitch a' Chairn, Saddle of the Cairn

Peak Fitness: No change since 1891 Tables.

The four Munros of the Geal-Charn Group line up in a row across the Bealach Dubh from Ben Alder. The eponymous peak of the group, though not the highest, rivals Ben Alder for the character of its vast summit plateau, while the other three Munros and an intervening Top punctuate the skyline to either side. Though nowhere a scramble, the ridge that connects the four Munros is quite narrow at one point and gives **a superb ridge walk in scenic country**, high above the surrounding flatlands.

Viewed from Culra, the most eye-catching peak of the group is, intriguingly, not one of the Munros at all, but the beautiful, conical summit of Sgor Iutharn, the dramatically named peak that was described in the 1891 Scottish Mountaineering Club Journal as '*the* peak of the Central Highlands'. Hidden behind this Top stretches the huge, unseen summit plateau of Geal-Charn, which in turn hides the steep-sided summits of Beinn Eibhinn and Aonach Beag further west. Carn Dearg, the runt of the litter, is a more lacklustre Munro that crouches on the moor east of Geal-Charn, directly above Culra bothy.

Rising to Sgor Iutharn beside the path to the Bealach Dubh, the eye-magnet that is the Lancet Edge pierces the sky like the keel of an upturned ship, eclipsing even the attractions of nearby Ben Alder. Despite appearances, and like its rivals the Long and Short Leachas across the glen, the narrow crest yields to an exciting yet easy scramble that gives access to the Munros above.

Climbing all four Munros of the Geal-Charn Group in a single day from Culra is a considerable expedition. If you intend to cycle in from Dalwhinnie first, it's an even more considerable expedition. If you intend to walk in, it's an inconsiderately considerable expedition. Breaking the four down into smaller groups gives more practicable options.

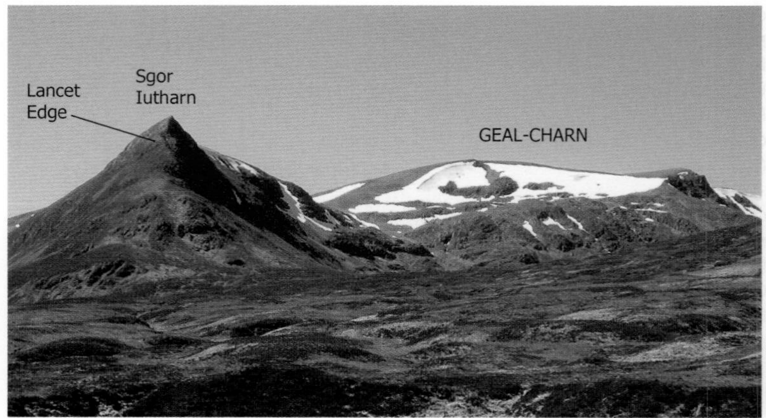

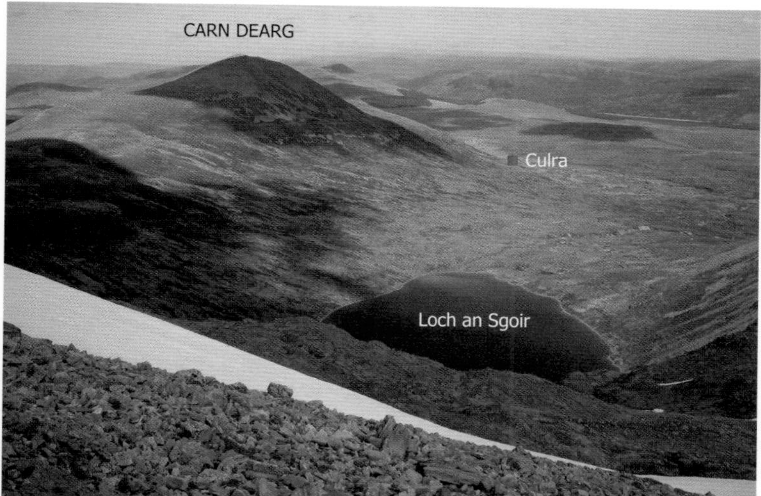

The two eastern peaks, Geal-Charn and Carn Dearg, are connected by a scenic 2½ml/4km ridge walk that can be reached from Culra by a scramble up the Lancet Edge (Route 100a). As a day walk from Dalwhinnie, this classic round may be just about possible for you. The two western Munros, Beinn Eibhinn and Aonach Beag, can be added if time permits. Non-scramblers have other ascent options that avoid the Lancet Edge (Route 100a Alternative Ascent).

As Carn Dearg is detached from the other three Munros by that 2½ml/4km ridge walk, another route option is to bag those three together and leave Carn Dearg for a separate trip, either from Culra, Dalwhinnie or Glen Spean (Route 100b).

On the opposite (north) side of the Geal-Charn Group to Culra, a network of Land Rover tracks and stalkers' paths runs southwards from the A86 in Glen Spean to the Ardverikie Trio (Section 22) and beyond, making Glen Spean a viable alternative starting point for ascents of the four Munros. It's a long approach to the mountains but, unless you're staying at Culra, it's shorter than from Dalwhinnie.

From Glen Spean, you may well be able to reach the two western Munros of Beinn Eibhinn and Aonach Beag without needing a torch, especially if you cycle the first part (Route 100c). Geal-Charn can be added without too much extra effort (Extension 1).

GiGi: Whoever named these Munros must have run out of ideas. Geal-Charn, Carn Dearg and Aonach Beag all have namesakes in the Central Highlands, making odd-one-out Beinn Eibhinn well deserving of its own name.

Carn Dearg can be added with considerable extra effort (Extension 2). Alternatively, as from Culra, it can be left for a separate trip.

Note that the three Munros of the Ardverikie Trio can in turn be reached from Culra (Route 110b).

Finally, Beinn Eibhinn, the most westerly Munro of the Geal-Charn Group, has two even more westerly Tops that are seldom visited. Top baggers will note, however, that an approach from Corrour station makes possible an ascent of Beinn Eibhinn via a round trip over both (Route 100d), while the other Munros can be bagged as add-ons.

Confused? You should be. The Geal-Charn Group lies at the secret heart of the Central Highlands, which at the same time makes it accessible from many points of the compass but difficult to reach from any. Which is the best ascent option? If you enjoy a wee scramble, there's no argument: climb the Lancet Edge above Culra (Route 100a). If you wish to avoid all scrambling, the Glen Spean approach is the shortest (Route 100c).

If you deem it more propitious to divide the group into smaller chunks, break out the map and, with the *Ultimate Guide's* words of wisdom to inspire you, start planning.

Needlepoint: In cloud, Geal-Charn's featureless summit plateau is even more difficult to find your way around than Ben Alder's. Its undulations make it one of the most difficult navigational problems in the Highlands. If you reach the craggy rim of Coire na Coichille at the north-west edge of the plateau, that makes a useful route-finding aid as the summit cairn lies not far back from the rim highpoint.

The other three Munros are easier to navigate, from whatever angle they are approached, although the number of radiating ridges, and the breadth of some of those ridges, encourage constant attention. On the ridge that connects the four Munros, navigation in cloud is aided by the presence of a good path.

The main opportunity for error occurs when trying to find the rocky rib that descends from the Geal-Charn plateau towards Carn Dearg. The safest option here is to find the rim of Coire Cheap, then follow it right until you come to the rib, but look for traces of path to make sure you don't stray onto dead-end buttresses.

Chilly Willy: As with Ben Alder, one of the main problems in winter is simply reaching the summits when daylight is short. Again as with Ben Alder, Geal-Charn's summit plateau is no place to be when night falls.

In perfect conditions, the Lancet Edge becomes a knife-edge of snow in its upper reaches, which means that it is no place for non-climbers. Elsewhere, if approached by any of the routes described in the following pages, the main problem in reaching the skyline in winter is not technical difficulty but length of route. Carn Dearg, especially, remains a straightforward winter hill walk if tackled by its mostly gentle north-east ridge above Loch Pattack (with ice axe and crampons, of course).

Difficulties multiply on the ridge that connects the four Munros. Steep snow may be encountered in several places, especially on the narrow sections of ridge between Aonach Beag and Beinn Eibhinn, and on the rocky rib that descends from Geal-Charn towards Carn Dearg. Here, snow slopes build on the upper walls of the corries to both left and right, overlap in the middle and submerge the rib completely, often barring progress until late spring.

Route 100a The Geal-Charn Group from Culra: The Lancet Edge M122/123

G4 ***** Geal-Charn + Carn Dearg round trip: 8ml/13km, 1020m/3350ft
All four Munros: 12ml/19km, 1510m/4950ft (including return trip from Geal-Charn to Aonach Beag + Beinn Eibhinn: 4ml/6km, 490m/1600ft)

From Culra bothy, take the Bealach Dubh path along the west bank of the Allt a' Chaoil-reidhe to the foot of the Lancet Edge, whose foreshortened crest looms overhead ever more improbably. Leave the path a short distance beyond the Allt Loch an Sgoir, the stream that flows down from Loch an Sgoir (*Loch an Skaw-ir*, Loch of the Peak) in the corrie behind the Edge. You'll complete the round of the corrie rim later in the day.

Pick your way up the hillside of grass and heather that rises to the foot of the ridge proper. As height is gained and the ridge steepens, the heather dies back and traces of path become more distinct. The first rock band goes direct or can be bypassed on a gritty little path to the left. Above lies a brief narrow section, exposed but of little difficulty, then a bouldery scramble leads up to the final upsurge of rock that is the most exciting part of the ascent.

Broken rocks rise to a very narrow crest on which there is no room for a bypass path. The scrambling is technically easy but the exposure is such that we predict an adrenaline surge. The less footsure have been known to seek improved stability by bottom-shuffling along the crest. Immediately beyond lies the Δsummit of Sgor Iutharn, where there is time at last to enjoy the prospect of Loch an Sgoir directly beneath your feet. Well? Does the peak deserve its name?

Beyond the Sgor, the character of the route changes immediately. Swathes of boulder-strewn heath descend gently to a broad saddle before steeper, more broken slopes climb to Geal-Charn's summit plateau. A stroll across the rising tableland of grass and moss leads to the ▲summit cairn, perched at the cliff edge overlooking a large open corrie to the north (Coire na Coichille, *Corra na Chochilya*, Corrie of the Cowl).

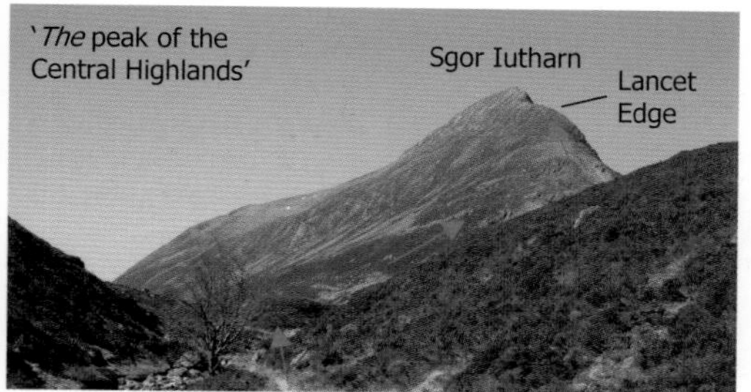

'*The* peak of the Central Highlands'

Now it is time to decide whether to make the return trip to the two western Munros. Viewed from Geal-Charn, both pyramid-shaped Aonach Beag and wedge-shaped Beinn Eibhinn look temptingly close, but those intervening bealachs are deep

GiGi: The Lancet Edge was named for its fanciful resemblance to the sharp blade of a surgeon's knife. It was given its name by Joe Stott, editor of the first Scottish Mountaineering Club Journal, following a visit in the 1880s.

enough to make the prospect of crossing them twice (there and back) somewhat less tempting. And it *is* a long walk back, especially with Carn Dearg still to come.

Heading south-west from Geal-Charn's summit along the cliff edge above Coire na Coichille, the plateau extends a shoulder from which a path descends easy grass slopes for 115m/370ft to the bealach below Aonach Beag. The ensuing 99m/325ft ascent to Aonach Beag begins on gentle grass slopes, steepens on loose rocks, then eases off again onto the table-top ▲summit, an eyrie at the apex of three ridges.

The route onwards to Beinn Eibhinn crosses a deeper gap as it rims the head of a second great northern corrie – the delicately named Coire a' Charra Mhoir (*Corra Charra Voe-ir*, Corrie of the Big Scab or Scurvy, named only on OS 1:25,000 map). The c.140m/460ft descent into the gap is in two stages. Easy-angled grass leads down to a steeper, narrower section, where a stony path descends among grass and rocks to the bottom.

The ensuing c.130m/420ft ascent to Beinn Eibhinn is a mirror image of the descent. From below, the crest looks rockier and more intimidating, flanked by the mottled outcrops that give the corrie its name. Yet the ascent is without difficulty. The first stage is quite steep and narrow, with a gritty path left of the crest, then the ridge continues over a minor dip before grassier slopes curve up to the half-dome ▲summit. The cliff-top summit cairn is the second highpoint on the craggy corrie rim.

Further west lie Eibhinn's two awkwardly sited satellite Tops, which even Top baggers may wish to leave for another day (Route 100e). But you'll want to take time out to admire the extensive view across them to Loch Ossian and Corrour before contemplating the return trip.

Back at the summit of Geal-Charn, heading north-east towards Carn Dearg, the plateau descends slightly to a marshy saddle before a minor rise. The obvious continuation goes left of the rise, where a prominent ridge heads north, but this takes you off route (see Route 100c Extension 1). Instead, bear right (north-east) towards Carn Dearg, whose summit can now be seen in the distance.

Soon you find yourself on the

The descent from the Geal-Charn plateau

craggy rim of Coire Cheap (*Corra Chyepp*, Carp Corrie), which narrows to become a rocky rib separating Loch Coire Cheap from Loch an Sgoir, nestling in their craggy corries to left and right. In Gaelic the rib is known as the Aisre (or Aisir) Ghobhainn (*Asher Gawin*, Blacksmith's Path). Its descent is steep and rugged but a path winds its way down without difficulty in a thrilling situation between the two lochs, with the Lancet Edge providing the perfect backdrop across Loch an Sgoir. Lower down, the angle eases and the descent ends with a pleasant little ridge walk to the next bealach.

On the far side of the bealach, the ridge continues gently on its way, broad and easy, with boulder-strewn heath underfoot. After reaching ΔDiollaid a' Chairn, the ridge becomes broader still, with even better terrain underfoot if that were possible, giving wonderful walking. After a slight descent to a saddle, the path leads up gentle slopes to a false rockpile summit, from where Carn Dearg's true ▲summit is revealed a few hundred metres further across the rubble.

Culra bothy lies directly below Carn Dearg's south-east slopes, but these are steep and stony at the top, such that a more roundabout descent route is more pleasant. After admiring Ben Alder across the moor (picture on Page 119), keep heading north-east along the continuing ridge. You'll soon leave the summit rocks behind and, on or off traces of path, be bounding down heath to a saddle. From here, a diagonal line back right, bearing left lower down, will find the easiest route through the grass and heather to the bothy.

Route 100a Alternative Ascent: via the Bealach Dubh Avoiding the Lancet Edge G2 **** M122/123

Geal-Charn + Carn Dearg round trip: 9½ml/15km, 1020m/3350ft
Beinn Eibhinn + Aonach Beag return trip: 13ml/21km, 920m/3000ft
All four Munros round trip: 12½ml/20km, 1270m/4150ft

The path from Culra to the Bealach Dubh continues over the bealach to facilitate a direct approach to Beinn Eibhinn at the west end of the Geal-Charn Group. The skyline can then be followed back over Aonach Beag, Geal-Charn and Carn Dearg to Culra. This is in fact the shortest way of bagging the four Munros as it involves least retracing of steps. Shorter variations of the route can be used to climb Beinn Eibhinn & Aonach Beag and Geal-Charn & Carn Dearg as two pairs.

From Culra, take the approach path past the foot of the Lancet Edge to the top of the Bealach Dubh. If opting for the shorter round over Geal-Charn and Carn Dearg, leave the path here. As with Ben Alder on the south-east side of the bealach (Page 128), easy slopes rise on the north-east side all the way to the top of Sgor Iutharn, only c.310/1000ft above, to join the Lancet Edge route (Page 139). Take a peek down the Edge and see what you think.

Easy route to Aonach Beag and Beinn Eibhinn

Viewed from the skyline

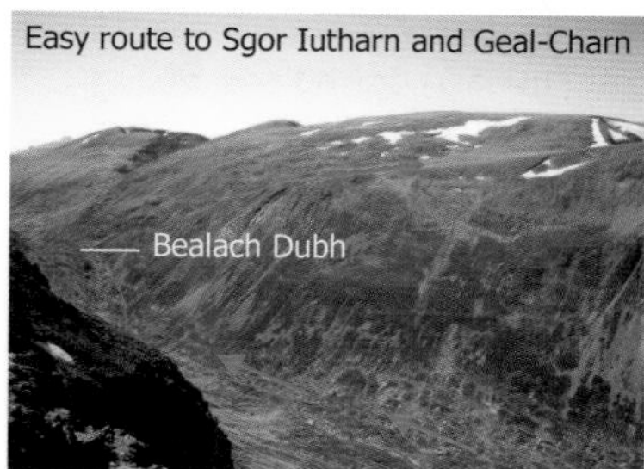

Easy route to Sgor Iutharn and Geal-Charn

To climb Beinn Eibhinn from the Bealach Dubh, walk a few hundred metres down the far side, cross the stream and contour into the grassy corrie on the right. This is Coire a' Charra Bhig (*Veek*, Little), a sizeable hollow but the little sibling of the even larger corrie on the north side of the mountain. Climb easy slopes, bearing left higher up, to reach the bealach between Beinn Eibhinn and Aonach Beag. With luck, you'll come across a boot-worn path at some point.

Once on the bealach, go left to bag Beinn Eibhinn and return, then go right to bag Aonach Beag (Page 140).

N.B. If you've had enough by now, omit Geal-Charn and Carn Dearg and descend by the route of ascent. Otherwise follow the ridge to those two eastern Munros (Page 141).

N.B. If you've had enough at the summit of Geal-Charn, omit Carn Dearg, descend to the Bealach Dubh and take the path back to Culra.

Route 100b Carn Dearg from Culra, Dalwhinnie or Glen Spean

From Dalwhinnie: G2 ** NN 634846, 21ml/34km, 820m/2700ft
From Culra: G2 ** NN 523762, 4ml/7km, 570m/1850ft
From Glen Spean: G2 ** NN 433831, 19ml/32km, 1270m/4150ft

We include a brief description of this route for those who wish to bag this outlying Munro alone, having climbed the other three Munros of the Geal-Charn Group by other routes. It is not the most uplifting ascent in the area, but you'll still get those incomparable Culra views.

If starting at Dalwhinnie, walk or cycle to the junction of Land Rover tracks at Loch Pattack, a few hundred metres west of Culra Junction. Take the left branch around the southern shore of the loch, branch right again after 100m and follow this track uphill to the foot of Carn Dearg's broad north -east ridge. The ridge rises at a gentle angle, rough at first but improving greatly with height. After reaching a rounded rise, where the summit is revealed ahead for the first time, excellent going leads to a saddle, then traces of path climb to the stony ▲summit plateau.

On descent, reverse the route of ascent all the way to the foot of the ridge or, after outflanking crags, take a short cut right down steeper slopes to reach the Land Rover track to Culra some way south of Loch Pattack.

If starting at Culra bothy, climb Carn Dearg by reversing the descent route described under Route 100a on Page 142. Do not make a beeline for the summit but find easier ground by aiming for the saddle at the foot of the upper north-east ridge (NN 513769), where you join the ascent route from Dalwhinnie. Return the same way or, if heading for Dalwhinnie, descend the north-east ridge as above.

From any road, the shortest approach to Carn Dearg begins in Glen Spean, as for the Ardverikie Trio. The first 3½ml/6km along Land Rover tracks to Lochan na h-Earba can be cycled. The mountain is climbed by its north-east ridge, as above, and the whole route is described on descent as Route 100c Extension 2.

Route 100c Beinn Eibhinn and Aonach Beag from Glen Spean

G2 **** NN 433831, 18ml/29km, 990m/3250ft M122/M180

As a day trip from a roadside starting point, Beinn Eibhinn and Aonach Beag, the two most westerly Munros of the Geal-Charn Group, are more easily bagged from the A86 in Glen Spean than from the A9 at Dalwhinnie. It is still a long walk-in, but tracks and paths are good and can be cycled part of the way. Given sufficient fitness and determination, you could bag all four Munros using this approach. You'll miss the magic of Culra and see nothing of the Lancet Edge, but there's no denying that the skyline still makes a great ridge walk.

The route begins as for the Ardverikie Trio (Route 110a), on a Land Rover track that bridges the River Spean just west of Moy Lodge. At a right-hand bend 300m beyond the bridge, branch left on a track that crosses the moor and climbs to a T-junction beside a wood. Take the right branch here to contour around Binnein Shuas and reach a fork in front of a small reservoir.

While Route 110a takes the left branch here, the route to the Geal-Charn Group takes the right branch across the moor beneath Beinn a' Chlachair. The track ends at the Allt Cam (*Owlt Caam*, Crooked Stream) near the ruined walls of the old homestead of Lubvan. You can cycle the 4ml/7km (and mere 130m/430ft of elevation gain) to here.

The next 2ml/3km stage of the trip follows a path beside the Allt Cam to the foot of the mountains. The path is in a fair state but we'd avoid it in wet conditions. Views are restricted by high riverbanks. The stream and path skirt Beinn a' Chlachair and eventually bear left around its back into An Lairig (*An Lahrik*, The Pass), the marshy defile that separates it from the Geal-Charn Group.

You now stand at the foot of Meall Nathrach (*Myowl Narach*, Hill of the Snake), the craggy nose that terminates Aonach Beag's north-west ridge. Further right is the north-west

Viewed from the A86

ridge of Beinn Eibhinn. The two ridges enclose Coire a' Charra Mhoir, whose headwall forms the Munros' connecting ridge. A round of the corrie skyline gives an aesthetically pleasing trip across the summits. By climbing Beinn Eibhinn first, you have the option of continuing beyond Aonach Beag to bag Geal-Charn (and Carn Dearg?), should the spirit move you.

At the foot of Meall Nathrach, it is tempting to leave the path, cross the Allt Cam and aim right, heading directly for Beinn Eibhinn, but the boggy, heathery terrain makes for arduous going. Instead, stick to the path as long as possible.

It follows the Allt Cam left (east) for a short distance, crosses the stream (stepping stones) and bears back right to climb across the lower slopes of Meall Nathrach beneath the crags. It becomes indistinct and even disappears a few times, but it is worth seeking out and keeping to as long as possible. When it becomes lost for good, continue the diagonal traverse up the moor into the huge, shallow bowl of Coire a' Charra Mhoir, where the going improves at last.

Between the craggy confines of the upper corrie and a small side corrie to its right (Coire Gorm, *Corra Gorram*, Blue Corrie), a steep rib climbs directly to the summit of Beinn Eibhinn. It looks a viable ascent route from below but is spoiled by a section of steep rubble higher up.

Much easier and gentler going will be found further right, across Coire Gorm, on the north-west ridge itself. You can climb to the ridge more or less anywhere, but for the best going make a shallow traverse up grass slopes to reach the skyline low down, at the top of the shoulder called Sron an Fhuarain (*Strawn an Oo-arin*, Nose of the Spring).

On good going of boulder-strewn grass and heath, the broad ridge rises gently to a highpoint then bears left across a shallow saddle at the head of Coire Gorm. If you stick to the crest, you'll find two picturesque little lochans nestling on the saddle. The ridge then broadens even more as it finishes up stony slopes to Beinn Eibhinn's cliff-edge ▲summit cairn.

Continue around the corrie skyline to ▲Aonach Beag, as per Route 100a,

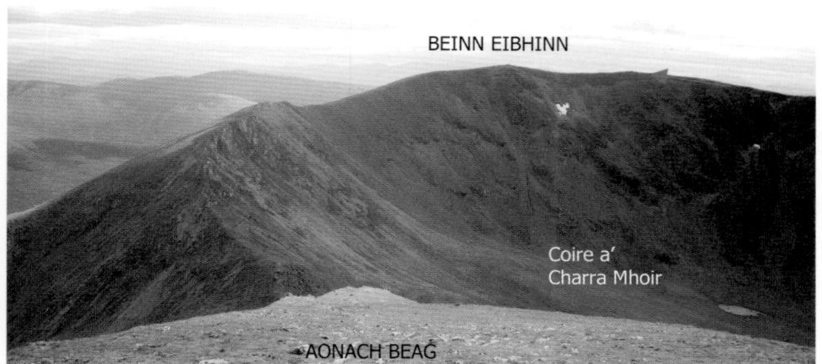

then begin the return trip to Glen Spean down Aonach Beag's broad north-west ridge. This is similar to Beinn Eibhinn's, except that there are more loose rocks around, including some remarkably brilliant white blocks of quartzite. Fortunately, there is also a lot of grass, which means that the rocks are generally avoidable.

Descend the ridge to a flat section before Meall Nathrach, then descend into the corrie on either side to avoid the craggy nose above the Allt Cam. Rather than descend left onto the tangled moors of lower Coire a' Charra Mhoir, which are perhaps still too fresh in the memory, it is easier to detour right into Coire na Coichille, whose slopes are almost totally devoid of heather.

Grass slopes lead down to boggy, tussocky ground beside the Allt Cam. The best strategy is to cross the stream and make use of its grassy right-hand bank, where there are traces of path. This leads back to Lubvan and the Land Rover track back to distant Glen Spean.

See also picture on Page 141

Route 100c Extension 1: Geal-Charn G2 ****

Add-on: 1ml/2km, 120m/400ft M122
All three Munros from Glen Spean: 19ml/31km, 1110m/3650ft

Geal-Charn is a relatively easy route extension. From Aonach Beag, as described in Route 100a, follow the skyline to ▲Geal-Charn, then continue north-east across a marshy saddle to the top of a rise.

Here Route 100a bears right around the rim of Coire Cheap in the direction of Carn Dearg, while the return route to Glen Spean bears left, down the gentle slopes of Geal-Charn's north ridge between Coire Cheap and Coire na Coichille. After a few hundred metres, bear left down easy grass slopes to reach the Allt Cam and the path back to Lubvan.

Route 100c Extension 2 Carn Dearg G2 ****

Geal-Charn to Carn Dearg: 2½ml/4km, 300m/1000ft M122/181
Return from Carn Dearg to Glen Spean: 9½ml/15km, 240m/800ft
All four Munros: 23ml/37km, 1650m/5400ft

Adding Carn Dearg to the route is a more serious extension than adding Geal-Charn, but the walk takes in the most spectacular scenery and turns the day into a round trip that avoids retracing steps to Lubvan.

From Geal-Charn, follow the ridge to ▲Carn Dearg as described in Route 100a. At the summit of Carn Dearg you are separated from Glen Spean by the bulk of Beinn a' Chlachair. Despite appearances to the contrary on the map, it is now less tiring to return around that mountain's eastern flank, via stalkers' paths around Loch a' Bhealaich Leamhain, than it is to return around the western flank to Lubvan, via the pathless marshy flats of An Lairig. This, despite an extra 240m/800ft of ascent.

From the summit of Carn Dearg, descend the north-east ridge, as described in Route 100b. Your goal is the end of the Land Rover track that runs from Loch Pattack to the Allt Cam (NN 519788), marked 'Ford' on the OS map (although it is no different from any other Highland stream crossing). N.B. This is not the Allt Cam that flows down the west side of An Lairig to Lubvan, but the Allt Cam that flows down the east side into Loch Pattack. Just to confuse Sassenachs, the canny Highlanders have given both streams the same name.

You could descend directly from the summit of Carn Dearg to the path along the eastern Allt Cam, but you'll find better going by staying on the north-east ridge all the way down. Near its foot, bear left across the moor to reach the ford, which you may have to paddle across to gain the stalkers' path on the far side. This excellent path climbs to Loch a' Bhealaich Leamhain, nestling in the steep-sided bowl between Beinn a' Chlachair and Geal Charn (the Ardverikie Trio's Geal

Charn, that is – keep up!).

Before reaching the loch, the path forks to send branches around each side to the Bealach Leamhain (*Byalach Leh-an*, Elm Pass) at its head. The right-hand path is best as it avoids an extra 60m/200ft ascent and descent taken by the left-hand path. Note that yet another path (also marked on the map) runs from the top of An Lairig to join the left-hand path on the shoulder of Beinn a' Chlachair, but this is harder to reach from the summit of Carn Dearg, harder to find and involves just as much ascent as the route via the ford and the right-hand path.

At the Bealach Leamhain, quit the right-hand path, cross a short stretch of ground to join the left-hand path and follow it down to Lochan na h-Earba and the track back to Glen Spean, as described in Route 109a.

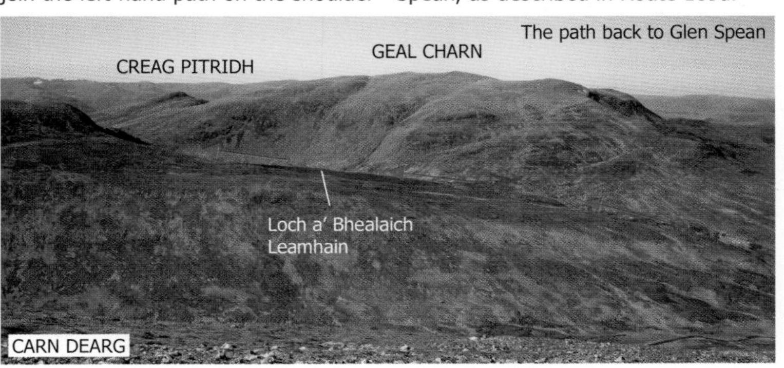

The path back to Glen Spean

Route 100d Beinn Eibhinn alone from Corrour

G2 *** Route Rage Alert NN 356664, 17ml/27km, 800m/2600ft M150

As with Ben Alder, the summit of Beinn Eibhinn lies closer to Corrour than it does to Dalwhinnie or Glen Spean. A Corrour approach is not an economical option for the Geal-Charn Group as a whole but it does have one advantage over others – it enables the easy bagging of Eibhinn's two awkwardly sited western Tops.

When viewed from the summit, these appear as nothing more appetizing than insignificant mounds. That's because they *are* insignificant mounds... guarded by a rough, clingy, almost permanently sodden moor. Nevertheless, their inclusion in Munro's Tables sure increases their baggability.

From Corrour Station, the approach is as for Ben Alder, along the shores of Loch Ossian and the glen of the Uisge Labhair (see Page 130 for details). You can cycle to the bridge over the Uisge Labhair at NN 418701. Less than a mile further along, the path crosses the stream that flows down shallow Coire Feith a' Mheallain (*Corra Fay a*

Vyalan, Corrie of the Bog of the Little Hill) between the two Tops.

The aim now is to make a round of the skyline via the broad, ill-defined ridges on each side of the boggy corrie. The two Tops form the high-points of the ridges, which coalesce behind the Tops to make a final rise to Beinn Eibhinn's summit.

Tackling the east side first, squelch your way up the moor to a brief levelling around the 730m contour. Above here the vegetation dies back for the final rise to the mossy summit dome of ΔMeall Glas Choire.

Continuing to Beinn Eibhinn, a short descent leads to a dip that goes by the grandiose name of Uinneag a' Ghlas Choire (*Oonyak*, Window). Curiously, the Top itself was known by this name until the 1981 Tables.

On the far side of the dip, climb easy grass slopes to join Route 100c from Glen Spean near the two small lochans on the saddle at the top of Coire Gorm. Wander up the final rise to the summit of ▲Beinn Eibhinn, then re-descend to the saddle. Easy slopes of boulder-strewn grass descend from here to a dip before making a short 30m/100ft rise to ΔMullach Coire nan Nead. On the brief ascent you'll pass

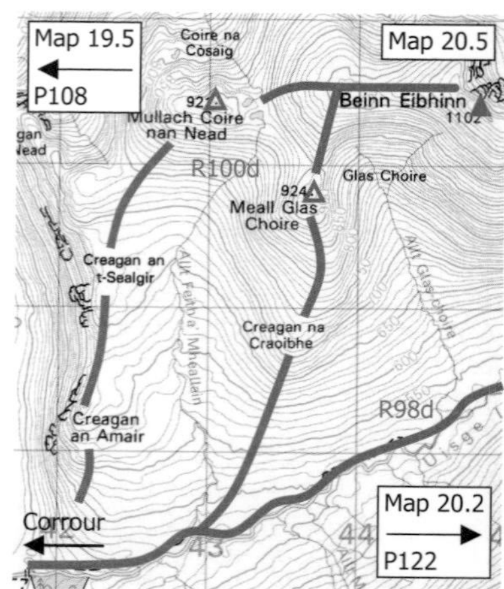

two large lochans, one of which flows north and one of which flows south.

To regain the Uisge Labhair path, descend the west side of Coire Feith a' Mheallain, staying close to the rim to outflank the corrie's vast peat hags. Just before reaching the final hillock, called Creagan an Amair (*Craikan an Ammer*, Rocky Hillock of the River-bed), you'll hopefully come across an ATV track. It's somewhat boggy but most welcome nonetheless as it will take you all the way back down to the bridge over the Uisge Labhair.

21 DRUMOCHTER WEST

East of Loch Ericht, squeezed between that great, glacially deepened fault line and the dreary defile of Drumochter Pass on the A9 further east, a triangle of nondescript country forms the Central Highlands' loneliest outpost. Separated by the loch from the rest of the Central Highlands, its rolling plateau summits have more in common with the Cairngorms still further east and are even located within the boundaries of the Cairngorms National Park. Unfortunately they lack one commodity that the Cairngorms have in abundance: scenic interest.

Notwithstanding its inclusion in the national park, the time-honoured corridor of Drumochter Pass has long been considered the dividing line between the Central Highlands and the Cairngorms. Hence the Munros to the east of the road are described in *Volume 4: The Cairngorms*, while those to the west of the road are described here.

It has to be said that the four Drumochter West Munros are lacklustre lumps half-hidden behind the even duller humps of the Sow of Atholl and the Boar of Badenoch. The Sow (NN 624741, 803m/2635ft) and the Boar (NN 621763, 739m/ 2425ft) are more interesting in name than in nature, such that their little visited summits remain chiefly the preserve of those completing non-Munro hillwalking lists.

Two of the four Munros have steep faces but, let's face it, they'd rate no more than a passing glance out of the windscreen were it not for their Munro

GiGi: Traffic Scotland maintains real-time CCTV cameras facing both north and south along the A9 at Drumochter Pass, and these can be accessed to obtain current weather information. View live images at www.trafficscotland.org/lev/index.aspx.

All routes are subject to possible access restrictions during the stalking season. Current contact number for local information: 01528-522-200.

status. When cloud rolls around their summits, as it often does, their best feature is the A9 itself, which speeds northwards past them in search of more interesting fare. Even under clear skies, the mountains' convex forms, dull colour, featureless hillsides and encircling moors induce lethargy. And if you overcome that, the road and railway, in sight and earshot on all ascents, to say nothing of the line of giant electricity pylons that march through the pass, do little to facilitate communion with nature.

Now for the good news. Thanks to the 452m/1483ft height reached by the road, you get a maximum of Munro for a minimum of effort in these parts. Moreover, once on the skyline, plateau summits and broad ridges, characterised by gentle angles and easy terrain, do much to compensate for the mountains' indifferent welcome. Go on a sunny day, without expectations, and you may well find yourself enjoying a strangely Tolerable Traipse across the Tops.

The four Munros fall naturally into two groups of two: Beinn Udlamain & Sgairneach Mhor (Route 104a) and A' Mharconaich & Geal-charn (Route 106a). You may prefer to make the extra effort and get them all out of the way in a single trip (Route 106b).

F-Stop: The one redeeming feature of the Drumochter West Munros is the eastern view they command over Loch Ericht to Ben Alder and other Munros around Culra. Beinn Udlamain and Geal-charn overlook the loch and have the best views.

GiGi: Drumochter Pass has a long history as an important access corridor from the north to the south of Scotland. During clan times drovers brought huge herds of cattle this way to the great market at Crieff.

The first road was built by General Wade in 1727-30 to give access from the south to Ruthven Barracks near Kingussie. At least modern users are spared the toll that was levied at Dalnacaroch between 1821 and 1878 (some malcontents jumped the toll gate on horseback).

The railway was opened in 1863 after many years of protest. 'The old charm is disenchanted, The old Highlands are no more', bewailed poet Principal Shairp, proving that there is nothing new in the battle between progress and conservation.

▲104 Beinn Udlamain **119** 1011m/3317ft (OS 42, NN 579739) *Ben Ootlaman*, obscure, often translated as Joint or Unsteady Mountain (from Gaelic *Udalan*, meaning a Swivel Joint), but a more appropriate derivation may be from Gaelic *Udlaidh*, meaning Gloomy

▲105 Sgairneach Mhor **155** 991m/3251ft (OS 42, NN 598731) *Scarnyach Voar*, Big Stony Place

Peak Fitness: No change since 1891 Tables although, owing to inexact Victorian maps, Sgairneach Mhor's summit was originally listed at NN 595728 on the south-east ridge.

Despite an intervening dip of only 14m/47ft, the lowly rise of Mam Ban (919m/3016ft, White Rounded Hill), 1ml/1½km south of the summit at the end of the south-east/south ridge, is a candidate for Top status in any future revision of the Tables.

If the well-chosen Gaelic names of this pair do little to inspire, neither does the roadside prospect, but there are worse things to do in life than stride out along their broad ridges. The summits lurk at the head of Coire Dhomhain (*Corra Ghoe-in*, Deep Corrie), the long, steep-sided defile that cuts west into the hills between the Sow and the Boar. A Land Rover track up the corrie gives easy access through the heathery drumlins at its mouth. Although traditionalists may object to such a man-made intrusion, we're more than grateful for the improvement it makes to the otherwise tedious approach walk (Route 104a).

Route 104a Beinn Udlamain and Sgairneach Mhor from Coire Dhomhain (A9)

G2 ** (*** if sunny) NN 632756, 9½ml/15km, 750m/2450ft M155

We suggest a clockwise round of the Coire Dhomhain skyline, climbing Sgairneach Mhor first, in order to leave the option of adding a third Munro (A' Mharconaich) at the end of the day. Begin at the lay-by on the A9 at the mouth of the corrie. The Land Rover track up the corrie begins on the far side of the railway line and is reached by a railway underpass. This will be found by walking a few hundred metres south along the old road that runs parallel to the A9. At the first stream south of the lay-by, a path takes a short cut, but following it would involve crossing (i.e. trespassing on) the railway line.

Walk up the undulating corrie track, past the Sow, until you reach a small trackside cairn (NN 615750). Take the path that descends from here to cross the Allt Coire Dhomhain. You may have to paddle across, or even cross higher up if the river is in spate.

On the far side, a path climbs the uniform, gentle, heathery hillside on the right-hand (west) bank of the stream that comes down from the saddle between Point 758 and Sgairneach Mhor. From below, this is seen as a dip on Sgairneach Mhor's north-east ridge, west of the deeper bealach that separates Point 758 from the Sow.

The path will be springy if you're lucky, boggy if you're not. Higher up, it bears right beside a streamlet to reach the crest of the north-east ridge some way above the dip. If you lose it, head for the ridge to pick up an ATV track that climbs the crest. Path and track join to continue up gentle slopes of rock-strewn turf to a small, cairned rise at the rim of Coire Creagach (*Corra Craikach*, Craggy Corrie), for which the mountain may be named. Sgairneach Mhor's ▲summit lies a short distance away around the rim.

Continuing to Beinn Udlamain, a twisting descent follows the lie of the land south-west, then north-west, then south-west again, to the 809m/2655ft bealach at the head of Coire Dhomhain. You should come across a path that crosses the right-hand edge of the peaty bealach (N.B. not the one that veers south towards Mam Ban and leads nowhere). Good going makes the path redundant on descent, but it proves useful on the rougher ascent to Udlamain's stonier,

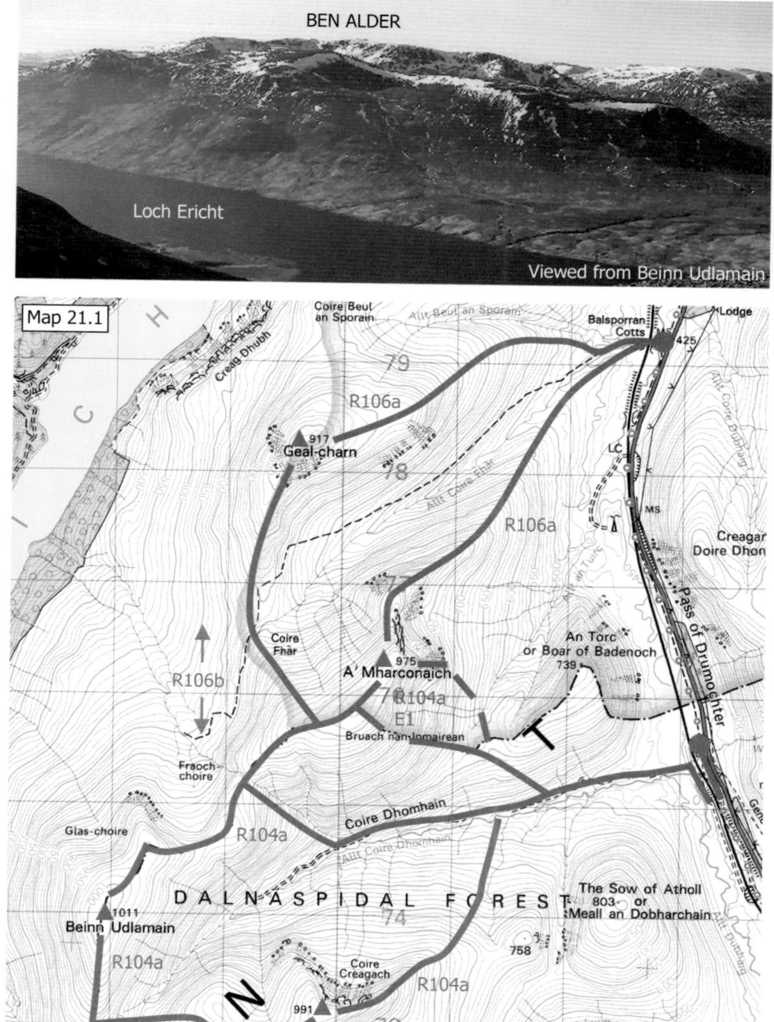
BEN ALDER
Loch Ericht
Viewed from Beinn Udlamain
Map 21.1
Coire Beul an Sporain
Allt Beul an Sporain
Balsporran Cotts
Lodge
425
Creag Dhubh
R106a
917
Geal-charn
LC
Allt Coire Fhar
R106a
MS
Creagan Doire Dhon
Pass of Drumochter
Coire Fhar
R106b
975
A' Mharconaich
An Torc or Boar of Badenoch
739
R104a
E1
Bruach nan Iomairean
Fraoch-choire
Glas-choire
R104a
Coire Dhomhain
Allt Coire Dhomhain
DALNASPIDAL FOREST
The Sow of Atholl
803 or
Meall an Dobharchain
1011
Beinn Udlamain
R104a
758
Coire Creagach
R104a
991
Sgairneach Mhòr
Allt Coire Luidhearnaidh
N

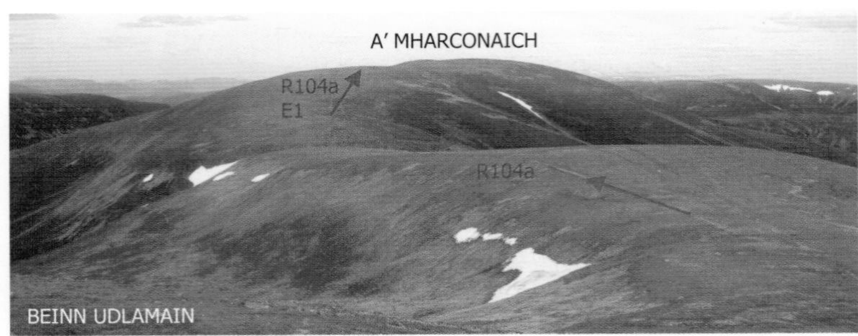

easy-angled south ridge. Once on the ridge, with views opening up across Loch Ericht to Ben Alder, follow a line of old fence posts past a substantial stone shelter to the plateau ▲summit.

Over the summit, the broad ridge continues north-eastwards, back towards the A9, with perfect turf going and an excellent path. Still following the fence posts, it twists gently down over a couple of brief rises and reaches the 861m/2825ft bealach below A' Mharconaich. Unless you decide to continue to this easily reached third Munro (Extension 1), descend from here.

The track back down Coire Dhomhain lies only 250m/800ft below and is easily reached by descending well right of the main stream. In order to find the least steep and least heathery line down, plan the descent route from across the corrie while at the summit of Sgairneach Mhor.

Needlepoint: The broad, undulating, twisting ridges that characterise the skyline of Coire Dhomhain make routefinding difficult in cloud. Good paths and a line of fence posts minimise the possibility of error, but the Drumochter hills really are driech in foul weather.

Two spots demand particular attention. On the convoluted, pathless descent from Sgairneach Mhor to the Beinn Udlamain bealach, two major changes of direction conspire to lead the unwary astray.

The descent from Beinn Udlamain to the A' Mharconaich bealach makes similar changes of direction atop the ridge's two minor rises. At the first especially, take care not to follow the lie of the land north onto difficult ground.

Chilly Willy: Even more than most, the Drumochter mountains are immeasurably more attractive under snow, both to view and to climb. As insiders know, peaty terrain is easier to negotiate when the ground is frozen. If you've never set foot on snow and ice, this route is a good place to practise use of ice-axe and crampons.

Route 104a Extension 1: A' Mharconaich

G2 ** (*** if sunny) Add-on: ½ml/1km, 120m/400ft M155

The broad ridge that runs along the north side of Coire Dhomhain from Beinn Udlamain ends at the outpost of A' Mharconaich above the A9. From the bealach between the two Munros, from which Route 104a descends to the track down the corrie, the climb to A' Mharconaich's summit is little more than a gentle stroll with a small gain in height. The descent that follows is less congenial than a descent from the bealach, but few hillwalkers resist the temptation to bag another Munro for so little effort.

The summit plateau consists of two rounded tops separated by a shallow saddle. The first top reached is the south-west top, called Bruach nan Iomairean (*Broo-ach nan Immeran*, Slope of the Ridges). The line of fence posts from Beinn Udlamain descends south-east from here, following the boundary line shown on the OS map (see below). The second top (the north-east top at the rim of the eastern corrie) is slightly higher and sports two cairns. The second, larger cairn marks the true ▲summit.

A direct return from the summit to the roadside is blocked by the Boar, so the first objective on descent is to reach the intervening bealach. It is tempting to descend straight over the summit but the spur that descends from here is very steep and in any case bottoms out on the north side of the bealach (the Coire Dhomhain track is on the south side). If you manage to work your way down the steep grass and rubble, you'll still have to cross that peaty bealach.

For a better way back, return to A' Mharconaich's south-west top and descend from there in the direction of the Sow, following the fence posts and seeking grassy patches to ease the heathery going. Stay right of the bealach to reach the track below.

▲106 A' Mharconaich 179 975m/3199ft (OS 42, NN 604762) *A Varkanich*, The Place of Horses

▲107 Geal-charn 279 917m/3008ft (OS 42, NN 598731) *Gyal Charn*, White Cairn
(not to be confused with namesakes ▲100, ▲111 & ▲116)

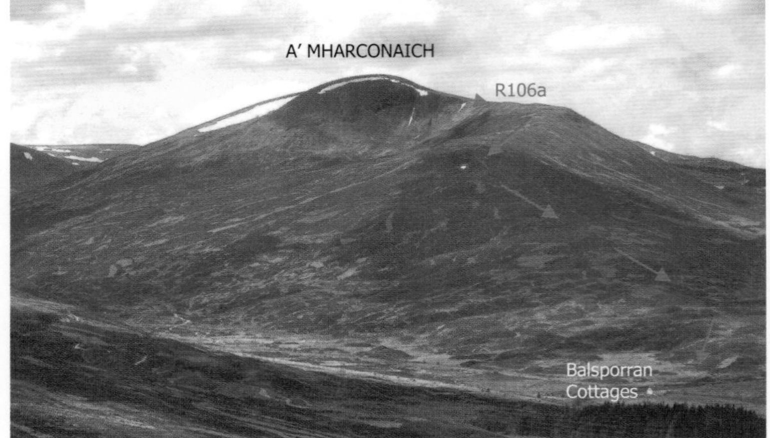

Peak Fitness: Early maps spot-marked only the south-west top of A' Mharconaich (Bruach nan Iomairean), which was originally thought to be the summit. The correct grid reference of the true summit (north-east top) did not appear in the Tables until 1974.

Immediately north of Sgairneach Mor and Beinn Udlamain, these two accomplices form the highpoints on either side of Coire Fhar (poss. meaning Winding Corrie). This is another long, feature-free defile that runs parallel to neighbouring Coire Dhomhain.

As befitting the general tenor of the area, Geal-charn is the lowest of the four Central Highland Munros that bear that name. A' Mharconaich at least looks more interesting from the roadside, with a high eastern corrie whose well-defined rim promises a narrower ridge walk than might be expected hereabouts. Unfortunately, it turns out to be just as broad as all the others. To reduce Route Rage among the peat hags at its foot, we prefer to use it as a descent route and climb Geal-charn first (Route 106a).

Route 106a A' Mharconaich and Geal-charn from Balsporran Cottages (A9)

G2 ** (*** if sunny) NN 628792, 7ml/11km, 730m/2400ft M155
Geal-charn alone return trip: 4ml/7km, 490m/1600ft

To match the Land Rover track up Coire Dhomhain, a good ATV track climbs to the head of Coire Fhar, giving easy access to the summits. From the car park at Balsporran Cottages (former railway cottages), follow the track across the railway line and up the corrie for a few hundred metres, to the Allt Beul an Sporain (*Owlt Bay-ul an Sporran*, anglicised to Balsporran, Stream of the Mouth of the Sporran or Pouch).

Subsidiary ATV tracks branch right to climb the hillside on both sides of the stream. Ignore the first branch (on the near side of the stream), follow the main track across the bridged stream, then take the next branch, about 130m beyond the bridge. The track climbs onto the broad, gentle north-east ridge of Geal-charn and gives an easy ascent.

The going is boggy at first but improves with height as the track becomes a broad path across heathy terrain. The only distraction of note is the view back across the A9 to the lumpen mass of A' Bhuidheanach, a Drumochter East Munro in *Volume 4: The Cairngorms*. After reaching a rounded rise, the path becomes less distinct on ever more gentle slopes that continue to the flat, twin-cairned, bouldery summit plateau. The far (west) cairn marks the ▲summit, where the view opens up across Loch Ericht to the Ben Alder group.

Bouldery ground persists on the ensuing descent, south-west then south, to the 739m/2425ft bealach below A' Mharconaich, at the head of Coire Fhar. Despite the rocky terrain,

the ridge is again broad and gentle, which makes for an easy descent. On the way down, you'll pick up a path and then rejoin the Coire Fhar ATV track, which continues to the bealach.

At the low point of the bealach there's a fork. The main track continues right, to traverse the hillside into Fraoch-choire (*Freuch Coire*, Heather Corrie) below Beinn Udlamain. Leave it to branch left on a rougher path that climbs steeper slopes of rocks and heath. The path becomes indistinct as the angle eases onto the south-west ridge of A' Mharconaich, but you can gain the skyline easily at any point.

Once up, a short and speedy trip along the grassy ridge brings you to A' Mharconaich's summit plateau. As noted in Route 104a Extension 1, the ▲summit is the second top reached, beyond a shallow saddle, at the far north-east end of the plateau.

To descend, go left (north) around the rim of the eastern corrie. After an initial steep descent on stony ground, the going eases as the ridge curves right above Coire Fhar. A path leads down the ridge and crosses the boggy moor at its foot, staying on the right side of the Allt Coire Fhar all the way to the railway bridge at Balsporran Cottages. If the moor is sodden enough to induce Route Rage, you may well be tempted to ford the river and pick up the ATV track.

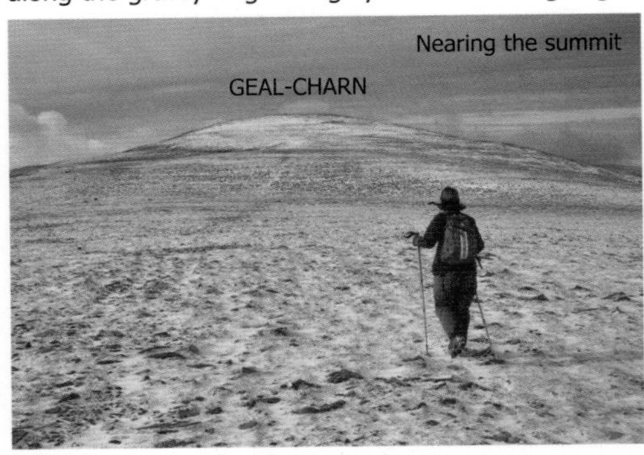

Nearing the summit

F-Stop: Another reason to tackle this route in an anti-clockwise direction is to maximise views over Loch Ericht. The most scenic viewpoint for the loch and its Munros is the top of Creag Dhubh (*Craik Ghoo*, Black Crag, NN 586786), but as this lochside crag lies more than 300m/1000ft below the summit of Geal-charn, it is rarely visited.

Needlepoint: On the broad summit ridges, two spots may cause especial confusion in cloud. The correct route off the rounded summit of Geal-charn is not initially obvious, and remember that the summit of A' Mharconaich is the *second* top reached on its summit plateau. The main path bypasses the first top.

Chilly Willy: A return trip to the summit of Geal-charn, up and down the north-east ridge, is one of the easiest winter ascents in the Central Highlands. If continuing to A' Mharconaich, care is required on descent from each summit as the windswept stony ground tends to become iced. This is especially true on A' Mharconaich owing to the initial steep descent around the rim of the eastern corrie.

Route 106a Extension 1: Beinn Udlamain

G2 ** (*** if sunny) Add-on return: 3ml/5km, 150m/500ft M155

Beinn Udlamain is connected to A' Mharconaich by a broad 2½ml/4km ridge that crosses a high 861m/2825ft bealach. Just as A' Mharconaich can easily be appended to the round of Sgairneach Mhor and Beinn Udlamain (Route 104a Extension 1), so Beinn Udlamain can easily be appended to the round of Geal-charn and A' Mharconaich.

On the map, the shortest way to Beinn Udlamain from the bealach between Geal-charn and A' Mharconaich follows the ATV track into Fraoch-choire and makes a beeline for the summit from there. However, the going is steep and rough once you leave the track. You'll find better going at an easier angle by getting onto the ridge as soon as possible. From the bealach, take the path that climbs towards the ridge, as described above, and bear right to gain the ridge in the vicinity of the Mharconaich-Udlamain bealach. Turf slopes continue up to Udlamain's ▲summit. From there, return along the ridge and continue to A' Mharconaich as per Route 104a.

Route 106b All Four Drumochter West Munros from Balsporran Cottages (A9)

G2 ** (*** if sunny) NN 628792, 12ml/19km, 1070m/3500ft M155
+ 2½ml/4km roadside walk

Bagging all four Munros in a single trip doesn't involve an overlong day but it does require a 2½ml/4km walk back from end point to start point on the cycleway alongside the A9. You could do the route either way round. As with Route 106a, we recommend an anti-clockwise direction.

From Balsporran Cottages, follow Route 106a over ▲Geal-charn to ▲A' Mharconaich, then reverse Route 104a over ▲Beinn Udlamain and ▲Sgairneach Mhor to regain the A9 at the mouth of Coire Dhomhain.

22 LAGGAN AND SPEAN

Between the A9 at Dalwhinnie/ Kingussie and the west coast at Fort William/Spean Bridge, the A86 runs alongside Loch Laggan reservoir and through Glen Spean, bisecting the Central Highlands from east to west. To the south of the road is the great tract of roadless country described in Sections 17-21. To the north is another great tract of roadless country crossed by a number of ancient trails but containing fewer Munros.

Three of the Munros to the north form the miniature mountain range of Creag Meagaidh, which is sufficiently complex to merit a section all on its own (Section 23). Further east, the four Munros of the Monadh Liath form

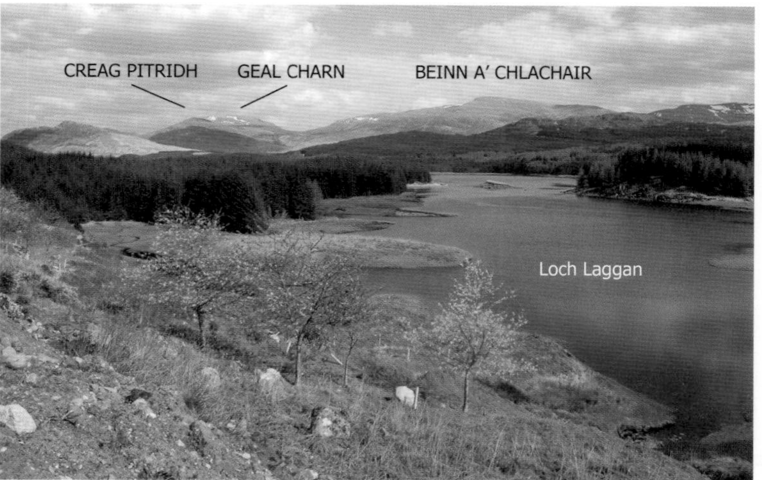

Baffies: When the tops are in cloud, try two rewarding short walks at the east end of Loch Laggan.

Pattack Falls plunge 12m/40ft into a rocky gorge beside the Land Rover track that leaves the A86 around a mile east of Loch Laggan (NN 554898). The 2½ml/4km return trip can be extended to the Linn of Pattack and other waterfalls upstream.

Dun da Lamh (*Doon da Laav*, Fort of the Two Hands) is a dilapidated but still enormous 130m x 70m Iron Age fort that crowns the hill-top west of Laggan village, 180/600ft above the valley floor (NN 582929). It is reached by forest track and path and the views are considerable.

For Monday-Saturday access restrictions during the stalking season, see www.ardverikie.com and roadside notices.

another distinct unit (Section 24). This section describes the remaining five Munros accessible from the roadside, of which two lie to the west of Creag Meagaidh and three to the south.

The two Munros west of Creag Meagaidh are Beinn a' Chaorainn and Beinn Teallach, whose nondescript southern slopes drop to the roadside to give easy access (Routes 108a & 108c). To add more interest, Beinn a' Chaorainn can be climbed by an exciting scramble (Route 108b), and the two peaks can be connected by their intervening bealach to make a round-trip two-bagger (Route 108d).

Further east, on the south side of the road, the three Munros of Beinn a' Chlachair, Geal Charn and Creag Pitridh form a compact cluster in the Ardverikie deer forest and are known as the Ardverikie Trio. The shortest approach to them is from Culra further south (Route 100b) but, as Culra is difficult to reach, the normal approach is from the A86 (Route 110a).

The balmy shores of Lochan na h-Earba

Torpedo: Above Roybridge at the west end of Glen Spean, **Glen Roy** cuts through the hills to a hidden valley packed with scenic interest. The most famous sights here are the Parallel Roads – long hillside terraces that are the successive shorelines of an ancient ice-bound lake.

Beyond the road end at Brae Roy Lodge are the **Falls of Roy** and the **White Falls** on the River Roy, plus a **natural bridge** and numerous waterfalls on the Burn of Agie. A Land Rover track along the north bank of the Roy leads to remote grassy flatlands and vast moors, across which a good path continues past Luib-chonnal bothy to Melgarve and the minor road to Laggan village.

If you can arrange transport at both ends, Brae Roy Lodge to Melgarve is one of the most rewarding but least known wild walks of the Highlands (one-way trip: 9mlk/15km, 200m/650ft).

▲108 Beinn a' Chaorainn 80 1052m/3453ft (OS 34, NN 386851) *Ben a Cheurin,* Mountain of the Rowan (not to be confused with namesake ▲166 in the Cairngorms)
∆South Top 1049m/3442ft (OS 50, NN 386845)
∆North Top 1043m/3423ft (OS 50, NN 383857)

▲109 Beinn Teallach 283 914m/3000ft (OS 34 or 41, NN 361859) *Ben Tyallach*, Mountain of the Forge or Fireplace, perhaps named for the appearance of its steep eastern corries

Viewed from across Glen Spean

Peak Fitness: No two mountains, cantankerous neighbours in more ways than one, have caused so much trouble for Munro's Tables. Beinn Teallach wasn't even a Top before resurveying elevated it to the magic 3000ft mark in 1984.

Its status was ratified by a 2009 survey that re-measured its height as 914.60m (3000.80ft), since when it has replaced Ben Vane, re-measured at 915.76m (3004.60ft), as the lowest Munro of all.

Beinn a' Chaorainn's summit plateau, with three highpoints of similar elevation, has caused even more trouble over the years. Both current summit (Centre Top) and South Top were listed at 1049m in the 1997 Tables. Prior to then, between 1974 and 1997, the Centre Top was listed at 1052m, and this is currently the case again on OS maps. It has been suggested that cornice formation may contribute to differing height measurements.

In Tables history, the South Top was the Munro between 1891 and 1974. The Centre Top was a Top in 1891, was deleted from the Tables completely in 1921(!) and was reinstated as the Munro in 1974, which it has been ever since. We suggest you climb both, just in case.

These two most westerly Glen Spean Munros stand on the north side of the A86, where their retiring summits offer little of note to distract attention from the more compelling mountainscapes on the south side of the road. Their dull southern slopes give easy if laborious ascents.

More positively, both mountains harbour craggy corries on their hidden north and east sides. Beinn a' Chaorainn in particular is a triple-topped, deeply ice-gouged peak that harbours two great eastern corries. They can't match Coire Ardair of Creag Meagaidh in stature, but they do have two attractions that corrie doesn't: a cliff-edge rim walk and a rocky spur (the east ridge) that separates them. While the normal ascent route up the broad south-west ridge is a feature-free footslog (Route 108a), the scramble up the east ridge is nothing less than a minor **Central Highland classic** (Route 108b).

Unlike its near namesake, the redoubtable An Teallach in the Northern Highlands, Beinn Teallach has no such redeeming features. If future geological re-alignment resulted in its diminution by a mere foot, it would be no great loss to the Tables. We can but hope. Steep northern and eastern corries (Coireachan Garbh, *Corrachan Garrav*, Rough Corries) attempt to alleviate the monotony but, approached by its south ridge from the A86, the mountain is little more than one humongous, wet, sprawling heap (Route 108c).

The two Munros are separated by the glen of the Allt a' Chaorainn, whose head forms a 614m/2015ft bealach between them. In keeping with the general nature of the terrain hereabouts, the bealach is one humongous, wet, sprawling hollow, but crossing it in either direction is easy. A combined ascent saves having to make a return trip and, more importantly for aficionados of the Highland landscape such as your good self, takes you close to the heart of the scenery (Route 108d).

Route 108a Beinn a' Chaorainn from Roughburn: South-west Ridge

G2 *** NN 377814, 6ml/10km, 850m/2800ft M168
North Top return trip add-on: 1ml/1½km, 90m/300ft

Much of this ascent is a head-down plod, with only the view behind across Glen Spean to distract from the effort. We nevertheless award the route three stars for the redeeming summit ridge walk around the rim of the eastern corries.

Begin at the car park at the bridge over the Allt a' Chaorainn near Roughburn on the A86, just east of Laggan Dam. Take the forest track into the trees and, c.200m beyond a sharp right-hand bend, branch left at a fork. N.B. Ignore the path and the forest break on the bend itself.

Around 100m along the left branch, a cairn marks the start of a boggy path that tunnels up a forest break to reach open ground at a stile. The arboreal quagmire at the start can be avoided in the trees on the right.

Above the forest, Chaorainn's broad south-west ridge climbs all the way to the South Top, although at first the crags of Meall Clachaig (*Myowl Clachak*, Rocky Hill) block the way. Indistinct paths fork left and right at the stile. To avoid rocky ground, take the left-hand path, even though it contours much further left than seems warranted before turning to find a way up the hillside.

It is not the driest of paths and may be difficult to follow in places, but it is infinitely less tiresome than the heather on either side. It stays below the crest of the ridge until petering out on approach to a level section behind Meall Clachaig (NN 375835). Note this spot for the return trip.

Now on the broad ridge crest, another indistinct path leads onwards and upwards. The top seen ahead is only a shoulder of the mountain, but the South Top isn't far beyond. As height is gained, more and more rocks litter the hillside. The path is reduced to traces then gives up altogether, but the going remains good on grass and turf among the rocks.

At the ΔSouth Top the scenery changes dramatically. With the main effort now behind you, you can relax and enjoy your reward – the broad ridge walk around the rim of the eastern corries. Remember that the Centre Top is currently the Munro although, from the South Top, the 6m/20ft lower North Top looks higher. As the finest part of the walk is between the Centre Top and the North Top, it would in any case be remiss of you not to visit the latter. Distances between the three Tops are not great.

Beyond the South Top, the ridge rims the first of the two eastern corries and gives good views of the east ridge (its far bounding rim). The corrie is named Coire Ban (*Corra Bahn*, White Corrie) for its foaming stream.

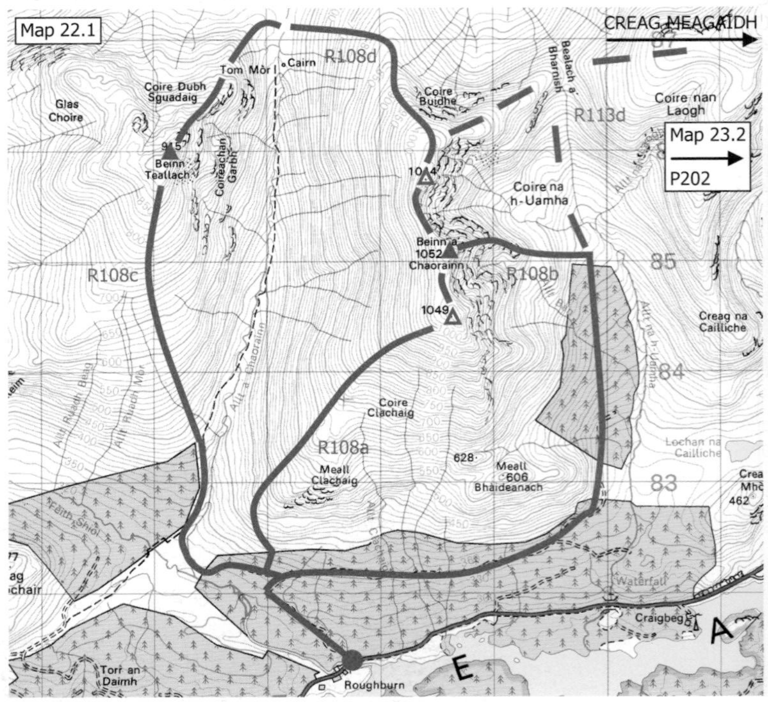

Beinn a' Chaorainn's ▲summit (Centre Top) is perched at the top of the east ridge, overlooking the second, even grander corrie. This comes complete with lochan and is named Coire na h-Uamha (*Corra na Hoo-aha*, Corrie of the Cave) for a cave at NN 400820, just above the roadside waterfall marked on the OS map.

The sky-high stroll to the ΔNorth Top, along a narrowing grassy ridge above the corrie depths, is just recompense for the effort of the ascent. To descend, unless continuing to Beinn Teallach (Route 108d), reverse the whole route.

The correct line of descent off the dome of the South Top is not initially obvious. Aim in the direction of the conical summit of Creag Dhubh (*Craik Ghoo*, Black Crag, NN 323825), seen across the Allt a' Chaorainn, until the south-west ridge opens up below you.

Around 390m/1300ft down, at NN 375835, you'll reach the level section noted above. The path down descends to the right of the little hillock on the far side.

F-Stop: From their isolated vantage point on the north side of Glen Spean, both summits offer a striking panorama of the mountains on the south side of the glen. The view of fjord-like Loch Treig, entrenched between its steep flanking Munros, is especially diverting.

The northern vista includes the rarely trodden upper reaches of Glen Roy, while from Beinn Teallach's summit you can gaze at the Western Highlands and make promises to yourself.

Torpedo: From Beinn a' Chaorainn's North Top there are two ways to extend the day and avoid retracing steps. The normal extension is to cross the intervening 614m/2015ft bealach to the west to Beinn Teallach (Route 108d), but an alternative option is to cross the intervening 824m/ 2705ft Bealach a' Bharnish to the east to Creag Meagaidh.

Broad, gentle ridges of moss and grass flank each side of this high bealach, giving an easy crossing, although you'll then have to descend Meagaidh's south ridge (Route 113c) and cross the Allt na h-Uamha to regain the forest road to Roughburn. Be advised also that we'll never speak to you again unless you then re-climb Meagaidh on another day via Coire Ardair.

GiGi: The name Bharnish is one of the more peculiar misspellings of many on OS maps of the Scottish Highlands, being an odd mixture of Gaelic and English. The Gaelic is Bhearnais, pronounced *Varnish*, meaning Notch.

BEINN A' CHAORAINN

Needlepoint: In cloud, take care when navigating across Beinn a' Chaorainn's broad summit plateau, and on descent make sure to take the correct line off the South Top.

Chilly Willy: Beinn a' Chaorainn's south-west ridge offers a straightforward winter ascent to view some spectacular snow scenery. On the summit plateau, the curving corrie rim between South Top and Centre Top, and between Centre Top and North Top, around the head of the two eastern corries, can become heavily corniced in winter, so stay well back from the edge.

In a white-out, both arcs will be difficult to navigate safely; a direct compass bearing between Tops would take you over the edge. Accidents have happened here.

Route 108b Beinn a' Chaorainn from Roughburn: East Ridge

G4 or G5 **** NN 377814, 8ml/13km, 820m/2700ft M168

Separating Beinn a' Chaorainn's two deep eastern corries, the east ridge occupies an enviable situation, rising in a series of rock steps directly to the ▲summit (Centre Top). To make it an even more seductive line of ascent, the schist rock is tilted up at an inviting angle, giving holds that were simply *intended* for fingers to curl around. This enables you to enjoy situations that elsewhere might be a tad *too* exciting. Any experienced scrambler who foregoes an ascent of the east ridge for an ascent of the south-west ridge should have his or her scrambler's badge revoked.

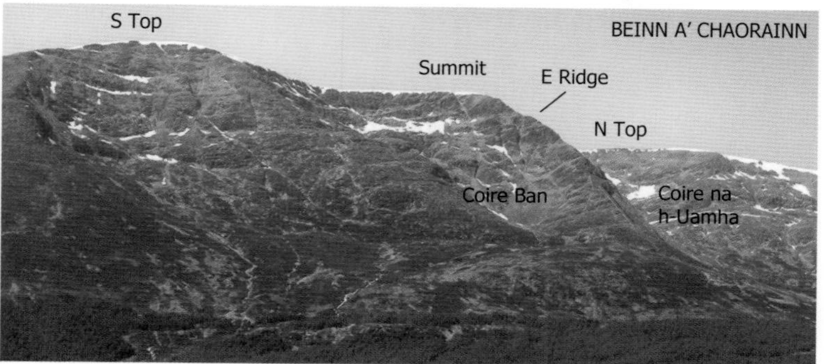

The route begins on the Roughburn forest track, as per Route 108a. Stay on the main track and it will turn eastwards to take you all the way around the foot of Beinn a' Chaorainn and up the glen of the Allt na h-Uamha beneath the eastern corries. Once out of the glen's upper forestry plantation, the foot of the ridge is close at hand across rising moor.

Initial steep heather slopes rise to a levelling at around 800m/2600ft, above which the upper ridge rears skywards. Dotted across grassy slopes, outcrops large

The East Ridge looms overhead

and small pile on top of one another. There are plenty of variations, depending on which particular rock problems you choose to tackle or avoid. Some sections of the ridge are quite exposed, but the scrambling need never be hard unless you wish it to be. Buttresses, walls, corners, cracks… choose your playground and enjoy.

Return from Beinn a' Chaorainn's ▲summit down the mountain's south-west ridge (Route 108a) or continue to Beinn Teallach (Route 108d).

Did I really climb that?

Route 108c Beinn Teallach from Roughburn: South Ridge

G1 ** Route Rage Alert NN 377814, 8ml/13km, 690m/2250ft M168

If the ascent of Beinn a' Chaorainn from the A86 is a plod, the ascent of Beinn Teallach from the same direction is a megaplod that will fully test the waterproofness of your boots. The elevation gain is 120m/ 400ft less and an ATV track further helps reduce the effort involved, but this is more of a bogtrot than a hill walk.

Begin on the Roughburn forest track and branch left c.200m beyond the right-hand bend, as for Beinn a' Chaorainn (Route 108a). Follow the track to the forest edge, where the dreary slopes rising to the summit of Teallach can be seen for the first time.

Note that the forest edge can also be reached by following a more picturesque riverbank path beside the Allt a' Chaorainn from the A86 car park. This is an especially tempting option on the return trip, but the path is rough, seems to go on forever and will cause only frustration and regret.

Beyond the forest edge, a path continues across a field to the Allt a' Chaorainn. Cross the river on flats below a small gorge to join a fairly good path along the far bank. Unless the river is low, it may require a watersplash or paddle.

The path climbs to join a boggy ATV track beside a forestry plantation. At the upper forest fence, when the track bears right to continue up the glen between Teallach and Chaorainn, climb straight up the hillside ahead on a more overgrown, even boggier track-cum-path. To call it wet is an understatement. Its line is not always obvious but it is worth following if at all possible. Leave it and you'll soon find out why – the gentle angle of the hillside has turned this side of the mountain into a vast marshy moor of clinging grass and heather.

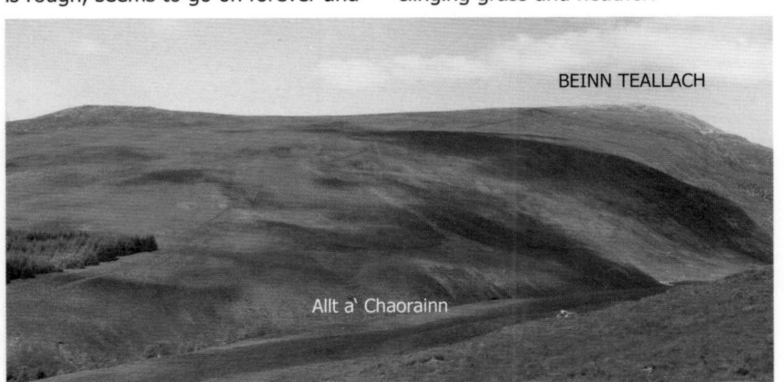

Poor terrain lower down

Good terrain higher up

As height is gained, the track gives increasing respite from the flanking terrain and eventually offers good walking as moor gives way to dry heath. As the angle eases even more, the track becomes lost on turf and boulders, but the going now is everywhere excellent as you approach the summit.

The ▲summit cairn overlooks the first (only?) interesting feature of the day – the northern corrie of Coire Dubh Sguadaig (*Corra Doo Skoo-atak*, meaning obscure), with its broken buttresses and remote loch. Unless continuing to Beinn a' Chaorainn (Route 108d), descend by the route of ascent. If you are able to ignore the squelchiness underfoot, this can be a surprisingly pleasant descent route, with fine views of Loch Treig across Glen Spean to speed you homewards.

Top of NE Ridge

Needlepoint: As with Beinn a' Chaorainn, Beinn Teallach's simplicity of form makes it an easy objective in cloud. The only cause for confusion is a cairned rise to the east of the summit, at the top of the north-east ridge. The true summit lies 150m west of here, just off the main spine of the mountain.

Chilly Willy: A winter climb up Teallach's south ridge is among the easiest in the Central Highlands. When the boggy terrain is iced, the ascent is infinitely more pleasant than in summer and gives good cramponning practice for beginners.

On the other hand, if the boggy hillside is merely covered by soft snow, Teallach is a mountain best left to those with a predilection for masochism.

Route 108d Beinn a' Chaorainn and Beinn Teallach (Round of both Munros) from Roughburn

G2 *** Route Rage Alert NN 377814, 10ml/16km, 1180m/3850ft M168

On their hidden north sides, the two Munros drop easy ridges to a 614m/2015ft bealach whose crossing enables both summits to be bagged on a round trip. Unfortunately, in either direction, the actual crossing of the bealach is about as absorbing as the normal route up either mountain. Using the standard southern approaches from Roughburn for ascent and descent, the big decision to be made is which summit to bag first.

If you climb Teallach first you'll save the best scenery till last, on the rim of Chaorainn's corries. However, you could well miss the path down Chaorainn's south-west ridge and find yourself on steep ground below Meall Clachaig. If you climb Chaorainn first you'll have an easier crossing of the bealach and an easier bogtrot down from Teallach at the end of the day, so we'll describe the crossing in this direction first.

Chaorainn to Teallach

After climbing ▲Beinn a' Chaorainn (Route 108a/b), continue to the North Top. From here, an attractive swathe of moss curves gently down to the junction of the north and north-east ridges, which enclose Coire Buidhe (*Corra Boo-ya*, Yellow Corrie), Chaorainn's remote northern corrie. On turf-&-boulder terrain, continue down the broad north ridge around the corrie rim, with good views across the bowl of the corrie to the remote north side of Creag Meagaidh.

The main decision to be made now is when to leave the ridge to descend left to the bealach, so note that the going will deteriorate as soon as you quit high ground. The bealach and flanking hillsides are rough and marshy, so we leave it to you to pick a good way across (hint: there isn't one). Just south of the bealach's highpoint is a cairn and a spot named Tom Mor (*Towm Mor*, Big Knoll) on the OS map, although it is unclear what feature this refers to.

Once across the bealach, gain Teallach's complex north-east ridge at a convenient point (steeper to the left, easier to the right). The ascent of this ridge, with grass and proper rocks underfoot, together with a surprisingly good path, gives the best walking on the whole mountain. It's hard to believe but, from below, the top of the ridge even masquerades as a commanding highpoint above the steep broken face of Coireachan Garbh. From the cairn at the top, the ▲ summit lies 150m to the west across a shallow dip. Descend the south ridge (Route 108c) to regain Roughburn.

Teallach to Chaorainn

In the direction Teallach to Chaorainn, first cross to the cairned top of Teallach's north-east ridge to find the path that descends to the bealach. When this becomes lost on boggy ground, cross the bealach and gain Chaorainn's north ridge as soon as possible, to find better going on high ground. Follow the ridge up around Coire Buidhe and across the swathe of moss to Chaorainn's summit.

Needlepoint: Finding the featureless bealach in cloud requires pinpoint navigation... and the abominable going is the stuff of Route Rage. Respect is due to all who persevere.

Chilly Willy: The steep, wet slopes that rise on each side of the bealach require care when iced if an unexpectedly rapid descent is to be avoided.

The Ardverikie Trio:

▲110 Beinn a' Chlachair **56** 1087m/3566ft (OS 42, NN 471781) *Ben a Chlachir,* Mountain of the Stonemason

▲111 Geal Charn **81** 1049m/3442ft (OS 42, NN 504811) *Gyal Charn*, White Cairn, probably named for the colour of its quartzite summit (not to be confused with namesakes ▲100, ▲107 & ▲116). Also known (and originally listed in the Tables) as Mullach Coire an Iubhair (*Mullach Corran Yewvir*, Summit of the Corrie of the Yew)

▲112 Creag Pitridh **264** 924m/3031ft (OS 42, NN 487814) *Craik Peetry,* meaning obscure, possibly Petrie's Crag or from Gaelic *pit* (farm) and *ridhe* (field), or perhaps a corruption of its name in the original Tables: Creag Peathraich (*Craik Perrich*, Sisters' Crag)

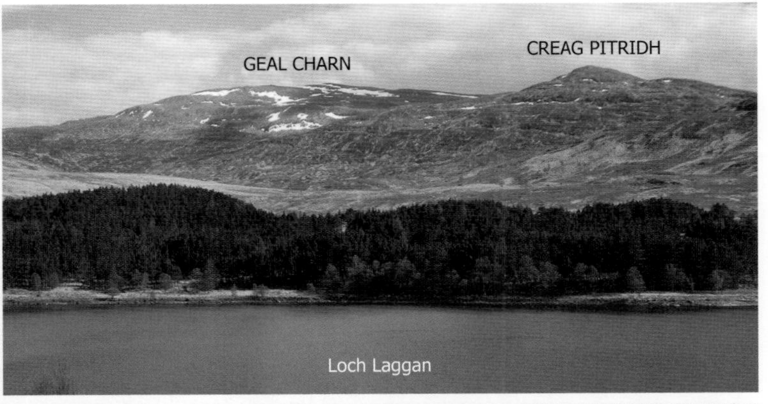

Peak Fitness: No change to Munros since 1891 Tables. Sron Garbh (NN 509810, *Strawn Garrav*, Rough Nose) was a Top of Geal Charn until 1981.

The Ardverikie Trio (aka The A-Team) is a compact triangle of Munros in the Ardverikie Forest on the south side of Loch Laggan. The forest is not a tree forest but a 'deer forest', as shooting estates were known in Victorian times, and no area of the Highlands is so richly endowed with stalkers' paths that give easy access to the heights.

It's more difficult to enthuse about the off-path terrain. Beinn a' Chlachair and Geal Charn are bulky mountains whose summit plateaus are encrusted with sharp quartzite rocks that make boulder-hopping the *de facto* mode of locomotion. Creag Pitridh is a contrastingly conical little hillock that should consider itself very lucky indeed to be revelling in Munro status. From the bealach that separates it from Geal Charn, the elevation gain to the summit is a mere 105m/345ft. What was Sir Hugh thinking of? Still, it's one of the easiest ticks in the Highlands... and it does make a great viewpoint over Glen Spean.

If the three summits are no great shakes individually, the group as a whole is considerably better than the sum of its parts. The mountains are set in complex country far from the roadside, are approached by excellent paths, are adorned by crags and lochans and are connected in a way that makes for an absorbingly intricate round trip.

A three-bagger from the A86 is a considerable outing of some 16ml/26km, but it is the normal way to climb the trio (Route 113a). For shorter trips, bag close neighbours Geal Charn and Creag Pitridh together and leave Beinn a' Chlachair for another day. On the hidden south side of the group, stalkers' paths criss-cross the mountainsides from the vicinity of Culra and offer a further variety of ascent options if you're staying there (Route 110b).

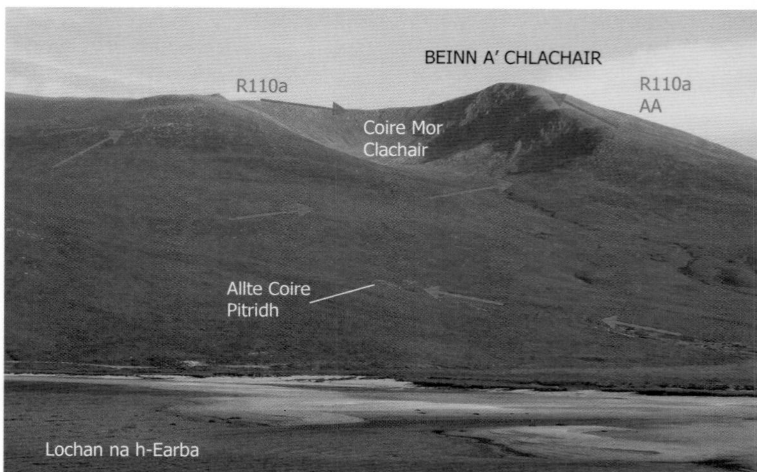

GiGi: Queen Victoria loved this area. She stayed at Ardverikie House in 1847 and considered purchasing it as a base (the present baronial building at NN 508876, seen across Loch Laggan from the A86, was built in 1877). However, the weather was 'dreadful' and the following year she fell in love with Balmoral. If the sun had shone that rainy August, perhaps Royal Deeside would now be Royal Lagganside.

Route 110a The Ardverikie Trio: Beinn a' Chlachair, Geal Charn and Creag Pitridh from Glen Spean

G2 *** NN 433831, 16ml/26km, 1270m/4150ft M180/181
Beinn a' Chlachair alone: 12ml,19km, 840m/2750ft
Geal Charn and Creag Pitridh alone: 14ml/22km, 910m/3000ft

The route begins at the bridge over the River Spean just west of Moy Lodge, at the west end of Loch Laggan (park in the lay-by beside the bridge). The first part of the trip is a 3ml/5km walk or cycle along Land Rover tracks to Lochan na h-Earba (*Lochan na Herba*, Lochan of the Roe). This is a 4ml/7km double loch (lochan?) that is hidden in a great trench behind the craggy lumps of Binnein Shuas (*Been-yan Hoo-as*, Upper Peak) and Binnein Shios (*Been-yan Hee-os*, Lower Peak).

At a right-hand bend 300m after crossing the River Spean bridge, branch left on a track that crosses the moor and climbs to a T-junction beside a wood. Take the right branch here to contour around Binnein Shuas to a fork in front of a small reservoir. Take the left branch here to reach the sandy shores of Lochan na h-Earba at the foot of Creag Pitridh.

The elevation gain to the loch is only 100m/330ft, so a brisk walk should get you there in about an hour. In front of you the whole way are the northern slopes of Beinn a' Chlachair, indented by the deep scoop of Coire Mor Chlachair (Big Corrie of the Stone-mason), the mountain's finest (if only) feature of note. The standard ascent route climbs to the corrie's near (north-east) rim and wanders around the corrie head to the summit, situated at the top of the far (south-west) rim (but see Alternative Ascent Options).

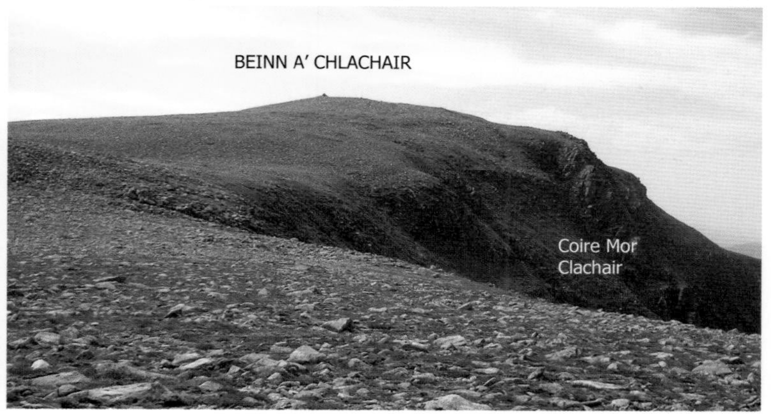

After crossing the bridge at Lochan na h-Earba's inflow stream, ignore the shortcut that goes straight on and stay on the main track, which curves right then back left, eventually to run along the far shore of the loch. After c.400m (cairn), branch right on a grassy track that crosses to the Allt Coire Pitridh, the stream that comes down Coire Pitridh from the bealach between Geal Charn and Beinn a' Chlachair (Bealach Leamhain, *Byalach Leh-an*, Elm Pass, named only on 1:25,000 OS map).

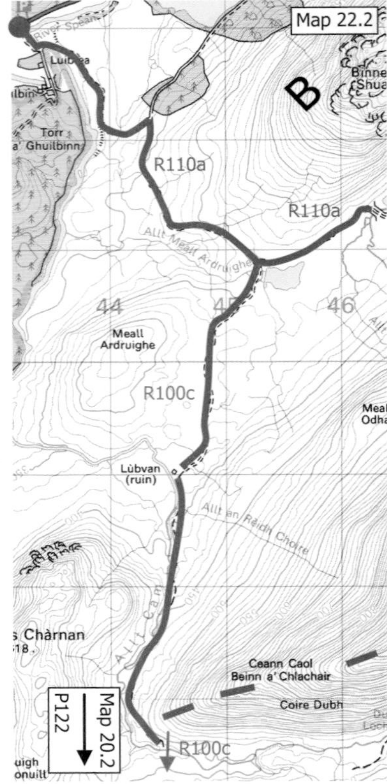

Once the track reaches the stream, it becomes a stalkers' path that climbs over the bealach to Culra and all points east and south. As far as the confluence with a stream that comes down from the left (NN 473804), the path has been renovated so well that the surface gives even better walking than the approach track (really!).

Above the confluence, the path becomes grassier but remains in excellent condition. It's a pity that you'll have to leave it at some point to tackle the uninviting moorland that rises to the near rim of Coire Mor Chlachair on the way to Beinn a' Chlachair's summit. The path veers left, away from the corrie, and the longer you stay on it the further you'll have to walk across the moor. It's a judgement call.

The Stonemason's leavings

Once you take the plunge, at least the going turns out to be less horrendous than feared. Heather gives way to grass as the angle steepens before easing again onto the corrie's

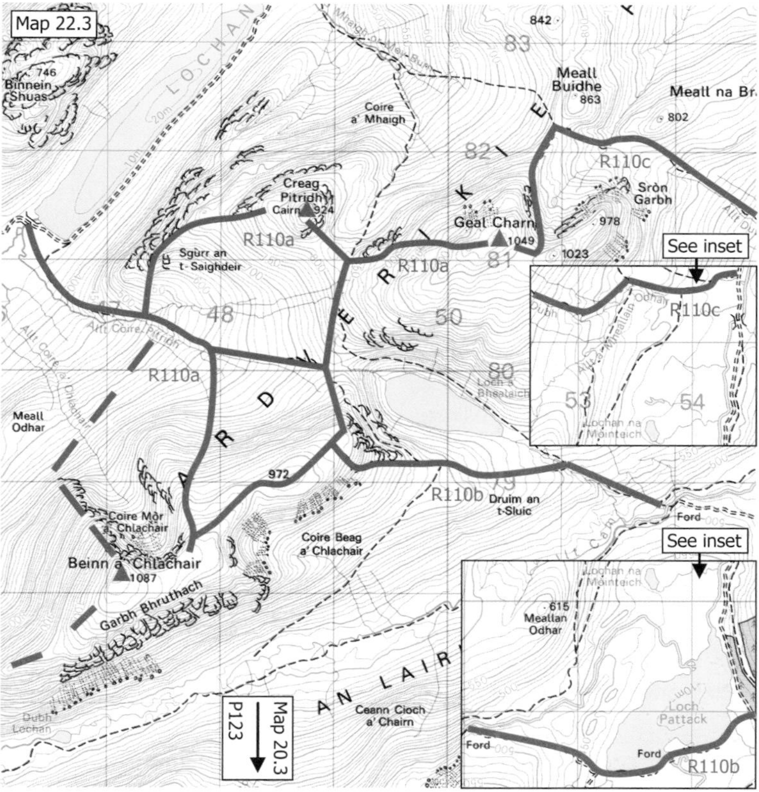

Map 22.3

Map 20.3 P123

north-east rim, to reveal an imposing view of the summit atop the craggier south-west rim. Note the parallel gullies that drop from each side of the summit.

Follow the corrie rim to the summit. The angle remains gentle but the terrain becomes much

rockier as you round the head of the corrie and join the plateau-like north-east ridge. Seek out pockets of greenery, where grass stabilises the quartzite, then boulder-hop up the final ankle-twisting rockpile that forms the ▲summit.

The summit cairn is suitably large, but then it's not as if there's a shortage of construction material. The mountain's name is a rare example of humorous geographical nomenclature. Whoever the Stonemason was, he sure left the place in a bit of a state. Across the deep glen to the south, the inviting Culra Munros seem deceptively close at hand… for another day.

Next up is Geal Charn. Begin by retracing steps around the head of Coire Mor Chlachair, then continue all the way down the north-east ridge. Once off the summit rocks, there's enough grass around to carry a path and give welcome respite from boulder -hopping. If only it lasted. More of the Stonemason's leavings return to slow down the gentle descent to a dip, after which the rocks fade away to give improved going again.

Beyond the dip is a rise of 29m/95ft to the cairned East top, restored to its former height of 977m/3206ft on the latest OS maps (and a candidate for future Top status in the Tables?). Go over or around it to find grass slopes descending to an abrupt end at a cliff face overlooking Loch a' Bhealaich Leamhain, situated in the corrie on the east side of the Bealach Leamhain.

At a distance of 1½ml/2½km from the summit of Beinn a' Chlachair, this is a fine spot to pause and contemplate the great whaleback of Geal Charn, which rises on the far side of the loch, and the more mammary Creag

Pitridh to its left. The descent to the Bealach Leamhain is nowhere near as steep or as difficult as it looks at first sight. Descend the hillside left of the crags, weaving an intricate route down grass among small outcrops. If you're lucky you'll find a small path that takes you down to the stalkers' path that crosses the bealach.

Turn left to follow the stalkers' path a short distance downhill to a fork just west of the bealach. The left branch is the Allt Coire Pitridh path you left earlier and which you will later rejoin further down. For now, take the right branch, which climbs around the foot of Geal Charn to the 819m/2686ft bealach between it and Creag Pitridh. You could climb Geal Charn's south-west ridge direct from the Bealach Leamhain, on going similar to that on Beinn a' Chlachair's north-east ridge, but the stalkers' path is just too good not to use.

Viewed from Creag Pitridh

From its highpoint, just right of the lowest point on the Geal Charn-Creag Pitridh bealach, the stalkers' path continues down the far side to Lochan na h-Earba, while a baggers' path crosses the bealach laterally to climb each Munro. Don't be fooled by the proximity of Creag Pitridh into thinking Geal Charn will be a doddle. This far into the day, the convoluted 230m/755ft ascent, with the summit hidden from sight until the last moment, will seem like a fair old climb.

The path is intermittent and hard to follow, but the slopes of heath and rocks (yes, more of the Stonemason's leftovers from Beinn a' Chlachair) are climbable anywhere. Take a shallower diagonal line up than seems warranted, first along the edge of the corrie on the far side of the bealach, then up a complex hillside of bouldery knolls and grassy terraces. The terrain becomes rockier with height, but it's never as bad as on Beinn a' Chlachair.

Eventually you'll reach the broad south-west ridge, which comes up from the Bealach Leamhain. Follow it across a minor rise to reach the ▲summit at its far end. Surprisingly, there's an ever larger cairn here than on Chlachair. If energy permits, take a stroll down to the rim of the deep north-east corrie (Coire an Iubhair

Mor, named only on OS 1:25,000 map), the mountain's finest (if only) feature of note and from which it derives its original name. See if you can spot the admirable stalkers' path that ascends the corrie (Route 110b).

After returning to the bealach below Creag Pitridh, that third Munro awaits the imprint of your boots. You may well be slowing down a bit by now, so remind yourself that it is the last ascent of the day and that it is only 105m/345ft to the summit. The path is initially indistinct as it crosses the bealach laterally, passing a small lochan, but it becomes better defined as it makes a beeline for the summit up Pitridh's grassy eastern slopes.

At a final steepening, the path eases the angle by taking a dog-leg left and right. After the boulder plateaus of the two previous Munros, the ▲summit is an attractive rocky eyrie with a glorious view over Lochan na h-Earba and Loch Laggan to Creag Meagaidh, to say nothing of limitless views up and down Glen Spean.

There's a choice of ways back down to the Allt Coire Pitridh stalkers' path. If you've had your fill of off-path terrain, the most effortless way back, even though it's not the shortest, is to re-descend to the Geal Charn bealach and join the stalkers' path network there. For a more direct descent, go down Creag Pitridh's south-west ridge, which leads to the outpost of craggy Sgurr an t-Saighdeir (*Skoor an Sijer*, Peak of the Soldier) above the shores of Lochan na h-Earba.

A path leaves the summit to head down the south-west ridge but it becomes intermittent. If you lose it, you may never find it again as the ridge becomes broader and more complex. You can continue all the way out to Sgurr an t-Saighdeir and descend from there around outcrops, but the going on the ridge-crest becomes so tussocky that you may well give up on the endeavour.

Left of the ridge, broad slopes of tussocky grass descend to the stalkers' path beside the Allt Coire Pitridh. If you can find no path down to it, aim for the stream's northern tributary, where you'll find a developing path along the bank. This joins the stalkers' path at the stream confluence, at the top of the resurfaced section.

The ensuing swift descent to the lochside leads you to the most difficult act of willpower of the day – tearing yourself away from a sandy-shored sojourn for the 3ml/5km walk back to the roadside (picture on Page 164).

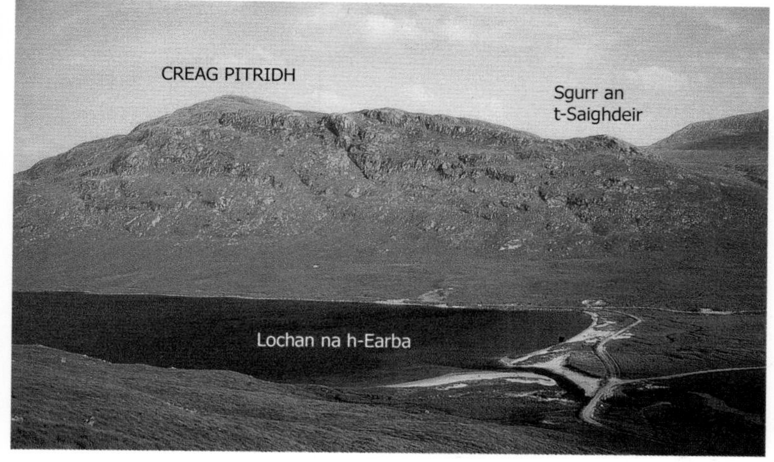

Route 110a Beinn a' Chlachair: Alternative Ascent Options G2 ***

The normal route up Beinn a' Chlachair involves a climb across heathery moorland from the Allt Pitridh stalkers path to the north-east rim of Coire Mor Chlachair, then the negotiation of the summit boulderfield on both ascent and descent. There are two alternative ways up. You can decide if you wish to take either of them *en route* to Lochan na h-Earba.

(1) Leave the Allt Pitridh stalkers' path lower down, cross the mouth of Coire Mor Chlachair and climb the far south-west rim directly to the summit. This involves more moor work to begin with but leads to better going on the corrie rim, on less ankle-twisting terrain than on the north-east rim and with close-up views of the corrie's main crags. (No extra mileage/ascent; see picture on Page 178)

(2) Approach the summit via the long, grassy south-west ridge, which gives a much more genteel ascent than either rim of Coire Mor Chlachair. To reach the foot of the ridge, leave the approach track to Lochan na h-Earba at the fork before the small reservoir and branch right on the Land Rover track to Lubvan (as described on Page 145). From Lubvan, the path used by Route 100c to reach the Culra mountains continues beside the Allt Cam around the foot of the south-west ridge. Go all the way to the foot of the ridge or take a short-cut onto it, then head skywards. (Add-on: 1ml/2km, zero ascent, see picture on page 186)

Terminator: On the shores of Lochan na h -Earba, take time out to study the towering south-east face of Binnein Shuas. Although the hill is a lowly 746m/2448ft high, there's nothing mediocre about those daunting crags. Hidden from the A86, they remained ignored until their discovery in the 1960s led to important developments in modern Scottish rock climbing. When it was first ascended in 1967, Ardverikie Wall, the great buttress of clean rock towards the right, became an instant classic.

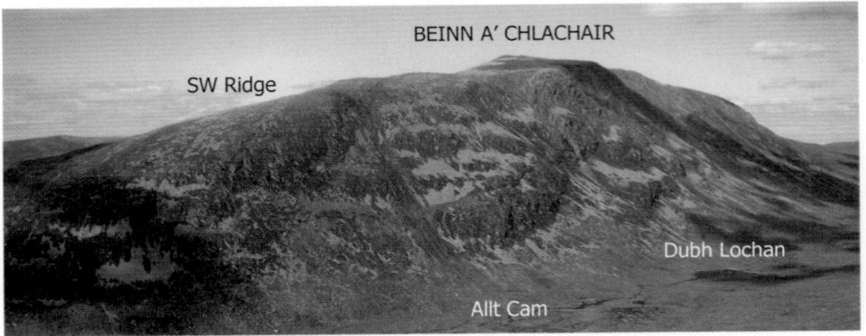

Needlepoint: Swirling cloud makes Beinn a' Chlachair seem even more like a Stonemason's quarry site than ever. As the highest point, the summit is easy enough to find, but routefinding on descent is more difficult because the north-east ridge is so broad. Geal Charn too is an awkward mountain to navigate in foul weather owing to its bouldery terrain, broad undulating summit ridge and the diagonal line required to reach it from the Creag Pitridh bealach. At least the large cairn means there's no mistaking the summit when you do finally reach it. Creag Pitridh is a much easier ascent but, taken together, the Ardverikie Trio in cloud is a navigational test-piece.

Chilly Willy: The complete round is a long winter's day, but the only problematic section is the steep descent from Beinn a' Chlachair's north-east ridge to the Bealach Leamhain. In hard conditions this will require care, while in soft conditions, on yielding snow among rocks, it will be sporting/infuriating (delete as applicable).

Route 110b The Ardverikie Trio: Beinn a' Chlachair, Geal Charn and Creag Pitridh from Loch Pattack (Culra)

G2 *** NN 433831, 12ml/19km, 1100m/3600ft + walk-in/out (see below) M181

The network of stalkers' paths in the Ardverikie Forest extends to the south and east of the three Munros to provide approach routes from the Culra area. The path over the Bealach Leamhain, between Beinn a' Chlachair and Geal Charn, makes both flanking peaks as accessible from Culra as from Glen Spean (although first, of course, you have to get to Culra – see Page 114 for access).

The ascent of all three summits from the Culra side begins at the junction of vehicle tracks at the south end of Loch Pattack ((NN 531784), 2ml/3km north of Culra bothy. From a roadside, this is 7ml/11km south-west of Dalwhinnie along the Loch Ericht track (NN 634846) and 8ml/13km south of the A86, at the east end of Loch Laggan, along the River Pattack track (NN 554898).

From Loch Pattack, take the track west to the Allt Cam and the start of the stalkers' path to the Bealach Leamhain. The path climbs towards Loch a' Bhealaich Leamhain in the depths of the pass and forks to climb each side of it. The left branch climbs to Beinn a' Chlachair's north-east ridge. Follow it to a fork at the crags overlooking the loch, then branch left on a steepening path to gain the north -east ridge above the crags.

Walk and boulder-hop up the ridge to ▲Beinn a' Chlachair, then return and continue to ▲Creag Pitridh and ▲Geal Charn as per Route 110a. Climb Geal Charn last, so that you can then descend south-east down easy grass slopes to regain the approach path below Loch a' Bhealaich Leamhain.

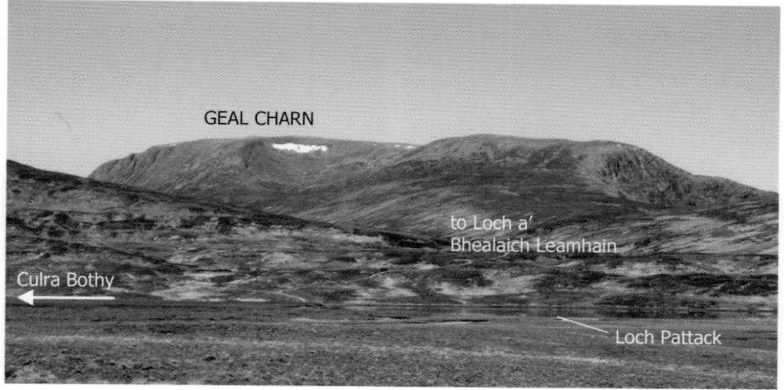

Route 110c Geal Charn from River Pattack (Culra): The Coire an Iubhair Mor path

G2 **** NN 544816, 7ml/11km, 620m/2050ft + walk-in/out (see below) M181

On the Culra side of the Ardverikie Trio there's an enticing little ascent route that's worth considering as an idiosyncratic way of bagging Geal Charn. On the normal approach from Loch Laggan, the mountain's finest feature, its north-east corrie (Coire an Iubhair Mor), is hidden from view all the way up. Yet not only is it an impressive scoop in the hillside, but it also hosts the most beautifully realised stalkers' path in the area, which climbs through it almost all the way to Geal Charn's summit.

The route begins in the valley of the River Pattack (NN 544816), 5½ml/9km from the A86 at the east end of Loch Laggan. From here a stalkers' path climbs across the mouth of Coire an Iubhair Mor to a bealach on its far side, at the foot of Geal Charn's north-east ridge, from where it descends to Lochan na h-Earba.*

The Coire an Iubhair Mor path branches left on the bealach. It starts up the north-east ridge but soon leaves it to make a diagonal ascent beneath rock outcrops on the corrie's craggy western wall. Eventually it climbs out of the head of the corrie to end on a grassy saddle between Geal Charn's summit and the rounded former Top of Sron Garbh. From here, a mere 60m/200ft of ascent on heath separate you from the summit.

*The path on the Lochan na h-Earba side of the bealach can be used to approach the Coire an Iubhair Mor path from the A86 and so give an interesting, if roundabout, round trip over Geal Charn and Creag Pitridh from Lochlagganside.

Chilly Willy: North-facing Coire an Iubhair Mor holds snow late into the year. It is rarely visited and, seen distantly from the A86, often intrigues those who think they know the Central Highlands well. When the corrie is snowbound, the steep snow climb to its head is naturally an altogether more difficult proposition than in summer.

23 THE CREAG MEAGAIDH GROUP

The Creag Meagaidh Group is named in honour of its reigning peak, which rivals Ben Nevis and Ben Alder as **one of the great mountains of the Central Highlands**. Deeply demarcated by the glens of the River Roy and River Spey to the north and by Loch Laggan to the south, its three Munros and seven Tops are slung out along an undulating skyline.

To the north, remote ridges drop to rarely trodden moors around the headwaters of the Roy and the Spey, which reward exploration when the tops are in cloud (see Page 164). Lovers of solitude can consult the map and plan ascent routes from here, but the northern approaches are in general much longer and less scenic than from other directions.

Creag Meagaidh itself is easily climbed from the south (Route 113c) and south-west (Route 113d), but all of its subsidiary Munros and Tops, to say nothing of its finest scenery, lie to the east and south-east, where craggy Coire Ardair bites deep into the sprawling summit plateau (Routes 113a, 113b & 113e).

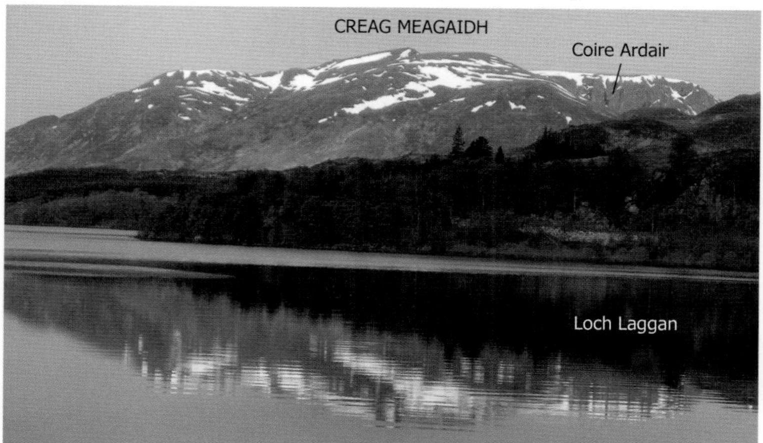

GiGi: In 1985 Creag Meagaidh was purchased for the nation by the Nature Conservancy Council (now Scottish Natural Heritage) to prevent it from being planted with conifers by the then owner. In 1986 it became a National Nature Reserve.

All routes except 113d and 113e are located within Creag Meagaidh NNR and are not subject to access restrictions during the stalking season.

The Creag Meagaidh Group

▲113 Creag Meagaidh 30 1128m/3701ft (OS 34 or 42, NN 418875) Craik Meggy, possibly Crag of the Boggy Place

△An Cearcallach 993m/3259ft (OS 34 or 42, NN 422853) *An Kyercalach*, The Rounded Place

△Meall Coire Choille-rais 1028m/3917ft (OS 34 or 42, NN 432862) *Myowl Corra Chulya Rash*, Hill of the Corrie of Shrubwood? (*Choille* = Wood and *Rais* = Shrub). Alternatively, Choille-rais may derive from the former name Choille na Froise. *Froise* (*Freusha*. Shower) is derived from *Frois* (Shaking)... perhaps referring to autumn trees?

△Puist Coire Ardair 1071m/3514ft (OS 34 or 42, NN 437872) *Poosht Corr Arder*, Post of the High Corrie

△Sron a' Choire 1001m/3285ft (OS 34 or 42, NN 448878) *Strawn a Chorra*, Nose of the Corrie, formerly Sron a' Ghaothair (*Gheuhar,* a bagpipe mouthpiece). Alternatively, Gaothar = Windy or Flatulent.

▲114 Stob Poite Coire Ardair 76 1054m/3459ft (OS 34 or 42, NN 428888) *Stop Potcha Corr Arder*, Peak of the Pot of the High Corrie (the 'pot' being the bowl of the corrie)

△Sron Coire a' Chriochairein 993m/3259ft (OS 34 or 42, NN 447899) *Strawn Corra Chree-ocharan*, possibly Nose of the Corrie of the Boundary or Stonechat

▲115 Carn Liath 127 1006m/3301ft (OS 34, NN 472903) *Carn Lee-a*, Grey Cairn (not to be confused with namesake ▲120 in the Cairngorms)

△Meall an t-Snaim 969m/3180ft (OS 34, NN459904) *Myowl an Try-im*, Hill of the Knot

△Stob Coire Dubh 916m/3006ft (OS 34, NN 496916) *Stop Corra Doo*, Peak of the Black Corrie

Evening in Coire Ardair

Peak Fitness: A point 0.7ml/1.1km north-east of Creag Meagaidh at NN 428881 was listed in the Tables as its East Top from 1891 to 1921.

Creag Mhor (Craik Mhor, Big Crag, NN 442873) on Coire Ardair's southern arm was a Top from 1891 to 1981. Sron a' Ghaothair, a Top in 1891, was deleted from the Tables in 1921 but restored and renamed Sron a' Choire in 1981, when it replaced Creag Mhor.

Until promoted to Munro status in 1921, Stob Poite Coire Ardair was a Top named Creag an Lochan. Also in 1921, Crom Leathad (*Crome Lyat*, Sloping Ridge), a Munro in 1891, was demoted to Top status and renamed Stop Poite Coire Ardair East Top (NN 437892), only for it to be deleted from the Tables altogether in 1997.

A' Bhuidheanach (*A Vooyanach*, The Yellow Place, NN 481907) lost its Top status in 1981.

The summit of Creag Meagaidh forms the hub of a complex Catherine Wheel of supporting ridges divided by corries. And what corries! If you like big, dramatic scenery, Coire Ardair bows only to Coire Leis on Ben Nevis for scale and grandeur. Here, forming a soaring backdrop to lonely Lochan a' Choire, are nearly 2ml/3km of cliffs up to 450m/1500ft high, with towering buttresses split by great gullies (called *posts*).

To add to its appeal, the corrie is tucked away at the end of a curving 4ml/6km glen that was specifically designed to hide it from the roadside. The name Ardair is usually translated as High, but it is derived from the Gaelic *Ard Dhoire* (High Grove or Wood), perhaps referring to Coill a' Choire in the lower glen.

Two other Munros, Stob Poite Coire Ardair and Carn Liath, together with two intervening Tops, are found on the northern arm of the corrie/glen. The southern arm sports two more Tops and still more are dotted around the massif: two on the rims of deep corries adjacent to Coire Ardair and one north -east of Carn Liath.

In such a sprawling miniature mountain range, it is impossible to see all there is to see on a single outing. You could make a raid on the three Munros and bag them together, but they deserve better than a ticking trip. On a first visit, it would be remiss not to approach Creag Meagaidh via Coire Ardair (Route 113a). You could still bag nearby Stob Poite Coire Ardair (Extension 1) and return over Carn Liath on the corrie's northern arm. However, we would leave these for another day (Route 113b) and return instead along the corrie's southern arm, which is shorter and more scenic (Route 113a Alternative Descent).

And that's not all. The easiest routes up Creag Meagaidh climb ridges from the south (Route 113c) and south-west (Route 113d). They avoid Coire Ardair altogether but visit other corries and Tops and are not without merit.

The one Top not covered by these routes (Stob Coire Dubh) lies 2ml/3km north-east of Carn Liath. Interested parties can reach it from further east on a route that provides an unusual and interesting approach to Carn Liath itself (Route 113e).

Route 113a Creag Meagaidh via Coire Ardair from Aberarder

G2 ***** NN 483873, 12ml/19km, 900m/2950ft M193

The 4ml/6km path to Coire Ardair begins at Aberarder Farm car park on the A86 beside Loch Laggan. This path was at one time infamously boggy, but after Creag Meagaidh became an NNR it was improved dramatically using boardwalks made from railway sleepers. More recently still, the whole path has been upgraded to form a beautiful, well-gritted, perfectly formed, Alpine-style highway to the corrie – a textbook example of what can be achieved in the Highlands given the requisite resources. It now rivals the paths around Culra for superior access to inspirational scenery.

From the car park the path runs past the farm buildings and follows the glen of the Allt Coire Ardair all the way into the bowl of the corrie. It climbs the right-hand side of the curving glen well above the river, with an especially fine section that passes through the old birch wood of Coill a' Choire (*Culya Chorra*, Wood of the Corrie). Once around the bend of the glen, the great cliffs of Coire Ardair come into view and loom ever more impressively as the path approaches the imaginatively named Lochan a' Choire at its heart.

The route to the summit plateau traverses right beneath the cliffs to the curious nick in the skyline known as the Window (in Gaelic: Uinneag Coire Ardair, *Oonyak*). The renovated path ends abruptly at the far side of the lochan, leaving you with nothing but fond memories as you face the more customary boot-worn path that then continues up the hillside.

It climbs through an Inner Corrie on

grassy slopes to reach the foot of a boulder ruckle below the Window. To find the best going, a stony path climbs right of the boulders then traverses left into the Window itself – a bouldery defile that forms the bealach between Creag Meagaidh and Stob Poite Coire Ardair.

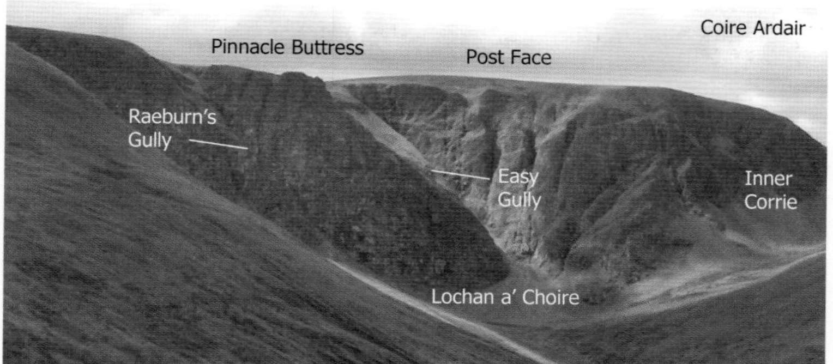

Terminator: The shore of Lochan a' Choire is a fine spot from which to study the cliffs of Coire Ardair. The most awesome feature is Pinnacle Buttress, which rises like a shark's fin behind the lochan. To its left is Raeburn's Gully and to its right is Easy Gully (only easy by comparison).

Further right is the Post Face, riven by the four vertical posts (gullies), and further right still, around the corner, is the Inner Corrie, through which you pass *en route* to the Window.

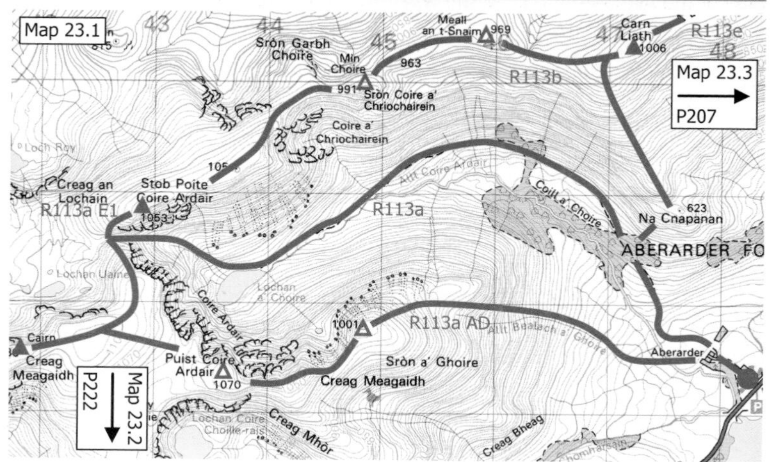

Turning left on the skyline, the path climbs a broad shoulder of grass and stones between the cliffs of Coire Ardair and the cliffs above Lochan Uaine (*Lochan Oo-an-ya*, Green Lochan), the largest of an attractive necklace of lochans on the north side of the mountain. Finally, you arrive on Meagaidh's extensive summit plateau. Ahead on the skyline, on the side of a rounded rise east of the summit, is the conspicuous large memorial cairn known as Mad Meg's Cairn. The smaller cairn that marks the ▲summit is on the rise just beyond, at the far end of the plateau.

Needlepoint: With its vast acreage and flanking crags, Creag Meagaidh's grassy, featureless summit plateau is no place for an afternoon stroll in the cloud. Even on the route up from the Window, gaps in the path could well lead you to conduct a more extensive exploration of the plateau than envisaged. The easiest foul-weather routes up the mountain are the south and south-west ridges (Routes 113c & 113d).

See also picture on Page 200
Mad Meg's Cairn
CREAG MEAGAIDH
Lochan a' Choire
Lochan Uaine
The Window
STOB POITE COIRE ARDAIR

Chilly Willy: After you've climbed Creag Meagaidh in summer, you simply *must* go again in winter and marvel anew at the scenery. The snowbowl of Coire Ardair was made to be seen at this time of year, with its frozen lochan as centrepiece and the Post Face in the condition that has made it a prime ice-climbing hotspot (coldspot?). You won't get up to the Window or summit without ice axe and crampons, but the corrie is a fantastic sight that makes a worthy destination in its own right.

Caution: Coire Ardair is renowned for its avalanches, especially on the route up through the Inner Corrie to the Window, so beware thaw conditions. The easiest routes in winter, as in cloud, are the south and south-west ridges (Routes 113c & 113d).

Route 113a Extension: 1 Stob Poite Coire Ardair

Add-on return trip: G1 *** 2ml/3km, 120m/400ft M193

From the Window a stony path climbs easily to the nearby ▲summit, which gives aerial views down into Coire Ardair. You could continue all the way along the corrie's northern arm to Carn Liath, but this route is best tackled in reverse to maximise views (see Route 113b).

Route 113a Alternative Descent: Coire Ardair Southern Arm

G2 ***** Compared to return via Coire Ardair:
1ml/1½km less mileage, 120m/400ft more ascent M193

The southern arm of Coire Ardair boasts two Tops on route, two more Tops off route and a narrow ridge that gives superb ridge walking with unrivalled views of the corrie. It even offers a shorter way back to Aberarder Farm. On the final descent you'll miss that renovated approach path but, if you can handle some temporary rough ground, the rewards more than compensate.

From Creag Meagaidh's summit, begin by wandering eastwards to the adjacent rise (the east top). It is tempting to continue in the same direction to the rim of Coire Ardair, in the hope of gaining great views, but the rim is unstable and views are awkward to obtain.

Instead, head south-east across

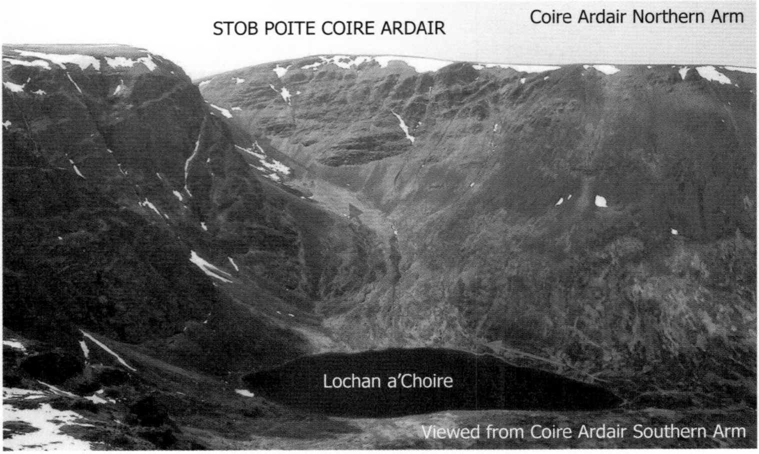

STOB POITE COIRE ARDAIR
Coire Ardair Northern Arm
Lochan a'Choire

Viewed from Coire Ardair Southern Arm

Viewed from Stob Poite Coire Ardair

the plateau on grassy terrain to the shallow dip at the southern corner of the corrie rim, below the rounded Top of ΔPuist Coire Ardair. At some point you'll come across one path or another. The main path circumvents the very top of the Puist but doesn't save much effort. It is worth going over the top for views down Raeburn's Gully, a classic winter climb that tops out just beyond.

Before continuing, it is also worth making a short detour south of the Puist to the rim of Coire Choille-rais (also named Moy Corrie on OS map). This has a perfect circular shape and boasts its own crag-encircled lochan to mirror Coire Ardair's. On its far side lie

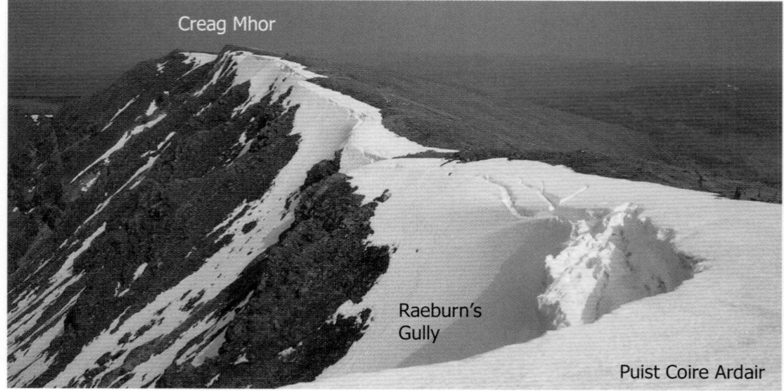

the two off-route Tops of ΔMeall Coire Choille-rais and ΔAn Cearcallach (see Route 113c Extension 1 for details).

Beyond Raeburn's Gully, the rim of Coire Ardair narrows and reaches Creag Mhor, a pointy cliff-edge peak (and former Top) that is the best-looking summit on the mountain and which gives the best views of the corrie's crags and lochan. Beyond this lies a slightly lower twin pointy peak, then the ridge broadens. Slopes of rock-strewn grass descend to a saddle before a short rise to the flat top of ΔSron a' Choire. On purely aesthetic grounds, it is a travesty that this uninspiring summit replaced Creag Mhor as a Top in 1981. To add insult to injury, the OS even continually misprints its name as Sron a' *Ghoire*.

Beyond Sron a' Choire, broad grassy slopes fan out towards a flat shoulder that marks the end of the ridge. Before reaching the shoulder, descend into the shallow corrie on the right, aiming for Aberarder Farm seen below.

On steeper slopes of grass and heather below the corrie mouth, keep left, beside the leftmost streamlet, to find an increasingly boot-worn path that makes a rough descent to the moor. If in doubt, you'll find the path lower down beside the main stream before it veers away left and passes a prominent boulder. The going is a tad on the damp side but the path gets the job done.

On the flat moor it crosses an ATV track and makes a beeline for the riverbank of the Allt Coire Ardair, which it follows down to a bridge at NN 476874. The last section of path is becoming overgrown but remains relatively dry and allows easy progress. The dual carriageway of the ATV track is a tempting alternative but is wetter overall.

Both path and track lead to the bridge, beyond which the track gives the driest route to Aberarder farm and the track back to the car park.

Needlepoint: As noted previously, Creag Meagaidh's summit plateau is notoriously difficult to navigate in foul weather. Save the southern arm for a clear day.

Chilly Willy: The southern arm isn't so narrow that it should cause major problems in winter. With proper equipment, it gives a good introduction to winter ridge walking, but stay well clear of cornices and take care on the steep final descent if the hillside is under snow.

Route 113b: Carn Liath and Stob Poite Coire Ardair via Coire Ardair Northern Arm from Aberarder NN 483873 M193

G2 ***** 10½ml/17km, 960m/3150ft
Carn Liath alone return: G1 *** 5ml/8m, 750m/24500ft

These two Munros are connected by a 3ml/5km ridge that forms the northern arm of Coire Ardair and gives excellent, easy ridge-walking throughout. It is best tackled from east to west, climbing Carn Liath first, in order to ease routefinding and obtain morning light on Coire Ardair. Creag Meagaidh can be added without too much extra effort (Extension 1).

Beginning at Aberarder Farm on Lochlagganside, as per Route 113a, take the Coire Ardair path up to the birch woods of Coill a' Choire, where two rough paths leave the main path to climb Carn Liath. Path 1 begins immediately before the first trees; look for a small cairn where a ditch turns right up the hill. Path 2 begins c100m further along; look for an iron fence post and a cairn just beyond.

Historically, Path 2 is the more well-used and therefore the more distinct and boggy. It follows a line of rusted fence posts, initially by burrowing through the trees (definitely to be avoided when wet). After reaching open hillside, it climbs diagonally left of Na Cnapanan (*Na Crapanan*, The Lumps) to reach Carn Liath's broad south-east ridge.

Path 1 begins on less claustrophobic but still rough ground and is in places less distinct. Improving with height, it climbs to a dip left of Na Cnapanan then bypasses a rock bluff on the right before cutting back left to join Path 2 on Carn Liath's south-east ridge.

As vegetation and going change with time, it is difficult to recommend either path over the other. Which do you prefer: something easier to walk on (Path 1) or something easier to follow (Path 2)?

Once on the ridge, the going improves on grass and scattered rocks. The fence posts continue to the summit but the path stays left of them, below the crest, giving views into Coire Ardair. It eventually becomes lost on Carn Liath's south-west shoulder a few hundred metres from the rounded, stony ▲summit.

Heading west from Carn Liath, the broad northern arm of Coire Ardair undulates invitingly over a number of flat tops with minor intervening dips. A pleasant trot across the moss brings you to ΔMeall an t-Snaim, then a stonier rise is crossed *en route* to ΔSron Coire a' Chriochairean. The dips before the two Tops are smaller versions of the Window above Coire Ardair and are marked as Uinneag (Window) on the OS 1:25,000 map.

Beyond Sron Coire a' Chriochairean, the ridge narrows around the rim of craggy Coire a' Chriochairean to climb the long summit ridge of Stob Poite Coire Ardair. A cairned rise on the shoulder may lead to confusion in cloud. Further along is the cairned east top and further still, across a shallow dip, is the ▲summit. Occasional detours left of the crest will give excellent views over Lochan a' Choire to the cliffs of Coire Ardair.

Beyond the summit, a path descends stony slopes to the Window, from where Route 113a is reversed to descend to Lochan a' Choire and the path back to the car park.

Torpedo: The outlying Top of ΔStob Coire Dubh lies 2ml/3km east of Carn Liath, in the opposite direction to Stob Poite Coire Ardair. The gentle route to it along the broad mossy ridge of A' Bhuidheanach and around the rim of craggy Coire nan Gall, is a fine stroll that gets few takers. For full details, see Route 113e. Return trip 4ml/6km, 150m/500ft.

Needlepoint: Although nowhere near as difficult to navigate as Creag Meagaidh's summit plateau, the northern arm of Coire Ardair nevertheless requires concentration in cloud. The broad ridge has numerous rises and changes of direction, while the line of fence posts and the path itself are no more than intermittent.

Chilly Willy: Like Coire Ardair's southern arm, the northern arm gives a good introduction to winter ridge walking, with great views of the corrie at its most spectacular. The main danger, as noted under Route 113a, is the steep, avalanche-prone descent from the Window. If in doubt, return along the northern arm.

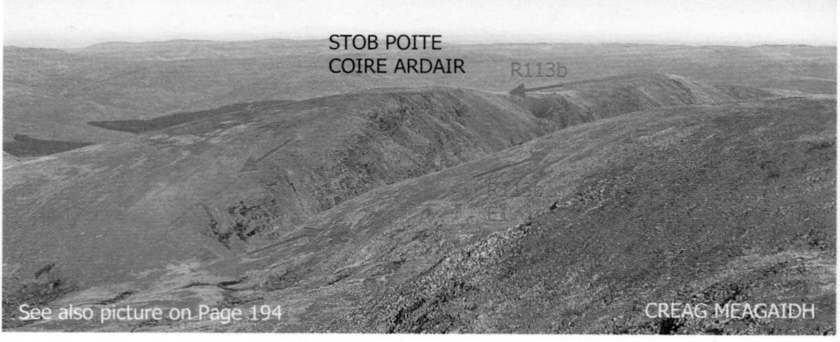

Route 113b Extension: 1 Creag Meagaidh

Add-on return trip: G2 **** 2ml/3km, 190m/600ft M193

Creag Meagaidh is an easy return trip from the Window (see Route 113a on Page 194 for description). From the summit you can return to the car park by Coire Ardair's southern arm (Route 113a Extension 1), a tempting option that would amount to a complete skyline circuit of Coire Ardair (Total trip: G2 ***** 9½ml/15km, 1040m/3400ft).

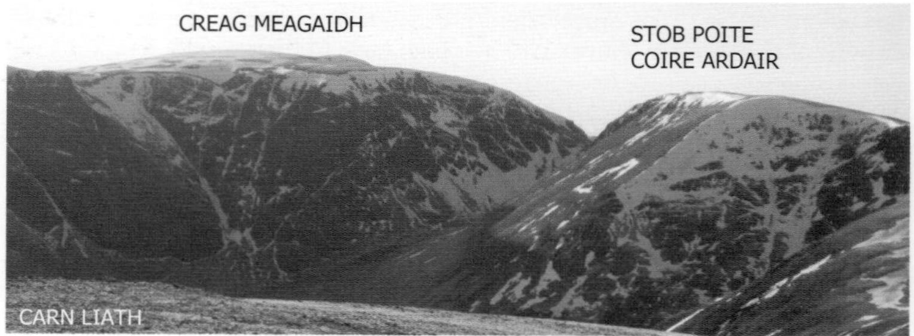

Route 113c Creag Meagaidh South Ridge from Moy

G2 *** Route Rage Alert NN 421827, 8ml/13km, 860m/2800ft M202

On its south side, Creag Meagaidh drops two ridges that provide the easiest ascent routes on the mountain: the south-west ridge (Route 113d) and the south ridge (described here). The gentle south ridge curves invitingly to the summit from the craggy outpost of Creag na Cailliche (*Craik na Kyle-yacha*, Old Woman's Crag) above the roadside. A small path runs along the broad crest beside a dry-stane wall that is a redoubtable feature in its own right. We call it the Great Wall of Meagaidh. If that isn't enough to tempt you, this route is also the shortest way to the summit. The only catch is a guarding tangle of moor that can induce Route Rage.

If you have already visited Coire Ardair, try the south ridge approach in winter or on a sunny day, when you can go a' wanderin' to your heart's content around Meagaidh's summit plateau and visit more corries and Tops (see Extension 1).

Begin opposite the entrance to Moy Lodge, 5ml/8km west of Aberarder on the A86, where a gate gives access to the pathless moor. An ATV track proves useful for a while, but soon you will be left to your own devices to battle across the tangle of marshy moor to the foot of Creag na Cailliche.

The Creag looks steep and rocky on approach but turns out to be no more scrambly than desired. For a hands-free ascent, make a shallow rising traverse over the left-hand skyline to reach the Great Wall. You'll find traces of path on its near side, and as an added bonus you'll get great views of the eastern ridges and corries of Beinn

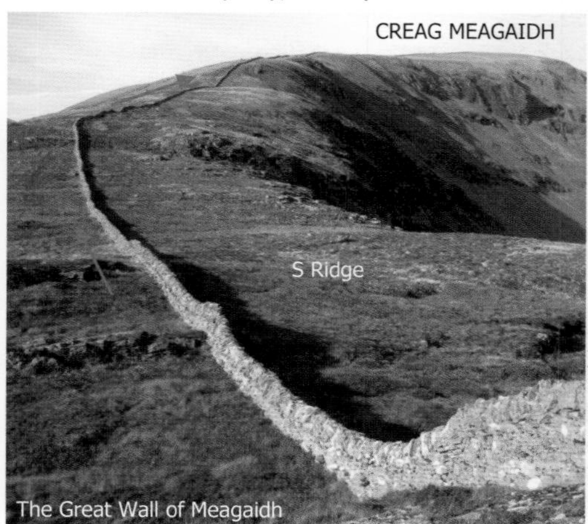

The Great Wall of Meagaidh

a' Chaorainn.

All ascent lines merge atop Creag na Cailliche, where the character of the route improves beyond all imagining. On easy-angled moss-heath, between the deep glens of the Allt na h-Uamha and the Moy Burn, the beautifully proportioned south ridge curves all the way to summit. The Great Wall points the way along the crest. For added fun, there's an easy rock step near the start, when the wall surmounts a small outcrop (easily bypassed).

When the wall ends, old wooden fence posts continue up the ridge to the junction with the south-west ridge. The final stretch beyond here bears right to round the head of the glen of the Moy Burn and level out on the highest rise on the plateau – Creag Meagaidh's ▲summit .

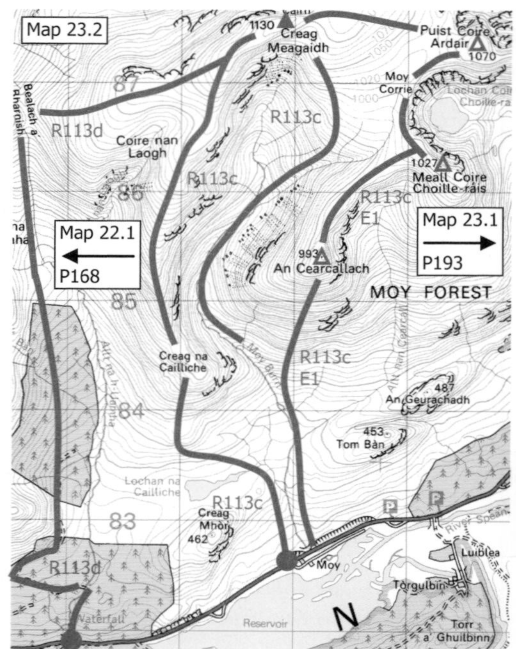

To make a round trip, return via the far (eastern) rim of the Moy Burn glen. Follow the summit plateau around the head of the glen to descend gentle slopes southwards towards ΔAn Cearcallach, a rocky companion to Creag na Cailliche across the mouth of the glen. When you reach the main stream that flows down to the Moy Burn (NN 427863), descend easy grass slopes on its right-hand (north) side (picture on Page 204). Once into the glen, follow the river down either side. The going is rough but pools and waterfalls add interest.

After the wall ends...

Lower down, with any luck, you'll come across an ATV track that takes a roundabout route down the left-hand side of the river, eventually reaching a roadside gate a few hundred metres from your starting point.

Needlepoint: As long as you keep to the wall and the fence posts, reaching the summit should pose no problem in cloud. A continuation across the plateau, in an attempt to find the descent route described, would require unwarranted optimism. Return by the ascent route. When the fence posts end, an indistinct little path continues to the summit. Make sure you don't miss it on the return trip.

Chilly Willy: An ascent by the south ridge and descent by the Moy Burn gives an easy winter round with ice axe and crampons. A direct descent from An Cearcallach (Extension 1) is best avoided when its steep slopes are under snow. The Great Wall shelters snow drifts until late spring, and that's the best time to explore the plateau for spectacular views of snowy gullies and crumbling cornices.

Route 113c Extension 1: Coire Choille-rais and Three More Tops

G1 or G2 **** Add-on: 1ml/1½km, 110m/350ft M202

On a sunny day you can enjoyably extend your sojourn at Creag Meagaidh's summit by a promenade around the plateau, visiting nearby Coire Choille-rais and maybe bagging some more Tops on the way. From the summit, first head south-east across the plateau to Puist Coire Ardair, as described on Page 195. You may wish to make the short return trip along Coire Ardair's southern arm to Creag Mhor (or even further to ΔSron a' Choire if you're an unrepentant Top bagger – return trip from Creag Mhor:

2ml/3km, 120m/400ft).

After taking in your fill of the scenery, head south-west then south-east around the curving rim of Coire Choille-rais, on the south side of the Puist (Coire Ardair is on the north side). As noted previously, the corrie is a perfect round bowl with craggy sides and a circular lochan at its heart. The going is excellent and soon leads to ΔMeall Coire Choille-rais, a sentinel at the south end of the corrie rim. From here the corrie and its lochan are seen to perfection, as is the great two-tiered waterfall that leaps over the headwall from the plateau.

Meall Coire Choille-rais separates Coire Choille-rais from a shallower corrie further south-west, on whose far rim stands ΔAn Cearcallach. An easy stroll around the corrie rim soon leads to this final Top, which is a superlative viewpoint over Loch Laggan and the Munros to its south.

Bidding a reluctant farewell to the heights, you now have a choice of two ways down. If you wish to descend in the manner to which you have become accustomed, on easy-angled terrain, use the Moy Burn descent route described on Page 202. To find this, return along the corrie rim and bear left to pick up the stream that flows down to the Moy Burn.

Alternatively, and more directly, it is possible to descend the south-west face of An Cearcallach directly to the mouth of the Moy Burn glen, where the stream is squeezed between the craggy noses of An Cearcallach and Creag na Cailliche. The descent looks steep when viewed from Creag na Cailliche on the outward journey but is much easier than it looks. Progress is slow and awkward, and certainly a shock to the system after the carefree skip around the plateau, but with judicious routefinding you can weave a way down steep grass among broken rocks without difficulty.

You'll encounter problems only if you allow the lie of the land to pull you too far right onto craggier ground. Aim in the direction of Moy Lodge, not Creag na Cailliche. Once onto the moor, keep an eye out for the ATV track mentioned previously, which will take you down to the roadside.

Route 113d Creag Meagaidh South-west Ridge

G1 * Route Rage Alert NN 400819, 10ml/16km, 830m/2700ft M202

Creag Meagaidh's south-west ridge gives the gentlest ascent on the mountain, but it lacks views and, owing to boggy ground, can be recommended only after a dry spell.

Begin at the bridge over the Allt na h-Uamha on the A86 just west of Craigbeg (roadside parking spaces). Cross a stile and take the boggy, waymarked path through the forestry plantation on the right-hand (east) side of the stream, passing a series of waterfalls. When the path reaches an overgrown forest track at a clearing, follow the track left across the stream (an easy paddle). (The path continues up the stream's right-hand bank to the upper forest boundary.)

Once across the stream, follow the track for several hundred metres, keeping right at a fork, to reach the main forest track from Roughburn. Turn right to follow this up the glen of the Allt na h-Uamha and through a second plantation, as for Route 108b to Beinn a' Chaorainn's east ridge.

Near the upper end of the second plantation, the track deteriorates into an ATV track that continues all the way up to the 824m/2705ft Bealach a' Bharnish between Chaorainn and Meagaidh. Unfortunately it is a quagmire for much of the way, forcing you to take to the rough moorland beside it.

Above the bealach, Meagaidh's south-west ridge rises as a broad, convex slope of moss and grass. Higher up, a line of fence posts runs to the junction with the south ridge, where Route 113c is joined for the last short stretch to the ▲summit. N.B. If you decide to return down the south ridge to avoid the boggy ATV track, you'll have to cross rough moorland at its foot to reach the approach path (but at least you won't have to ford the Allt na h-Uamha again).

A local on the SW Ridge

Needlepoint: Thanks to the ATV track and the line of fence posts, routefinding should remain easy in cloud.

Chilly Willy: This is the easiest winter ascent route on Meagaidh, especially when the boggy ground is frozen solid.

Route 113e Carn Liath alone from Spey Valley

G1 *** NN 532938, 9ml/14km, 800m/2600ft M207

Map note: OS 35 is needed in addition to OS 34.

This little-trodden route up Carn Liath is pathless and twice as long as the normal route from Loch Laggan (Route 113c), and until the summit is reached it manages to avoid views of Coire Ardair completely. Yet it makes **a great little training walk**. From a high starting point of 310m/1000ft, a gentle, spacious ridge climbs to the summit via a rarely visited Top, passing several features of interest along the way and boasting extensive views.

The route begins on the east side of the mountain, 5ml/8km along the minor road up the Spey Valley to Garva Bridge from Laggan on the A86. Park near the Uillt (or Allt) Fhearna (*Owlt Hyarna*, Stream of the Alder) and make a bee-line up the grassy hillside to Carn Dubh (*Carn Doo*, Black Cairn). The going is occasionally tussocky and boggy but not so much as to impede progress. To the right is the Dirc an Uillt Fhearna, which you may wish to visit on the return trip.

A fence goes all the way to the top of Carn Dubh but you may not wish to follow its gyrations. The same consideration applies to an ATV track that begins c.400m back along the road at NN 535936 and whose lower section is much churned up.

Grass gives way to heath and a fence-side path as the angle of ascent eases with height. The trig. pillar atop Carn Dubh commands a panoramic view over the Spey Valley and marks the start of a broad, 3ml/5km ridge that runs all the way to Carn Liath. At this point also the ATV track comes in from the right to provide excellent going beside a broken fence from hereon.

The ridge initially rises to the right around the rim of Coire a' Bhein (*Corra Venn*, Corrie of the Mountain), the first of three craggy corries to be passed. It reaches the rounded top of Point 903 then bears left again around the rim of equally craggy Coire Dubh. Moving from OS 35 to OS 34, it

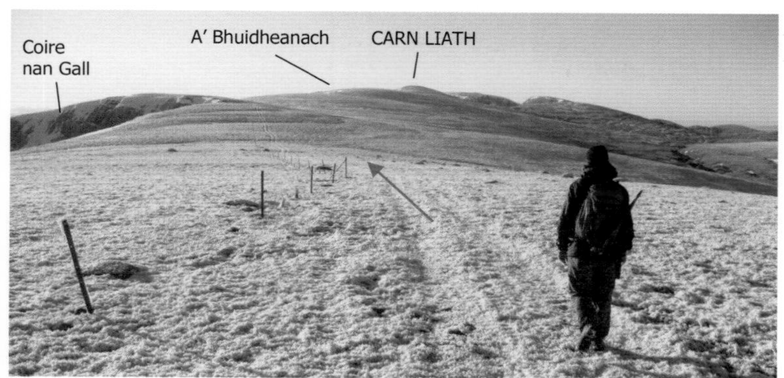

crosses a shallow dip and, at the far side of the corrie, reaches the Δsummit of Stob Coire Dubh. Note that the track bypasses the summit, but even non-baggers of Tops should make the short detour there for the view back over the corrie.

Veering right again, the ridge crosses another minor dip but one that marks an important boundary, because here you leave the Cairngorms National Park, whose western perimeter you have been following until now. Beyond the dip, the ridge rises to a long, almost level section that affords extensive views left over Loch Laggan and right over the Spey Valley to the rarely visited Monadh Liath backcountry. This scenic stretch is named A' Bhuidheanach (*A Vooyanach*, The Yellow Place) for its moss and grass.

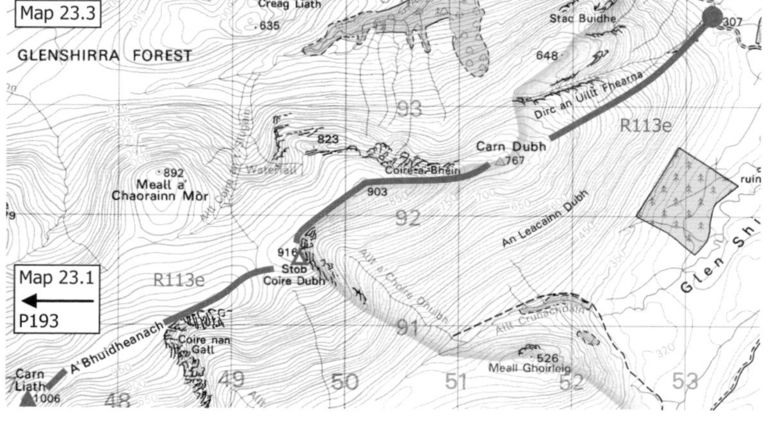

Above Coire nan Gall

A third craggy corrie is passed, the most impressive of the trio (Coire nan Gall, *Corra nan Gowl*, Corrie of the Stranger or Foreigner), and again it is worth leaving the track to wander (carefully) along the rim. The far side of the corrie marks another important boundary, as here you reach the eastern perimeter of Creag Meagaidh National Nature Reserve.

The fence ends at the foot of the final rise to Carn Liath's summit (NN 478906) but the ATV track continues until becoming lost on a final stretch of bouldery ground. The ▲summit cairn opens up views of Creag Meagaidh above Coire Ardair.

After returning to Carn Dubh, it is worth a slight dog-leg detour on descent to view the steep-sided glen of the Uillt Fhearna. Known as the Dirc an Uillt Fhearna (*Dirk*, Dagger), this great gash in the hillside is similar to An Dirc Mhor on Geal Charn (see Page 211). You'll find the ATV track running down beside it.

Needlepoint: Despite the twists and turns of the broad, featureless ridge, foul-weather navigation is made easy by the fence and ATV track.

Chilly Willy: A four-star winter training walk on easy angled slopes, yet with spectacular corrie scenery. Care is required around corniced corrie rims and ice axe and crampons are (of course) required in case of a slip or if the wet ground is iced.

Dirc an Uillt Fhearna

Torpedo: This route forms the first section of a rarely undertaken point-to-point long-distance ridge walk that links the five Munros on the north side of Glen Spean and Loch Laggan. From Carn Liath the route continues along the northern arm of Coire Ardair to Stob Poite Coire Ardair and Creag Meagaidh (Route 113b). It then crosses the Bealach a' Bharnish to Beinn Chaorainn and continues to Beinn Teallach before descending to Roughburn. One-way : 19ml/31km, 2060m/6750ft.

24 THE MONADH LIATH

North of Loch Laggan, extending almost all the way to Loch Ness, stretches the largest tract of roadless country in the Central Highlands. It is also the largest tract of featureless country in the Central Highlands, comprising over 400 square miles of dull moorland and glens.

Fortunately for Munro baggers in search of inspiring scenery, it is only in the south-east corner that the moorland need detain them, for it is only here that it heaves itself up to the 3000ft mark to form the Monadh Liath (*Monna Lee-a*, Grey Moor). The name highlights the difference between the area's mica-schist geology and the granite landforms of the Monadh Ruadh (*Roo-a*, Red) across the Spey valley, which are more widely known in English as the Cairngorms.

Although distinct and separate from the Cairngorms, the Munros of the Monadh Liath were included in the Cairngorms National Park established in 2003. The park boundary crosses their summits.

So many moorland rises top the 3000ft mark that compilers of Munro's Tables have had difficulty over the years in making up their minds about what counts as a Munro and what doesn't. There used to be six, but the editors of the 1981 Tables took pity on future generations and demoted two of them to Tops.

Of the four that remain, Geal Charn in the west is the most estimable and approachable (Routes 116a-116c). A' Chailleach and Carn Sgulain in the east are best done on autopilot (Route 118a), while all approaches to Carn Dearg in the centre are best not discussed in polite company (Routes 117a & 117b). The best route in the area, though lengthy, is the complete Monadh Liath Traverse across the spine of the plateau (Route 118b).

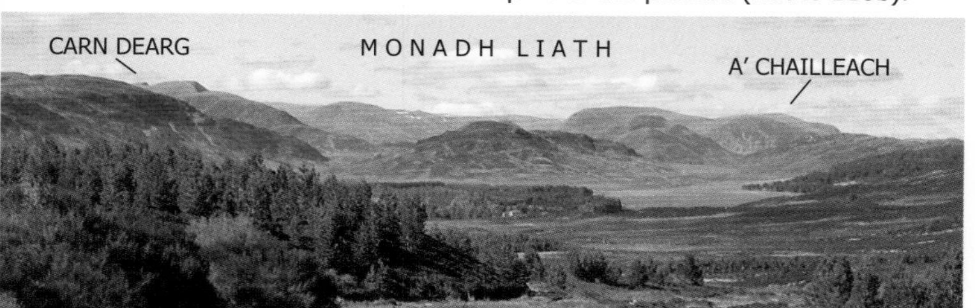

GiGi: Grey? Go in late summer or early autumn when the purple-heathered hillsides are picture-postcard pretty and serve up a fruit salad of wild strawberries and blaeberries.

Local estates dissuade access to the Monadh Liath during the stalking season. For specific access restrictions Monday-Saturday, see roadside notices.

▲116 Geal Charn 260 926m/3038ft (OS 35, NN 561987)

Gyal Charn, White Cairn (not to be confused with namesakes ▲100, ▲107 and ▲111, nor with other hills such as that just south-west of A' Chailleach)

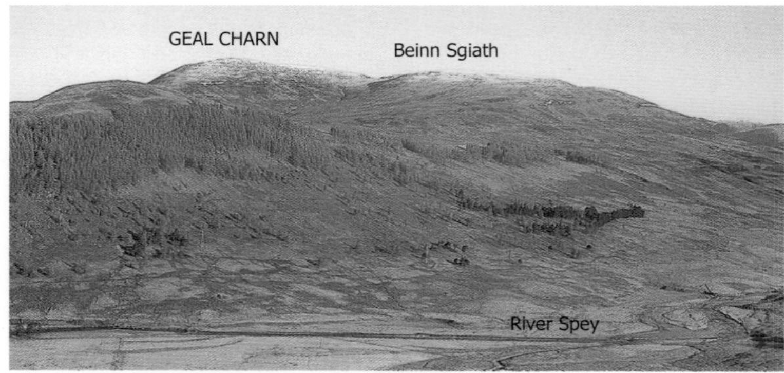

Peak Fitness: No change since 1891 Tables.

Approached from the road to the south, Geal Charn's featureless slopes fill the horizon but, for once in the Monadh Liath, appearances are deceptive. North-east of the summit lies a deep, craggy corrie floored by a lochan, imaginatively named Lochan a' Choire. A round of the corrie skyline, taking in the lochan, the waterfalls below it and the curious trench known as An Dirc Mhor (The Big Knife), gives a surprisingly diverting outing on a fine summer's day (Route 116a).

The route involves a ford of the Markie Burn, which may prove awkward if it is in spate. Routes 116b and 116c provide alternative but less interesting ascent routes.

GiGi: The minor road on which the three routes (+ Route 113e) begin is a former military road, built by General Wade in 1731 to link troop bases at Ruthven on Speyside and Fort Augustus on Loch Ness.

Beyond the Spey Dam, cars can be driven a further 8ml/13km to Melgarve, with much of historical interest to see along the way. Garva Bridge, where Route 116c begins, still stands and is one of Wade's finest constructions. Beyond Melgarve the road continues as a track over the historic Corrieyairack Pass.

Near the start of the road, crowning a hill-top 180m/600ft above the valley floor, is the ruined Iron Age fort of Dun da Lamh (NN 582929, *Doon da Laav*, Fort of the Two Hands). Visit it (by forest track and path) and marvel at its size (130m x 75m), its situation and its commanding views.

Route 116a Geal Charn from Spey Dam

G1 *** NN 584937, 10ml/16km, 710m/2350ft M212

Begin at the road bridge just before the Spey Dam, 2½ml/4km along the minor road that runs west from Laggan village on the A86 (roadside parking spaces). Take the riverside track to the dam and continue up Glen Markie for a few hundred metres. At the first tree (NN 581939) branch left through a gate on a side track that leads to the Markie Burn. The main track continues up Glen Markie and will be used for the return trip. The side track fords the Markie Burn, but you can cross dryshod, if somewhat indecorously, on an adjacent barrage of girders.

On the far side, grassy tracks head northwards across fields, aiming directly for Beinn Sgiath (*Ben Skee-a*, Wing Mountain), Geal Charn's subsidiary top. After reaching the corner of a forestry plantation that flanks the river, a diminishing ATV track runs beside the fence, but there's a better track within the forest. From a gate 50m right of the corner, this track runs through a tree-lined avenue, parallel to the fence, to reach another corner. Exit the forest here to follow its curving perimeter over rougher ground to the next corner, then keep going up open hillside.

Ahead, Beinn Sgiath's southern slopes are split by the deep horizontal gash of An Dirc Mhor (*An Dirk Voar*, The Big Cleft), which is barely off route and which it would be a shame to miss. If you keep heading in a northerly direction, you'll reach the stream that flows out of the Dirc's lower end. The curious craggy defile extends for around half a mile across the hillside and was

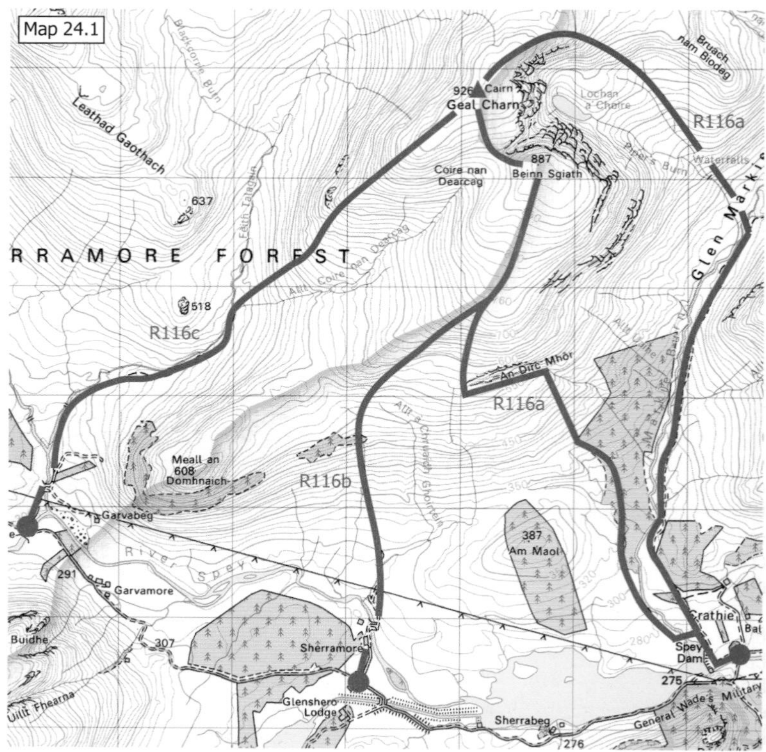

probably caused by a landslip. You can walk up its lower rim or clamber over the fallen rocks that litter its bottom.

Above the Dirc, continue up grass and heather to gain Beinn Sgiath's broad south-west ridge, where you'll find an ATV track to ease the rest of the ascent. The track goes all the way to the bealach between Beinn Sgiath and Geal Charn, with traces beyond, but first it's worth making the short detour to the mossy dome of Beinn Sgiath, whose summit lies near the rim of the crags of the north-east corrie.

The bealach that separates Beinn Sgiath from Geal Charn further around the corrie rim is a breach in the crags known as Uinneag a' Choire Lochain (*Oonyak a Chorra Lochin*, Window of the Corrie with the Lochan, named only on OS 1:25,000 map). This mirrors a similar feature on Creag Meagaidh further west. It sounds ominous, but the crossing couldn't be more gentle and soon leads you to the flat mossy ▲summit of Geal Charn.

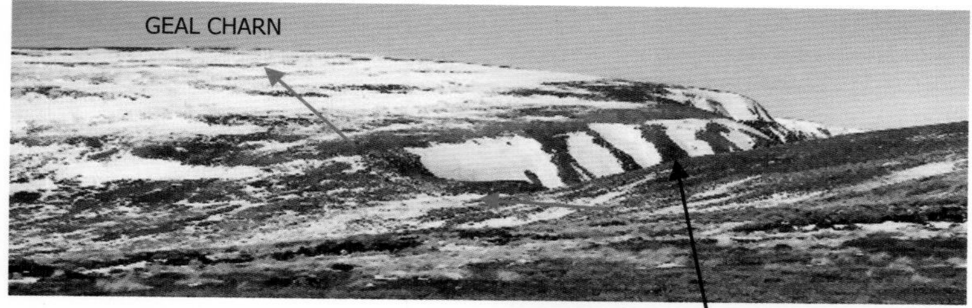

To continue the round of the corrie skyline, take the indistinct path that heads north-east from the summit cairn across the summit plateau, parallel to but well back from the corrie rim. After a few hundred metres, the path crosses a fence. A few hundred metres further along, a cairn will confirm that you're on the right line. Stay alert so as not to be misled by ATV tracks, broken fences and criss -crossing paths into going too far right (onto crags) or too far left (along the main spine of the Monadh Liath).

The path continues further along the corrie rim than seems warranted, but any short cut into the corrie will lead onto steeper ground. The path eventually descends into the eastern half of the corrie, well beyond Lochan a' Choire and its crags. The lochan is in any case not the most enticing stretch of water in the Highlands, nor is the tussocky moor that surrounds it the most inviting terrain.

The path becomes very indistinct as it descends into the bowl of the corrie. If you can follow it all the way down,

The summit dome of GEAL CHARN

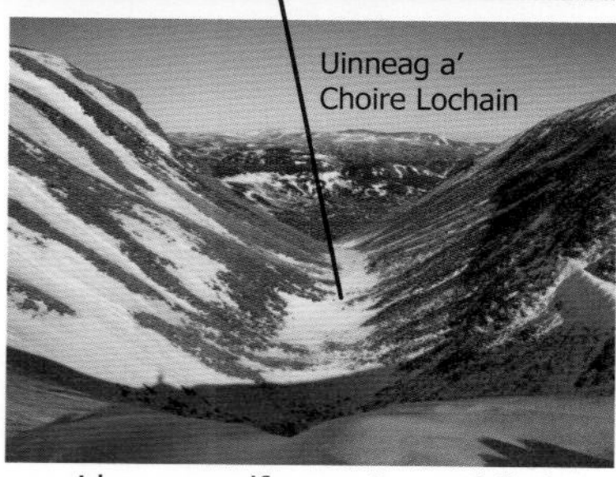

consider yourself a master pathfinder. Once into the corrie proper, rather than head for the lochan's outlet stream, known as the Piper's Burn, the path stays well left to descend the left bank of the leftmost burn in the corrie. If you lose the path, that burn is the one to aim for.

Lower down, the path reaches a gate in a fence and becomes an ATV track. Immediately below here, you'll pass a picturesque Y-shaped waterfall, which consists of a double series of upper falls feeding a series of lower falls. The track switchbacks down beside the fall and crosses the moor to reach the Glen Markie Land Rover track a couple of hundred metres above the confluence of the Piper's Burn and the Markie Burn.

The stretch of ATV track below the waterfall is quite marshy. A path finds better going on the left bank of the Piper's Burn. The Markie Burn normally requires a boulder-hop or watersplash (if in spate, it will be more awkward to cross). On the far side, an easy 3ml/5km walk along the Land Rover track will bring you back to your starting point.

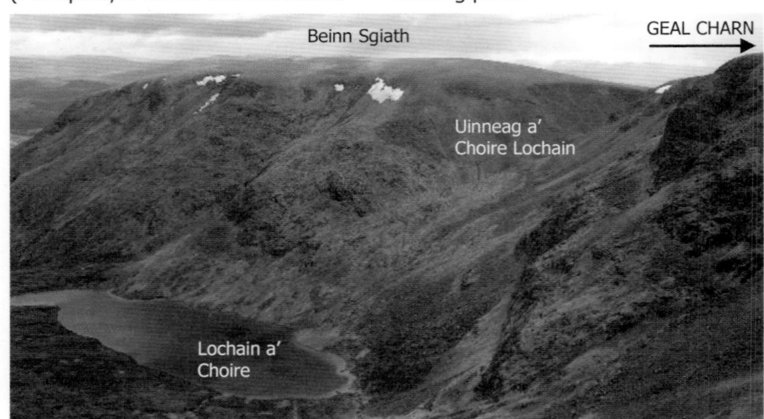

Needlepoint: In cloud, the wide-open spaces atop Beinn Sgiath and Geal Charn demand precise navigation, especially in the vicinity of the Window. On descent into the north-east corrie, if you can't find the path, be sure to take a wide berth around the crags above Lochan a' Choire.

The easiest way to bag the mountain in foul weather is to go straight up and down the south-west ridge (Route 116c).

Chilly Willy: This is an easy winter round, provided you take care in the vicinity of the Window and on the convex rim of the north-east corrie, which looks its best when under snow. The best views are obtained from Beinn Sgiath. On descent, as in cloud, make sure that you have outflanked all the cliffs before attempting to find a way down into the corrie.

If you judge the Markie Burn to be an unwarrantable winter obstacle, avoid the route and instead approach Geal Charn's summit using Route 116b or 116c, both of which give easy winter snow plods.

Route 116b Geal Charn from Sherramore

G1 ** NN 551934, 8ml/13km, 660m/2150ft M212

This route provides an alternative to Route 116a when the Markie Burn is in spate. From the roadside 5ml/8km west of Laggan village, walk up the drive to Sherramore Lodge and stay right on a farm track that bridges the River Spey. Ignoring a right branch after 100m, keep to the main track, which soon leaves the riverside to climb the lower slopes of Beinn Sgiath.

The OS map can't show the numerous tracks of varying definition that now criss-cross the hillside. Keeping right at all junctions, aim for the right-hand edge of the trees seen above. The track goes through the trees to a gate in a fence. Cross the short stretch of moor beyond to gain Beinn Sgiath's broad south-west ridge. Optionally, you could make a detour right to view An Dirc Mhor, but this would entail more moor work. Once on the ridge, the going eases and, further up, you join the ATV track used by Route 116a.

After reaching Geal Charn's ▲summit, return the same way or descend Route 116c, which deposits you at the roadside 2ml/3km from your starting point.

Route 116c Geal Charn from Garva Bridge

G1 * Route Rage Alert NN 521948, 8ml/13km, 630m/2050ft M212

This unscenic trudge on poor terrain manages to avoid completely everything of interest on the mountain. We include it because it is the easiest ascent route in foul weather and because you may wish to use it as a descent variation after ascending Route 116b.

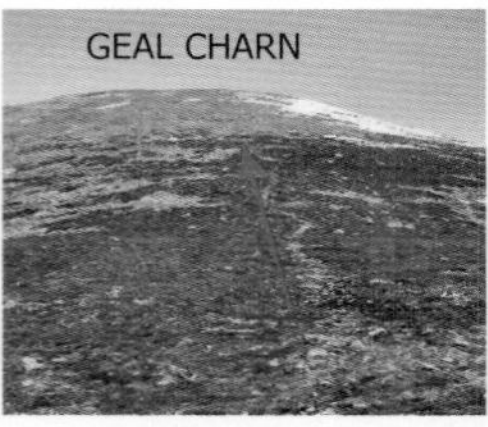

From the start of the route at Garva Bridge, 7ml/11km west of Laggan village, Geal Charn appears as nothing more appetising than a distant lump. Take the Land Rover track on the left-hand (west) side of the Feith Talagain to a bridge, then leave it for a path that runs up the right-hand (east) side of the river to the foot of the south-west ridge.

The approach seems straightforward on the map, but the path has seen better days and will see worse. Those unfamiliar with the ancient tongue are advised that Feith (*Fay*), here used as a river name, means Bog.

When the path ends, boggy moorland rises towards the south-west ridge. With height, the ridge becomes more well-defined and carries a path that eventually leads to excellent going (too late!) on mossy ground among boulders. The angle eases towards the ▲summit. If you wish to make the short trip to Beinn Sgiath for the views, you can make a direct descent from there to rejoin the approach path at the foot of the ridge.

▲117 Carn Dearg 225 945m/3100ft (OS 35, NH 635023)

Carn Jerrak, Red Cairn (not to be confused with namesakes ▲96 and ▲103, nor with a clutch of Corbetts and other hills)
ΔSouth-east Top 923m/3029ft (OS 35, NH 637017)
ΔCarn Ban 942m/3091ft (OS 35, NH 632031)
Carn Bahn, Pale or White Cairn
ΔCarn Ballach 920m/3019ft (OS 35, NH 643045)
Carn Ballach, Speckled or Spotted Cairn

Peak Fitness: No change to the three Munros since original 1891 Tables. Carn Ban (formerly Carn Mairg) was a Munro until it was demoted to Top status in 1981. In 1891 Carn Ballach's summit plateau boasted both a Munro and a Top. Since 1981 only a Top remains (see Page 230). Sneachdach Slinnean was an additional Top until it too was deleted from the Tables altogether in 1981 (see Page 221).

If you are of a delicate disposition, we suggest you sit down and take a potion, because Carn Dearg is a bagger's nightmare. It's not the summit itself. We like the summit. The summit is fine. It's reaching it that's the problem. On all approaches, a checklist of varieties of tough terrain await your pleasure.

On the map the landscape looks promising. South-east of the summit, a 1½ml/2km-long ridge promises an unusually scenic approach for this part of the globe. It is relatively narrow, is fringed by crags on its east side (Gleann Ballach) and harbours a lochan-filled corrie on its west side (Loch Dubh, *Loch Doo*, Black Loch).

From the Newtonmore direction, the map shows approach routes on both sides: a western path that leads to the lochan (Route 117a) and an eastern path that climbs over a low bealach into Gleann Ballach (Route 117b). What the map doesn't show is what lies underfoot.

Whichever of the two approaches you choose, the going is so bad that you'll be convinced the other must be better. Make use of such unwarranted optimism by going up one (117a) and down the other (117b).

Alternatively, minimise route rage by taking a longer approach from near Laggan village to the south (R117a Alternative Approach) or by crossing the Monadh Liath plateau from Carn Sgulain (Route 118b).

Route 117a Carn Dearg from Glen Banchor via Carn Macoul

G2 ** Route Rage Alert NN 693998, 11ml/18km, 740m/2450ft M218/219
Ascent only: 5½ml/9km, 740m/2450ft

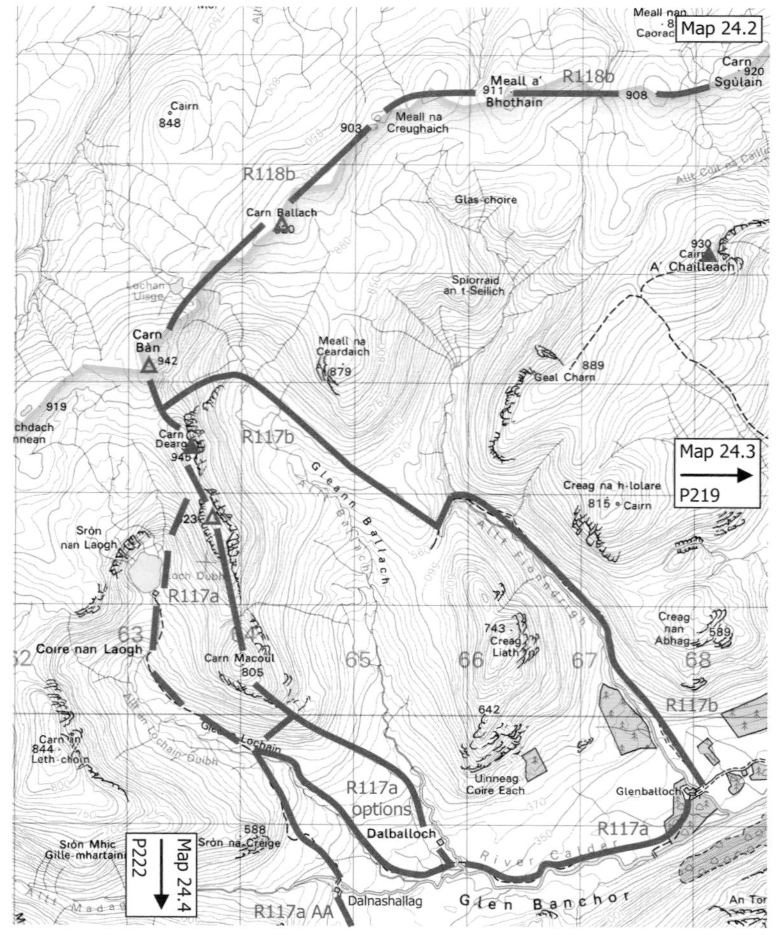

Upper Glen Banchor

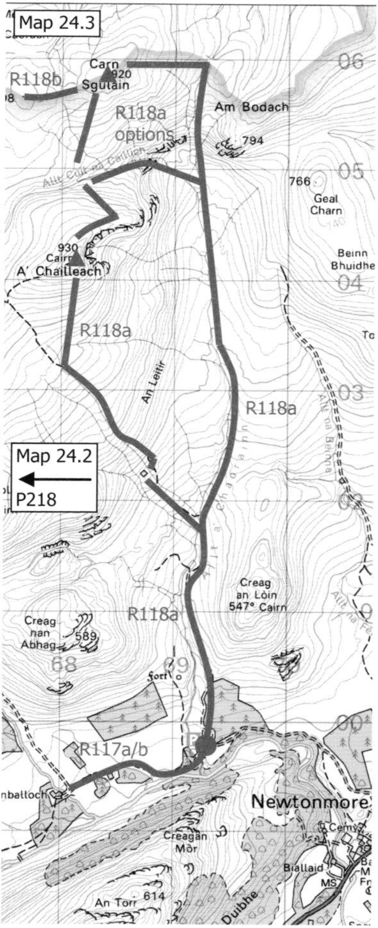

Map 24.3

Map 24.2 ← P218

The route begins at the end of the short road up Glen Banchor above Newtonmore. The road ends at the bridge over the Allt a' Chaorainn, where there's a car park. Follow the continuing Land Rover track along the glen to the boarded-up cottage at Glenballoch (which stands at the foot of the glen of the Allt Fionndrigh, not Gleann Ballach further west).

Leave the track here and go left to a gate in a fence, where you'll find a grassy track that continues westwards through new forestry. Keep right at a fork to reach the far side of the plantation and enter the great flat space of upper Glen Banchor. The track deteriorates into a boggy path beside the River Calder, but you ain't seen nothin' yet.

Below the ruined cottage of Dalballoch, at the foot of Gleann Ballach, the path fords the Allt Ballach (normally passable on stepping stones) to reach the Allt Madagain and its tributary the Allt an Lochain Duibh (the outlet stream of Loch Dubh). The riverside flats here sometimes become

GiGi: Before the River Spey was bridged in the eighteenth century, Glen Banchor was a major through route between Upper Speyside and all points south. A number of former townships testify to its importance. For a glimpse into the past, visit the ruins at Dail a' Chaorainn (*Dal a Heurin*, Rowan Field, NN 691999), a short distance along the west bank of the Allt a' Chaorainn.

so marshy that oars are more useful than trekking poles. The building seen in the distance is Dalnashallag bothy (see Alternative Approach).

The path follows the stream up to Loch Dubh but is reverting to nature now that ATVs prefer to motor up the other side of the stream. Above the loch, the rough, boggy slopes continue to Carn Dearg's summit but can hardly be recommended.

The alternative? Leave the path at the foot of Carn Macoul, the steep lump that terminates Carn Dearg's south-east ridge, and climb slopes of grass and heather to its summit. If the riverside flats are really sodden, you may prefer to climb Carn Macoul directly from Dalballoch. Follow traces of path beside the Allt Ballach to reach the south-west hillside.

As height is gained on Carn Macoul, matters finally improve. Both angle and going ease until you cross the summit on gentle heath-like terrain. The view from the summit, of Loch Dubh in its rugged little corrie, is better than that from the loch's shoreline, although anyone with rock-climbing sensibilities will be more taken with the great slab of clean rock in the next corrie to the left.

Beyond Carn Macoul, on good going now, continue across a dip and up the well-defined ridge that climbs to Carn Dearg's ΔSouth-east Top. A path is developing along the edge of the steep slopes that drop to Gleann Ballach. Over the Top, it is only a short stroll to Carn Dearg's ▲summit – a sheepishly fine spot atop a buttress of broken crags.

Needlepoint: The ridge from Carn Macoul to Carn Dearg is sufficiently well-defined to make it easily navigable in cloud, but reaching it in wet conditions will require a snorkel.

Chilly Willy: The approach march is best tackled in winter when the ground is frozen solid. Higher up, with snow on the ground, some may find the uniform slopes that climb to the SE Top unnervingly exposed above the drop into Gleann Ballach.

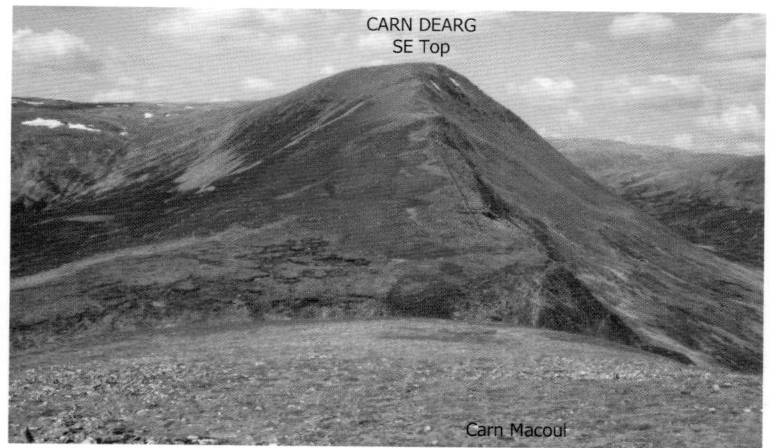

Torpedo: Once you've outwitted the guarding moor, Monadh Liath hillwalking has much to recommend it, with good terrain leading quickly to a smorgasbord of plateau highpoints. Sample the possibilities by heading out across the plateau from Carn Dearg, north then north-east, to ΔCarn Ban and ΔCarn Ballach, the poor Munros that were demoted to Tops in 1981 (return trip: 4ml/6km, 200m/650ft).

Sneachdach Slinnean, the Top that was completely lost from the Tables in 1981, lies to the north-west and is even easier to reach (return trip: 2½ml/4km, 80m/250ft). All three Tops: 6ml/10km, 220m/700ft. Reduce these estimates if you omit Carn Dearg's summit on return by descending Route 117b.

GiGi: Sneachdach Slinnean (NH 622027, 919m/3016ft) is no more distinguished a summit than any other Monadh Liath high-point. It is nevertheless worth a visit if you are of an idiosyncratic frame of mind, not only because of its former Top status and superb Gaelic name (*Shnech-kach Shlinyan*, Snowy Shoulder-blade), but also because it boasts a small lochan on its flat summit plateau. This has caused it to become known, with a little licence, as **Scotland's only underwater summit**.

Route 117a Alternative Approach from Cluny (A86)

G2 ** Route Rage Alert NN 693998, 12ml/19km, 880m/2900ft M218/222

This approach from the A86 to the south follows a Land Rover track to Dalnashallag bothy (NN 647985) west of Dalballoch. It is longer than the Glen Banchor approach, starts lower down, can't be combined into a round trip and avoids no more than a modicum of rough ground. Its main advantage is as a mountain biking route, as the track to the bothy can be cycled.

The track begins at a road bridge on the east side of Cluny Castle. It climbs through woodland onto rising moor and heads through a gap in the hills to the bothy. The one-roomed building has no bunks but provides welcome shelter on a driech day.

Above the bothy a grassy ATV track makes a rising traverse into the glen of the Allt an Lochain Duibh. Once it reaches the stream, it continues up the left-hand side, parallel to the path on the right-hand side. As it climbs it becomes increasingly boggy, circuitous and dreary. We recommend you leave it, cross the stream and climb over Carn Macoul, as per Route 117a.

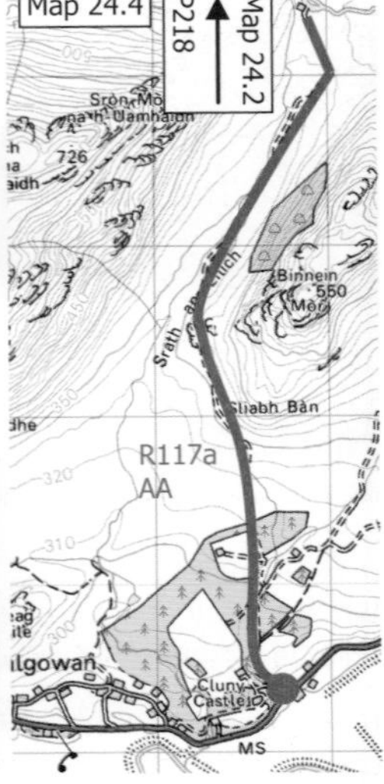

Baffies: If ever proof were needed that some mountains are better viewed than climbed, the Monadh Liath provides ample evidence. By far the finest features in the range are the roadside seats that flank the minor road up picturesque Glen Banchor.

Route 117b Carn Dearg from Glen Banchor via Allt Fionndrigh

G2 * Route Rage Alert NN 693998, 11ml/18km, 650m/2150ft M218/219
Ascent only: 5½ml/9km, 650m/2150ft

Begin as per Route 117a, on the Land Rover track to Glenballoch. On the near side of the bridge over the Allt Fionndrigh, just before the cottage, bear right on a grassy track through a field. This becomes a bulldozed track that climbs the dreary glen. Your goal is a footbridge over the river in the upper glen (NH 659019), where a small stream comes down from the bealach between Meall na Ceardaich (*Myowl na Kyardich*, Hill of the Forge) and Creag Liath (*Craik Lee-a*, Grey Crag). This bealach leads to upper Gleann Ballach and so to Carn Dearg.

The bridge is hidden from view at first, so here's how to find it. When the good track ends, continue along a grassier track for c.100m, then fork left (cairn) on an earthy/muddy path that crosses the hillside to the bridge.

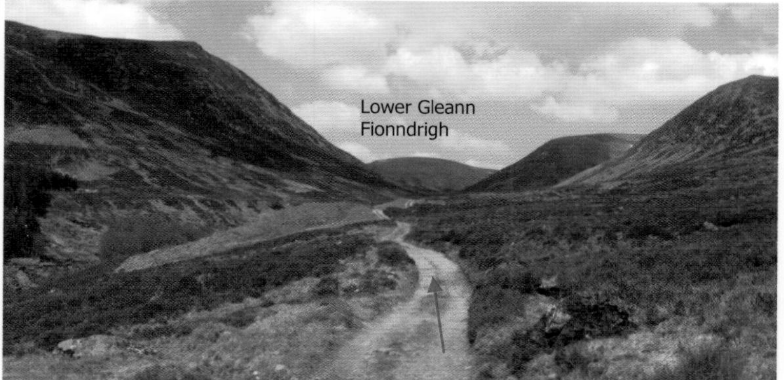

On the far side of the bridge, the path climbs beside a small stream onto the bealach that leads over to Gleann Ballach, becoming increasingly marshy with height. On the bealach itself, it turns right and climbs to a prominent cairned rock, after which you are left to your own devices.

The prospect ahead is less than enticing. 1½ml/2½km of peat-hag terrain separate you from the head of Gleann Ballach and the foot of Carn Dearg. The craggy east face is in view all the way up, but you'll be in no mood to appreciate it.

Gleann Ballach carries an old Right of Way over the Monadh Liath but it's hard to believe the route ever saw much traffic as the peat hags are abominable. To avoid the worst of

them, stay high above the Allt Ballach, aiming for the flat bowl at the head of the glen, below the steep headwall.

From here, climb back left up a broad, grassy shelf that rises above broken crags to the bealach between Carn Dearg and Carn Ban. It's not a great ascent, but it's no mean improvement on the route so far. As on any approach to Carn Dearg, the ▲summit comes as a relief.

Descent note: If descending by this route, rather than struggle through the peat hags all the way to the Meall na Ceardaich-Creag Liath bealach, you may be tempted to descend into the glen of the Allt Fionndrigh before reaching the bridge. There's a school of thought that says this is no bad thing: ford the Allt Fionndrigh and find better going on rough game tracks along the riverbank.

Needlepoint: In driech weather, upper Gleann Ballach is best left to budding orienteers and is likely to be appreciated only by masochists. There are few places where it is more enlightening to be able to see where you are going.

Chilly Willy: You want to climb this route in winter? You think deep heather and bog are easier to negotiate when blanketed by soft snow? You think the earth is flat?

▲118 A' Chailleach 251 930m/3051ft (OS 35, NH 681041)

A Chyle-yach, The Old Woman
(not to be confused with namesake ▲242 in the Fannichs)

▲119 Carn Sgulain 271 9320m/3018ft (OS 35, NH 683058)

Carn Skoolan, Basket Cairn

Peak Fitness: No change since 1891 Tables.

Unlike Ben Cruachan (▲47), the first Munro in the Central Highlands, these final two Munros are the kind of hills that give Munro bagging a bad name. Be honest: would you trudge to their rounded moorland summits if they didn't top 3000ft?

The best that can be said about them is that the terrain, though often boggy and best tackled after a dry spell, is not as bad as on nearby Carn Dearg. Apart from that, it is difficult to enthuse. We nevertheless disassociate ourselves from Terminator's disparaging translation of Carn Sgulain as Basket Case.

Needlepoint: The ascent path makes A' Chailleach an easy foul-weather climb, but manufacturing a direct line from there to the summit of Carn Sgulain will require supernatural intervention. If your idea of a good time is floundering around peat bogs in swirling cloud, head north and at some point you'll reach the fence that follows the spine of the Monadh Liath plateau across the summit.

The only safe descent route from Carn Sgulain follows the fence posts north-east then east, to the first bealach, where the Allt a' Chaorainn begins its journey (NH 693059). Follow the left bank down to reach the glen below.

Chilly Willy: Ditto Route 117b.

F-Stop: A camera is superfluous.

Route 118a A' Chailleach and Carn Sgulain from Glan Banchor

G1 * Route Rage Alert NN 693998, 9½ml/15km, 740m/2450ft M219

Begin as for Route 117a, at the end of the Glen Banchor road. Take the Land Rover track behind the car park, northwards past a forestry plantation into the wide-open glen of the Allt a' Chaorainn (*Owlt a' Cheurin*, Stream of the Rowan). The track starts on the right-hand side of the car park; alternatively, join it higher up using an excellent little path that starts on the left-hand side. A hidden wooden seat at the start of the path is a congenial spot to de-boot at the end of the day.

The glen of the Allt a' Chaorainn runs all the way along the eastern foot of the two Munros, passing A' Chailleach and reaching the bealach east of Carn Sgulain. The track penetrates the glen nowhere near far enough, but the route is still the shortest way back from Carn Sgulain. Tackling A' Chailleach first, your initial objective, hidden on its south-east hillside at NH 687022, is the old hut known as the Red Bothy (for the colour of its corrugated iron roof).

Don't do this: About 100m before the end of the track (NH 691013), a small cairn marks the start of a path down to a hidden bridge over the Allt a' Chaorainn. Old maps show a path from here to the bothy, but today there is nothing but tangled, marshy moorland.

When the track ends, a boggy path continues along the right-hand side of the stream. Follow it for a few hundred metres to a rusted gate in an old fence, then for a further couple of hundred metres to a point where an ATV track crosses the stream to climb to the bealach south-west of A' Chailleach. The track is marked on the OS map as a path but on the ground it is mostly boggy or non-existent, especially towards the skyline, where it is best avoided.

Boulder-hop or paddle across the stream and follow the track up to the hut, which can now be seen ahead on the hillside. When the track bears right to bypass the hut, avoid the wettest ground on a path that climbs directly to the hut.

GiGi: In the 1970s the Highland Regional Council conducted a survey of possible future ski areas to reduce congestion at the major centres. The report concluded that the extensive, easy-angled south-east slopes of A' Chailleach had the most potential, especially for beginners. Worth a thought as you ascend Route 118a.

Above the hut, the path continues diagonally up the hillside. It becomes intermittent on boggy ground but you really don't want to lose it. On a good, level section, it crosses the ATV track, which at this point climbs the hillside in better condition.

Follow the track up to peat bogs beside a small stream, where the path to the summit bears right to cross the moor without incident or scenic distraction. It is indistinct in parts on the peaty ground, but the final stretch can be seen ahead in the distance. The angle is gentle until that steeper final climb puts you at the rounded ▲summit, with its substantial cairn and (often welcome) windbreak.

Beyond the summit, a path descends left (north-west), making for the peaty bealach below Carn Sgulain. A more interesting path leads off around the rim of a steep east-facing corrie (Coire na Caillich) that is the mountain's most prominent (some say only) feature. When it too becomes lost among moss and peat bog, bear left down boggy ground into the steep little defile of the Allt Cuil na Caillich (*Owlt Coo-il na Kyle-yich*, Stream of the Old Woman's Back) and re-ascend through peat hags to the ▲summit of Carn Sgulain. It has to be said that the most appealing feature of this part of the route is its brevity.

The shortest and least fraught return route descends the glen of the Allt a' Chaorainn. A direct descent to its head is impeded by a hidden band of broken crags low down on the

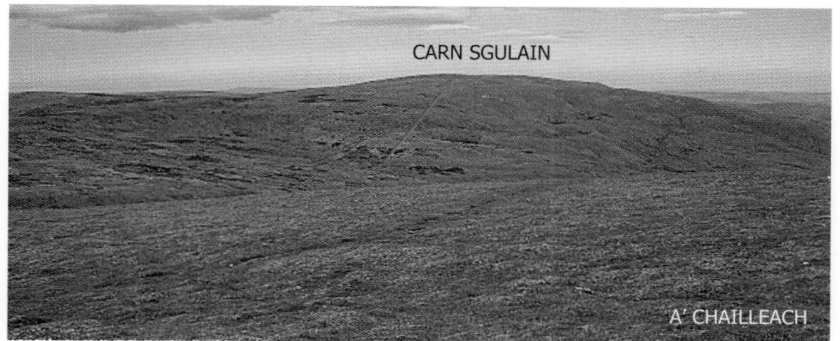

hillside south-east of Carn Sgulain's summit. This can be outflanked to either east or west. The west side adds a touch of adventure to an otherwise staid route. Return to the defile of the Allt Cuil na Caillich, which tumbles down a gorge between the crags. The descent of the right (south) bank of the gorge, high above the stream, is steep and rough (G2) but, this far into the day, some may find such terrain a welcome respite.

Easier ground, more in keeping with the rest of the route, will be found on the east side of the crags. From the bealach east of Carn Sgulain, simply keep to the left bank of the infant Allt a' Chaorainn. If in doubt about your bearings, see Needlepoint (Page 225).

Once onto the flat bottom of the glen, where the Allt Cuil na Caillich and the Allt a' Chaorainn meet, the north-east shoulder of A' Chailleach looks improbably pointy, a suitable spouse for equally pointy Am Bodach (*Am Bottach*, The Old Man) on the glen's other side. Below the stream junction, excuses-for-paths follow both banks. It's a long, boggy descent but, lower down, the left-bank path becomes surprisingly pleasant for a while on dry ground well above the stream. It's still a relief to reach the approach track again.

Baffies: On an off-day, lovers of wildlife should visit Insh Marshes, one of the most important wetlands in Europe. The entrance to the reserve is on the B970 north of Newtonmore. Go in autumn to see the aspens at their most colourful.

Route 118b The Monadh Liath Traverse: A' Chailleach, Carn Sgulain and Carn Dearg from Glen Banchor

G2 *** Route Rage Alert NN 693998, 15ml/24km, 1050m/3450ft M218/219

By combining Routes 117a/117b and 118a, you can bag the three eastern Monadh Liath Munros together. After climbing ▲A' Chailleach and ▲Carn Sgulain as per Route 118a, the 4½ml/7km walk across the undulating plateau to ▲Carn Dearg never dips below 850m/2800ft and is a good romp on mostly excellent terrain (yes, really!) with wide vistas. Admittedly the vistas are of nothing in particular, but they sure are wide.

The terrain is mostly grassy, with a number of boulder patches to pick your way around. Rusted fence posts mark the route all the way from Carn Sgulain to Carn Ban, but such is the confusing featurelessness of the plateau that you'll need to consult the map from time to time to verify your exact location. It's not a route that will be to everyone's taste but, once you've overcome the approach to the heights, there's no denying it's **a top-of-the-world stravaig** with a real feeling of airiness and loneliness.

From Carn Sgulain, the path keeps close to the fence as it crosses the bealach that marks the low point of the walk and re-ascends to Meall a' Bhothain (*Myowl a Vawan*, Hill of the Hut). There are two peaty sections, one just before a minor rise on the descent, and the other at the bealach itself, where a short detour may be necessary to avoid the morass.

Beyond Meall a' Bhothain the path crosses a plateau bump, named Meall a' Creughaich on the OS 1:25,000 map, and reaches the half-way point at a small lochan (NH 651054). If this contains water, it makes a good rest stop. Unfortunately, it tends to dry up in summer.

The start of the traverse: looking west from Carn Sgulain

Next underfoot are ΔCarn Ballach and ΔCarn Ban, with the east face of Carn Dearg now in view to draw you on. At Carn Ban you leave the high ground, which continues all the way to distant Geal Charn, to take the side ridge to Carn Dearg. All you have to do then is descend Route 177a or 117b to regain Glen Banchor.

Half-way lochan

GiGi: Where is the summit of Carn Ballach? The OS 1:25,000 map shows two 920m spot heights, one 300m SW of the cairn (NH 643045) and one 300m NE of the cairn (NH 648049). In the original 1891 Tables the SW summit was a Munro and the NE summit a Top. In 1921 the SW summit was deleted from the Tables and the NE summit became the Munro. In 1974 the NE summit was deleted from the Tables and the SW summit again became the Munro, demoted to Top status in 1981. Those interested in such weighty matters must await further clarification with baited breath.

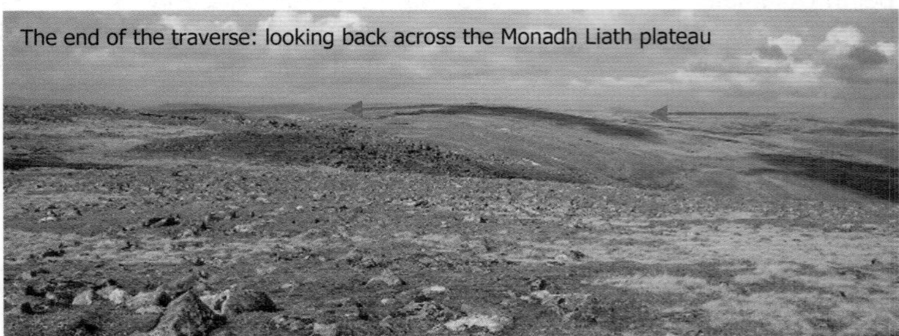
The end of the traverse: looking back across the Monadh Liath plateau

Torpedo: It is tempting to contemplate bagging all four Monadh Liath Munros in a single trip, but from Carn Dearg it is a further 7ml/11km and 220m/700ft across numerous minor tops to Geal Charn, and a descent from there would leave you requiring transport back to your starting point. The complete traverse would certainly amount to a memorable high-level trip if you could master the logistics.

Needlepoint: Thanks to the line of fence posts, you probably won't stray off-route in cloud, but it can seem like a long way across the plateau when there is no objective in sight. Furthermore, on the latter half of the route especially, the best ground is sometimes frustratingly too far from the fence posts for comfort.

Chilly Willy: Owing to its consistently high and gentle terrain, the Monadh Liath Traverse in winter often gives a wonderfully spacious romp across the white stuff. When combined with ascent and descent, the whole route is nevertheless a considerable undertaking, especially in soft conditions.

INDEX

On Geal-Charn (Culra)